Harold L. Raush

William A. Barry

Richard K. Hertel

Mary Ann Swain

COMMUNICATION
CONFLICT
AND MARRIAGE

Jossey-Bass Publishers
San Francisco • Washington • London • 1974

04425

COMMUNICATION, CONFLICT, AND MARRIAGE
Explorations in the Theory and Study of Intimate Relationships
        by Harold L. Raush, William A. Barry, Richard K. Hertel,
        and Mary Ann Swain

Copyright © 1974 by: Jossey-Bass, Inc., Publishers
                615 Montgomery Street
                San Francisco, California 94111
                        &
                Jossey-Bass Limited
                3 Henrietta Street
                London WC2E 8LU

Library of Congress Catalogue Card Number LC 73-18506

International Standard Book Number ISBN 0-87589-210-8

Manufactured in the United States of America

JACKET DESIGN BY WILLI BAUM

FIRST EDITION

Code 7404

The Jossey-Bass
Behavioral Science Series

Special Advisors

WILLIAM E. HENRY
University of Chicago

NEVITT SANFORD
Wright Institute, Berkeley

Preface

How do two people who are committed to maintaining an ongoing relationship handle the inevitable differences that are part of our human condition? Embodied within this question are the diverse fields of inquiry placed side by side in the title of this book—communication, conflict, and marriage. The book analyzes and investigates the communication processes involved in coping with interpersonal conflict in intimate and relatively enduring relationships.

One could hardly choose a conglomeration of themes for comment and research that entails more risks and has fewer boundaries. The rationale for our choice has at times seemed a psychological version of Hilary's reason for climbing Mount Everest ("because it's there"): "because life is like that." While communication, conflict, and marriage have perhaps been formally investigated most often by psychologists and sociologists, they are also themes of concern to and under scrutiny by clinicians—psychiatrists, psychologists, social workers, and other counselors—who in their practices face daily the ramifications of interpersonal conflict. Apart from their academic and professional interest, the three topics engage a fair (or unfair) share of our lives with one another.

The breadth of this book's subject matter is paralleled by its aspirations. We try to integrate diverse theories and coordinate these with consonant methods of clinical and statistical investigation. Surely this is too ambitious, and surely it does not ease the reader's task. The alternative, however, would have been oversimplifications untrue to the complexities of real life. We hope that in the course of the book the reader will gain increased understanding of the complexities of communication, interpersonal conflict, and marital development. We also hope that our approach to analysis may point to ways of examining other complexities of life.

A prologue suggests the book's directions. Part One presents the major themes. Parts Two and Three develop and interweave these themes with concrete findings. A final chapter offers a concluding commentary.

Like families, books have a developmental history, and we would like to acknowledge this book's genesis. The antecedents go back to studies begun at the National Institute of Mental Health. Wells Goodrich and Paul Blank created the Improvisations that formed the empirical base for our studies. Arden Flint, Robert G. Ryder, and Walter Sceery contributed to the early stages at NIMH.

In keeping with this age of high geographic mobility, the next developmental stage took place at the University of Michigan, aided by continued support from the National Institute of Mental Health to Harold L. Raush through USPH Research Grant, Communication Patterns, MH–10975, and by Public Health Service Fellowships to William A. Barry and Mary Ann Swain. At Michigan the network of influences expanded. The book profited from the contributions of Gary L. Coleite and Jeff A. Epstein initially and later of Margery Doehrman, Ethan S. Nebelkopf, and Elizabeth Hawkins. Eduardo N. Siguel deserves special mention for his patient and painstaking care with the computer programming. Jo-Anna M. Featherman, secretary par excellence, research assistant, humorist, and friend, nurtured the family through personal and interpersonal, budgetary, and statistical crises and a flood or two.

For the final stages of preparation, the book is indebted to the cooperation and support of Weston College School of Theology, Cambridge, Massachusetts, and the Psychology Department of the

University of Massachusetts at Amherst. Readings by and discussions with Sheldon Cashdan, Mona Fishbane, George Levinger, and George Magakis of the University of Massachusetts improved earlier versions. Very special appreciation goes to Jeffrey Baker who devoted many hours to critical examination, discussion, and editing of the manuscript. Lynn Swan at Weston College and Diana Veith and Diana Scriver at the University of Massachusetts typed faithfully and well. The final copy benefited from the skills, care, patience, and devotion of Sally Ives.

We have no doubt failed to mention some who contributed in one way or another: in the gathering of data; in the time-consuming, often tedious work of coding; in analysis, criticism, and editorial help. To them our apologies. As yet unmentioned is the group of helpers without whom—in the clichéd phrase—this book would not have been written: the young couples who contributed not only of their time but also of themselves.

February 1974   HAROLD L. RAUSH
Amherst, Massachusetts   WILLIAM A. BARRY, S.J.
                                                                  RICHARD K. HERTEL
                                                                  MARY ANN SWAIN

Contents

THREE: THE CONTEXTUAL SYSTEM
FOR COMMUNICATION AND CONFLICT

Communication
Conflict
and Marriage

Explorations in the Theory and Study
of Intimate Relationships

Prologue: Directions

After dinner Bob and Sue Smith settle down in the living room to talk and read the newspaper. Sue is pregnant, and she knows that at 9 P.M. channel 2 will be showing a special program—a panel discussion about the naming of children. Though she thinks Bob might not be happy about watching it, Sue expects he won't mind too much.

While Bob is reading the paper he notices that the NFL game of the week is on at nine. He knows that Sue doesn't like pro football much, but she has usually been a good sport about it—and besides she likes to read. He says, "The Vikings and the Packers are on at nine."

Sue replies, "Oh, no. I want us to watch a special about how children get named."

The incident is trivial and commonplace. Though topics may vary, the discovery and clash of opposing intentions is known

1

to all of us. Such conflicts are a part of our daily lives together. Sometimes, and in some relationships, they are resolved easily. Sue may say, "—but if you want to watch football, I'll read my novel," or Bob may say, "I didn't know that was on. We can watch it if you'd like to." Sometimes, as we all know, such minor incidents escalate far beyond their apparent triviality. Sue may say, "Damn it, you always watch what you want to see. You're always drinking beer and watching football. Nothing else seems important to you, especially my wishes." Or Bob may say, "Oh God, not that again. I don't know what you see in those dumb programs—a bunch of stupid loudmouths saying the same thing over and over." Among intimates, those who have made a commitment to live and interact with one another, the outcome itself—who wins and who loses in a specific interchange—is often of minor importance. What counts for the future is what gets said or is unsaid, by whom and to whom, when and in what way.

Winning and losing become even less relevant when issues directly involve the relationship itself. Consider a scene that is far less trivial at the start than disagreement over a television program. Bob is upset about Sue. Something about her personally or about something she has done or left undone has disturbed him deeply. He feels entirely estranged and alienated from her; at the moment, he wants nothing to do with her and can barely tolerate her presence.

Sue has become aware of Bob's distance. He is a stranger to her, no longer the person she married. Both her own peace of mind and the marriage are threatened, and Sue is resolved that this can go on no longer. Tonight she is determined to face the issue and to reestablish their closeness. In resolving or failing to resolve this scene, far more is at stake than questions of who dominates and who submits, who decides and who accedes, and who wins and who loses.

In 1959 under the direction of Wells Goodrich, the Child Research Branch of the National Institute of Mental Health at Bethesda, Maryland, began longitudinal studies of the early stages of family life. The initial researchers undertook an exploratory study with forty-eight couples who were fairly homogeneous in terms of socioeconomic factors and residential stability. The intent was to study each couple through interviews, questionnaires, and experimental procedures during the early months of their marriage, during the first pregnancy, and four months after the first baby was born.

In a procedure called Improvisations, conflict situations were devised as a means for studying the couples' interactions *in vivo* rather than through retrospective report.[1] The Improvisations were designed to engage couples in quasi-experimental, quasi-naturalistic interaction situations in which a conflict of interest was created through separate instructions given to each partner. The investigators hoped to evoke behaviors that would allow study of a couple's communications and modes of handling and resolving marital conflicts.

How does what Bob says or does affect Sue's response, and how do her acts affect his? Do their ways of handling conflict depend on the nature of the conflict situation? Do Bob's maleness and Sue's femaleness make a difference in the tactics they use with one another? Do their ways of dealing with interpersonal conflict change as they continue to live with one another and as they enter into parenthood? Does their view of themselves as happy or unhappy in their marriage make a difference in their interactions? What makes for constructive or destructive conflict in their marriage? Can we speak of creativity or stasis in a marital relationship?

Specific answers to such questions are lacking, although there is no dearth of research on marriage. Research studies proliferate annually. Many of these continue to center on peculiarly American cultural concepts—marital success, happiness, satisfaction, adjustment—as though these were absolute, permanent states, worthy goals to be strived for by each couple and to be achieved by a fortunate few. And, indeed, there are correlates of "success": "happy" couples share common attitudes; teenage marriages are more likely to dissolve than the marriages of older couples; "adjustment" in marriage is related to a husband's occupational status and job satisfaction; in "happy" marriages wives change, adapting to their husbands; there is some evidence that marital "satisfaction" declines during the first decade of marriage.[2] Such findings tend to

---

[1] Paul Blank and Wells Goodrich were the major developers of the Improvisations.

[2] Reviews and references can be found in Barry (1970) and Udry (1971). A sophisticated statistical survey and analysis of 216 middle-aged

remain at the level of isolated facts. We know correlates of what couples refer to as their marital satisfactions, but we have little or no explanation of why the correlations exist. Without such understanding, the facts themselves are empty, despite repeated confirmations. We do not know whether they represent fundamental aspects of intimate relationships or the vagaries of a passing era and its cultural definitions. Already some of these facts seem dated.

At an opposite pole from the atheoretical amassment of disconnected empirical facts about marriage and familial relations are the polemics. We are told that the family is dead, or that it should be. We are instructed on *the* way to resuscitate the moribund relationship—whether through different or better sex, fight-training, more open communication, greater personal freedom, fewer or newer or better "games." For the polemicist there is no lack of theory on what intimate relationships should be like. It is empirical evidence that is lacking, and in the absence of such evidence good-bad dichotomies flourish.

With rare exceptions neither the polemics nor the broad-gauge empirical researchers attempt to describe or explain the complexities that match our personal experiences of the interchanges characterizing continued close relationships. Reports by therapists who work with families convey a sense of these complexities, and there have been research reports that attempted to examine the specifics of intimate relationships. Most often the emphasis or study has been on the disturbed family.[3] It sometimes appears that, with very few notable exceptions, only novelists and playwrights describe marriage with any degree of veracity and depth.

The real work of understanding communication between intimates begins with decisions of what to look at and how to look at it. Those decisions are rooted in theoretical positions and investigative premises. Unfortunately, theories about interaction between intimates are neither sufficiently firm nor sufficiently specific at present to provide us with other than rough lines of guidance. In-

couples studied in 1970 tends to confirm some of these findings (Otto and Featherman, 1972).

[3] A current full list of references to such studies appears in Riskin and Faunce (1972), which also reviews methodological issues and research findings.

stead, our studies bring together three diverse sources: (1) communication theory, (2) conflict theory, and (3) object relations theory. These theoretical positions are discussed in the immediately following chapters.

It is appropriate for the reader to know at the start the investigative premises that govern this work. Some are the focus of later discussions, and our comments here can be brief.

Proposition 1. The intensive study of "normal" people is a worthwhile scientific endeavor. Most often intensive study seems to be reserved for the clinically disturbed; this is particularly true in the study of families. Much has been and is being learned from the study of families and couples who are patients. For the most part "normal" families and couples tend to be studied through simple, quick, "one-shot" methods. Just as the study of pathology may illuminate normal processes, so may the study of normal processes help us understand dysfunctions (see Handel, 1965).

Proposition 2. Studying what people say about themselves is no substitute for studying how they behave. Self-reports, particularly those given in brief questionnaires, are subject to massive distortion. Questionnaires and scales of marital satisfaction and dissatisfaction have yielded very little. We need to look at what people do with one another.

Proposition 3. Couples and families need to be studied as systems. To study Bob and Sue as isolated individuals is not equivalent to studying them as a couple. From the study of disturbed families it has become overwhelmingly clear that the behavior of each individual family member is directly related to the structure of the family as a unit and to the family's maintenance as a system.[4] This is not to deny the relevance of personal history. It does, however, imply that understanding a relationship requires knowledge of how the relationship functions.

Proposition 4. Longitudinal studies of continuing relationships are necessary. It is true that one can study families at various stages of development (the newlywed period, parenthood, the period when the children enter school, the launching of a new generation into adult life) by cross-sectional methods—sampling families at

[4] See especially Bowen (1971); Haley (1963); Jackson (1968); Minuchin and others (1967); Watzlawick and others (1967).

different stages simultaneously. Such studies cannot, however, tell us about continuity and change in individual families. Moreover, cross-sectional studies can too easily confound developmental with societal changes. For example, were we to compare newlyweds with contemporaneous couples who are sending their children off to college, we might be looking not only at changes in marriage, but at differences between generations growing up in different cultural eras. The investigation of stability and change, and of the correlates to these, requires longitudinal as well as cross-sectional study.

Proposition 5. Research methods should be congruent with the nature of the problems under investigation. To examine communication and interpersonal conflict in marriage, we chose real married couples rather than made-up pairings. Rather than maintaining a laboratory atmosphere, we tried to make our stage settings real, even modifying the instructions for different couples to achieve maximum involvement. The aim was toward naturalizing the investigative approach.

In one way, however, the Improvisations went counter to naturalism. For practical reasons, it would have been difficult to follow couples in their own homes, waiting for them to engage in different types of conflict in the presence of observers and recording equipment. The Improvisations method selects a limited range of conflict situations. Within the restrictions of these situations, however, the couples have considerable freedom. Unlike the usual laboratory situation, it is the subjects who produce, define, and extend the scale of events for one another. In terms of the two dimensions that Willems (1969) suggests for describing the range between laboratory experiments and naturalistic studies, the *manipulation by the investigator of antecedent conditions* is moderate and the *imposition of units on the behavior studied* is low.

The terms of these dimensions have implications for the findings of our studies. Since the investigators defined the conflict scenes, we cannot argue that the subjects would in their daily lives engage in the actions they produced in the Improvisations. Since it is the subjects who defined the repertoire of events for one another, however, we can premise that the relations between their acts were representative. That is, we do not know how often in real life Sue became threatening or Bob became coercive. But if, in our studies,

Sue got threatening when Bob got coercive, we are describing at least a possibility in their lives together. So, in our search for invariances, we bet here—as do some recent social psychological studies (Newcomb, 1965)—not on constancies of elements but on constancies of relations.

The aim for congruence between the research method and the problem presses for a naturalistic approach in studying communication and conflict in married couples. Naturalistic approaches to research have been discussed mostly in terms of how data are gathered (Willems and Raush, 1969). Insufficiently explored are the theoretical bases that underlie a move toward naturalistic, open-ended investigations and the analytic methods appropriate to such investigations. A shift toward naturalistic study implies an alternative view of scientific endeavors, one in which we do not have precise hypotheses or dependent and independent variables in the usual experimental sense. Such a state of affairs may be more typical than we usually think, even for older, firmer sciences. Thus, one observer suggests that even physics has come to be characterized by a *"multiple, probing, delineating* operationalism" in contrast to a *rigid, single* operationalism, and that "the firmness and relative unequivocality of our knowledge of distal constructs come through triangulation from two or more operations, no one of which has priority as the criterion or the definition, and no one of which would be unequivocal without the other" (Campbell, 1959, pp. 176–177). Rather than testing hypotheses unequivocally, the investigator triangulates toward generalizations, spirals in on data from different angles, checks the consistency of a finding with other findings, and searches for the ones that click together to make a coherent statement of principle.

Chapters Two through Five offer a theoretical base for such an alternative approach to research in human relationships. The analytic methods, clinical and statistical, in the chapters that follow aim toward congruence with both raw data and theoretical position. That is, they seek not to reduce or simplify, but rather to capture and explicate the complexities basic to living, interrelating systems.

II

An Adaptive Probabilism

Concepts of marriage are changing. Divorce is more common, former notions of marital roles and obligations no longer seem valid, and alternative arrangements for intimacy and communal living proliferate (see Constantine and Constantine, 1971). Though marriage still probably remains the longest and most significant relationship in most lives, its functions, as sociologists suggest (Udry, 1971), have changed. For the average American couple, basic subsistence no longer demands total preoccupation. Education and mass-media communications are increasingly shared by both sexes. Definitions of the division of labor between men and women thus are beginning to break down, role restrictions are becoming more relaxed, there is more questioning of traditionally defined modes of relation. New goals for marriage are emerging.

As practical exigencies lessen and as cultural guidelines and prescriptions for action and interaction weaken, there is more room for the interplay of personal, social, and circumstantial factors in couples' interactions. Modes of relation become matters to be worked out, rather than prescribed givens; emphasis shifts away from adjustment to what is given and toward creation of what is to be (see Raush and others, 1963). The high mobility of the contemporary American family creates circumstances in which that family may be the single source of stability and continuity in the relationships of its individual members; the working out of intrafamilial relationships consequently becomes not only an opportunity for creating congruous patterns of relations but a critical necessity for individual and group continuity. New kinds of rules—about who makes the rules, how they are to be made, and about what—become important in adapting to a rapidly changing world (Haley, 1963; Laing, 1972).

As the working out of its own modes of relation becomes a major function of the family, the contemporary couple, far more than earlier counterparts, faces issues of decision-making, conflict resolution, and mutuality of understanding. Increased attention is given to such interpersonal concepts as empathy, intimacy, and communication.[1] An age of constantly and rapidly shifting norms, with its absence of prescribed behaviors, allows—and for some couples may demand—increased growth through creative interaction, as we shall illustrate.

Probabilism and Determinism

Given the above conditions, a single-variable explanation of any phenomenon is difficult to come by. A host of factors, including situational requirements, individual requirements and their meshing, and prior interactions, may influence a couple's resolution of conflict; no single factor is determinative of what takes place. Marriage may allow a variety of alternative modes of dealing with conflict, each of which is associated with a probability of occurrence. At any given moment there is some doubt or uncertainty about which of these alternatives will occur. For example, let us say

[1] Lack of communication seems to have become the predominant complaint of couples who seek help for marital difficulties. See, for example, Lear (1972).

that in general the likelihood that Bob will insult Sue is very low; but if Sue mocks his mother, Bob insults her more often than not. Sue, however, only mocks his mother when she gets very angry in an argument—which does not happen often. Thus, a heated argument raises the likelihood of Sue's mocking Bob's mother, which in turn increases the likelihood of his insulting Sue. But these are probabilities, not certainties. In the heat of argument Sue does not always mock Bob's mother, nor does he always insult her when she does.

In the completely deterministic case, the connection or absence of a connection between two events is perfect. Knowledge of X eliminates uncertainty about Y: either X relates to Y in a specified way (every time Sue mocks Bob, Bob insults her), or it affects Y not at all (no matter what Sue does Bob never insults her). A wholly deterministic case is a special limiting case incorporated within a broader framework of probability. *"The single-valued, determinate, transformation is thus simply a special extreme case of the stochastic.* It is the stochastic in which all the probabilities have become 0 or 1" (Ashby, 1961, p. 165).[2]

The probabilistic model has at times been confused with indeterminism. The latter view holds that one can never account fully for an event or set of events. Something—call it irreducible error, magic, divine intervention, or freedom—prevents us from ever going beyond a probabilistic interpretation. Such a position of indeterminism has been reached in an area of physics. The behavior of a single atomic particle cannot be fully accounted for because of the fundamentally irreducible influence of observation; hence description must be content with probability statements. Such fundamental indeterminacy may be as true for psychology as it is at the bordering edges of physics, but this is not at issue here. The probabilistic determinism that is basic to this work is neutral with respect to the issue of basic indeterminacy.[3]

A position of probabilistic determinism has strong practical implications for empirical studies, particularly when these concern

[2] See also Ashby's section on Markovian machines (1961, pp. 225–243).

[3] For an earlier expression of probabilistic determinism in psychology, see Brunswik (1947).

human affairs. Take, for example, a study that finds that condition A leads to condition B in 75 percent of the cases studied and does not lead to B in the remaining 25 percent. From a position of absolute determinism such findings (if found to contain a statistically significant relationship between A and B) would lead to further experimental studies that attempt to eliminate confounding variables in order to come closer to the presumed "true" perfect relationship. The ideal is to isolate factors and vary them one at a time in order to reduce connections to their simplest elements.

Such methods are appropriate where systems permit reduction to simple, independent components. Where systems are complex, however, and especially where we are concerned with interactions among complex systems, the model given by the special case of absolute determinism is no longer appropriate. It is particularly inappropriate when there is likelihood of organization among variables, that is, when the effects of variables X and Y on variable Z are not simply summative (see Watzlawick and others, 1967, pp. 123–126; Raush, 1965).

An empirical case in point is furnished by the findings from four sets of studies of children's social interactions (Raush and others, 1960): in each study identification of both social settings and individual children yielded information about social behavior; but situational and individual effects were not summative. In all studies the informational gain was at least twice as much through identifying *the child in the setting* as through summing the setting and the child as independent factors. Certainly insofar as human interaction is concerned, our everyday experience is sufficient to tell us that an act can seldom be independent of the context of other events in which it is embedded. This is implied in the Virginian's famous phrase, "Smile when you say that." The model of absolute determinism is also particularly inappropriate when we deal with successive interchanges between systems over time, but we shall come to this issue a bit later.

The probabilistic approach has encouraged study of the effects of several variables on a system simultaneously; the network to be investigated is extended rather than narrowed. The movement toward extending rather than reducing it is suggested in Figure 1. The crossing network of lines suggests that we may inquire as to the

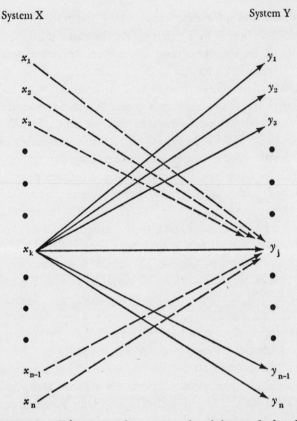

System X   System Y

FIGURE 1. Diagram of a network of interrelationships between two systems (modified from Fano, 1961, p. 10).

probability of any particular event in system Y given any particular event in system X. We may, however, also ask how a variety of events in X affect the probability of a particular event in Y and conversely how a variety of events in Y are affected by any particular event in X. Furthermore, a probabilistic model suggests that among the relevant features for investigation are the probability of the occurrence of any given x event among all x events and the probability of the occurrence of any given y event among all y events.

To illustrate, let us say that x_k is a threatening statement by one member of a couple ("If you change the TV program, I'll hit you"). Let us further assume that the other partner generally responds to x_k (threat) with y_1 (arguments) 10 percent of the time, with y_j (concessions) 20 percent of the time, and with y_n (counterthreats) 70 percent of the time. Provided that other x's ($x_1 \ldots n$, for example, rational arguments, expressions of affection, appeals to the other) do not yield the same array of responses, we gain information about y by knowing x. But we can go beyond this. The word *generally* in our assumptions meant "irrespective of other systemic properties in X that were also operative at the same time," such as sex of the threatener, length of time married, or whether the threatener is pregnant. These other properties of system X can be given the names x_1, x_2, x_3, and so forth. Each can be assumed to have an effect on the responses in system Y, and all together may load the probabilities in favor of y_j (concession) in a particular instance. To be concrete, let us assume that whereas generally a threat leads to a counterthreat, when the threat is made by a pregnant wife in a very happy marriage, the husband is much more likely to concede than to counterthreaten.

The direction implied in probabilistic determinism toward extending rather than narrowing the network of data suggests increased emphasis on naturalistic approaches. That is, the ecology of behavior (see Barker, 1968) becomes important. Although the inclusiveness of such approaches poses hard investigative problems, as compared to the exclusiveness of typical experimental designs it offers greater possibilities of legitimate generalizations about the phenomena under study (Bakan, 1967; Raush, 1969). As Moore and Anderson (1962) imply in a critique of some highly formalized and restricted treatments of social interaction, the study of social interaction that eliminates its ordinary complexities from possible examination rather misses the point. In the study of complex systems it becomes relevant to attend to the range of events produced, their organizational effects, their probabilities of occurrence under different conditions, and, in the case of interacting systems, the contingent probabilities between events or sets of events.

Out of such considerations arises the structure of the studies that follow. A range of conditions is set for our subjects, but essentially it is they who define the situations. Unlike the usual experiment, in these situations the subjects, not the experimenters, predominate in determining the events that take place. Some of the structural "looseness"—though indeed not all—is, therefore, deliberate, allowing subjects to express their input and output repertoires and to define the contingencies between the husband's and the wife's repertoires.

Too often in the past the use of multivariate approaches has been only technologically oriented—that is, applied as an efficient way to accomplish what might otherwise require a number of studies. The premises remain those of absolute determinism, and with these premises the power of multivariate methods to examine complex systems and their interrelationships is sharply attenuated. The issue here is not one of statistics but rather a matter of interpretation, orientation, and direction. To use an analogy to filming made by Menzel (1969) in comparing laboratory to field investigations, the orientation toward absolute determinism suggests a "zooming-in," the orientation toward probabilistic determinism a "zooming-out." If we zoom in too far, we may miss what goes on in complex organized systems and in the interrelations among such systems. Zooming out too far may confuse us with the variety of events under our lens. Multivariate probabilistic methods such as those provided by communication theory enable us to zoom out to a point where complexity and diversity can be comprehended.

Adaptive Probabilism

"Whereas the innate 'releaser mechanisms' of birds and animals give fairly definite, regular, automatic responses to certain simple signs, it is far less certain what a man will do when you address him, challenge him, or question him" (Cherry, 1966, p. 272). The automatic nature of stimulus-response patterns found in lower biological orders seems to give way in mammals to response variability. Behavior appears to shift from being wholly deterministic to becoming probabilistic (Beach, 1960).

Moreover, as one ascends the evolutionary scale, not only do exploration, curiosity, and play become increasingly relevant for describing the behavioral repertoire of a species but they also create manifold possibilities that may be tested for informational yield

(Berlyne, 1960; Thorpe, 1956, pp. 86–87). And, given a world in which conditions vary so that what is right one time is not necessarily right the next, such activities provide opportunities for testing contingencies under differing circumstances—that is, the likelihood of the same or differing outcomes under varying conditions. As Russell and Russell (1961) suggest, the flexibility of "exploratory" as contrasted with "automatic" systems has evolutionary advantages. It is this flexibility, based on responding probabilistically and leaving a residual uncertainty in the association between classes of events, that allows the formation of structures capable of adapting to diversity and change.[4]

The probabilistic position and the methods associated with it are peculiarly apt for studying evolutionary as distinct from stationary systems; that is, the relations between multivariate organized systems interacting with one another over a course of time seem fundamentally rooted in probability processes.

There are data suggesting that tendencies to respond probabilistically are indeed strong. For example, people act probabilistically in a probabilistic learning situation even when it is contrary to their best interests to do so (Estes, 1950). If a researcher randomly rewards one direction of behavior 70 percent and the other direction 30 percent of the time, subjects modulate their behavior over time to approximate these percentages, even though the payoff would be greatest if they responded all the time in the preferred direction.[5] Yet, responding probabilistically may have advantages in the long run in spite of its disadvantages in the short run. If subjects can be thought of as trying to beat the system, as trying to comprehend the order in a complex miniature world, they are better off varying their activities in attempts to match what is going on. But—and here is the paradox in these experiments—the attempt makes full

[4] Developments in terms of probabilistic rather than wholly deterministic associations can, furthermore, incorporate concepts such as equipotentiality (whereby one stimulus or response, is capable of substituting for another) and multiple determinism (a redundancy, to speak informationally, in which several events contribute to a single behavior). Again, each of these concepts can readily be thought of as adaptive functions in a complex and changing world.

[5] In other words, $(.70 \times .70) + (.30 \times .30) < (1.00 \times .70)$.

sense only if the world they are responding to *is* orderly, an assumption made false here by the experimenter's arbitrariness in randomization.

In a coherent world, then, playing with possibilities broadens one's way of gaining information about complex events. Even devices for maximizing chance, such as games, omens, and divinations, may serve as prescientific approaches to avoiding rigidity and to expanding experience (see Aubert, 1959). In such situations, as in the probability learning one, we behave as if nature were logical, orderly, and coherent, and the principles of the order are hard to figure out. It makes sense then to vary our hypotheses as to what is going on and to try to match these to the conditions nature presents to us.

Probabilistic modes of functioning become dysfunctional, however, in circumstances in which there is a premium on efficiency rather than flexibility. Stereotyped, one-to-one event relations seem called for, first, in activities that carry little investment, cathexis, or involvement. To weigh probabilities in relation to brushing one's teeth in the morning is obviously wasteful. Secondly, nonprobabilistic behavior is characteristic of activities that have undergone a high degree of overlearning. This appears in any achieved skill being expressed without interference. Thirdly, emergency situations involving immediate issues of survival call for primitive, stereotyped actions; an emergency allows only one best bet, and the choice must be the one act that offers the highest probability of success.[6]

But a great many of our activities, particularly those involving social interaction, suggest a strong preference for what might be thought of as probabilistic playfulness. The game a person always wins (or loses) or in which the moves are entirely predictable becomes utterly dull. A musical composition, a poem, a novel must carry or revive in us some measure of uncertainty if it is to hold our interest. An interpersonal relationship that is wholly predictable is apt to be boring. The delight in, the play with, and the search for resolution of uncertainty seem most highly developed in man.[7] Moore and Anderson (1962) speak of *autotelic* activities

[6] Even in the probability learning situation, when the stakes are high enough, choices tend to be entirely in one direction.

[7] Moreover, preferences for stimulation of high, as compared to low,

—activities undertaken by human beings solely because of their intrinsic interest—and they suggest that a model for social games comes far closer to representing human interaction than does the model used in the usual psychological experiment, which is appropriate to the physical sciences. Moreover, they point out that those "autotelic activities in which the rules are constantly changing may provide one way of acclimating people to a world of constantly and rapidly shifting norms" (p. 246).[8] It is in this sense that we see a probabilistic (rather than wholly deterministic) orientation to social interaction as having adaptive value.

In the studies that follow, therefore, our major concern is with the probabilities of behaviors of husbands and wives as they cope with interpersonal conflict. We examine how couples differ in their approaches to the uncertainties induced by conflict, including their acceptance or rejection of a probabilistic orientation. We explore the effects of various contexts—the uniqueness of the husband-wife pair, their orientation toward the marriage, the fact that they are male and female, the variations in the kinds of issues that are in conflict, the stages of their marriage—on the probabilities of modes of interaction.

Summary

We have here suggested a philosophical base for the study of human interaction. We argue that a position of adaptive probabilism characterizes much of human behavior, and we suggest that this position needs to be reflected in research approaches. The multivariate probabilistic methods of communication theory will enable us to treat the complex data of one such approach comprehensively.

---

variability increase with sophistication or training in the relevant field (see Munsinger and Kessen, 1964).

[8] See also Thorpe (1965, pp. 87–88) for a discussion of play in animals as a releaser from the binds of appetitive behavior and as a mode by which learning may be broadened. Bruner (1966, pp. 134–135), discussing the play of children, presents a similar argument, suggesting that the function of play in reducing "serious" external and internal pressures makes possible an intrinsic learning. Among some of our couples (see Chapter Eight) playfulness seemed to serve exploratory learning and relationship-strengthening functions.

III

Interpersonal Communication

If what I do has no effect whatsoever on you, then I have not communicated with you. Communication occurs when what I do affects you in some way. Communication in this sense is not limited to human beings or even to mammals. Machines can communicate. The work of Wiener (1948) and of Shannon and Weaver (1949) in developing mathematical approaches to the study of information and communication systems established a framework for examining the interplay between events or between systems and gave a new potential precision to the vague notions of interaction, communication, and information. And although the formulations developed out of a concern with machine and telecommunication systems, their implications extend far beyond these.[1]

---

[1] Dittmann (1973) presents an excellent nonmathematical explication of communication theory and its extension from telecommunication to the realm of interpersonal messages.

18

Consider Cherry's simple definition: "Communication . . . is essentially the *relationship* set up by the transmission of stimuli and the evocation of responses" (1966, p. 7). His use of italics puts emphasis not on the stimuli or the responses, but on the relationship set up between the transmission of one and the evocation of the other. It will be useful to examine several implications of this rather simple statement, and we shall do so in this chapter.

The words *stimuli* and *responses* are used by Cherry in a broad context. We would prefer to use the more neutral term, *event,* meaning anything that can be pointed to, delimited, set off from something else—a gesture, a statement, a state of weather, a political or social happening, a word, a poem—and to speak of the relationship between the events transmitted from a source (Sue says, "Let's watch the TV special") to the events received (or evoked) at a specified destination (Bob grimaces). In some kinds of communication one is interested in a high degree of equivalence between signals at the source and those at the destination (for example, in communication by telephone or television). But communication can occur when the events we observe at the source differ greatly from those we observe at a destination. We have already given an example between Sue and Bob above. Another occurs if I say, "Watch out!" and you jump. Your action and mine differ. It may be that you do not hear the words precisely or do not even understand English; in that case you would be responding to my gestures and tone of voice. Nonetheless we have communicated, since a relationship was set up between what I said and what you did.

Communication theory speaks of the flow of information between the two systems. Information refers to the surprise value of the event in system A that influences system B. That is, the less likely event X is in system A, the more information flows from system A to system B when X occurs.

Consider a rather prosaic example. If a husband asks his wife, "Where are the scissors?" and she says, "Oh, they're around," he has gained almost no information and hence undertakes no specific goal-directed behavior. Let us suppose that she says, "They're in the kitchen." If her husband knows that 95 percent of the time the scissors are in the kitchen, the statement tells him something, but not very much. He was leaning toward going to the kitchen already, and the information given easily determined that activity. If, under these probability conditions, his wife were to say, "Oh, they're in the bedroom now," he would know much more than he did before the statement, and there would be a marked change in the relative probabilities of his subsequent actions. The surprise value of the information might show itself in the startle as he shifted from a tendency to move toward the kitchen to moving toward the bedroom. In this instance, the less likely of two states of readiness is selected. It is evident that he has gained much more information than in the first situation.

Constraint

Now we can be more precise in our delineation of what communication is. We can say that information flows from system A to system B when a selection in system A (event X) reduces the degree of uncertainty about—that is, to some extent selects or constrains—what happens in system B. Cherry notes: "The information conveyed by signals is always relative; it depends upon the *difference* in the receiver's doubt before and after their receipt" (1966, p. 182). We may think of information gained as a ratio between a posteriori probabilities—Y, knowing X—and a priori probabilities —Y, not knowing X (Cherry, 1966, pp. 62–66). MacKay, relating communication to meaning, speaks similarly of the selective function and of the relational notion implied in communication. He adds the suggestion that "the basic idea behind 'communication' is *the determination of form*" (1961, p. 2), and he elaborates: "The effect of any information . . . is to determine the form of some aspect of the state of readiness or (conditional) orientation of the receiver—to select one such state from a possible range. This makes possible a definition of the *meaning* of a communication, which seems freer from philosophical objections than some others. Briefly, we can define meaning-to-the-receiver as the *selective function* of the communication on the range of his states of readiness for goal-directed activity—or for short, its *orienting function*. Without going into more detail, we may note that the definitive notion here is neither the *logical structure* of the message *per se*, nor its *effect* in the receiver, but the *relation* (orienting function) of which the effect is the exercise" (p. 24).

What MacKay is saying, it seems to us, is that the actual occurrence of event x in system A determines (that is, selects) one of a number of possible states of system B. B has certain expectancies (states of readiness) and the occurrence of x selects one of these. For example, take the case of the coin that is biased to fall tails 90 percent of the time. I expect with a high degree of certitude that it will fall tails, but before this particular toss I bet that it will fall heads and get good odds. I do not expect to win, but I have a chance. When it falls heads, I give a whoop. If it had fallen tails, I would have paid my bet without grumble. What has happened? The actual event x has selected one state in me—a potential for gleefulness at winning. My whoop is the exercise of this selective function of the information flow.

Thus, an event yields information if it selects or "gives shape to" some possibilities from among a set of possibilities. Statements such as, "The plane left at 8 P.M.," "My son is ten years old," and "The two cars crashed," select one more or less precise possibility from a manifold realm. Unless an event gives shape to some possibilities from among others, it can have no meaning for us.

Kuhn (1962) points out that, until the Copernican revolution, astronomers in Europe did not "see" stars that Chinese astronomers with no better equipment had been discovering at much earlier dates. European astronomers with their Ptolemaic paradigm did not expect change in the heavens whereas the Chinese, who had no such theory, were able to perceive changes. In communication terms, even though an event may have high informational value within system A, the flow of information will depend on the capacity of the event to effect a change in system B.

The European astronomers' perceptual blindness suggests that a major problem for human communication is nonrandom, systemic distortion. Such systemic properties, which distort messages, must be distinguished from "noise." Noise, which is a problem of telephone or machine communication, is random in character. It is generally systemic rather than random distortion that creates the problems of communication between humans. The systemic aspects in human face-to-face communications are complicated, as Dittmann (1973) notes, by the fact that (unlike those of the tele-communication system) the system components are not inde-pendent. That is, source, source encoder, and channel encoder are all in the sending person, and channel decoder, user decoder, and user are all in the receiving person. If system B does not have the possibility of receiving event x from system A, event x is not received —at least not as event x. As the scholastic philosophers put it, what-ever is received is received according to the manner of the recipient.

Not only does communication theory provide a model for clarifying our thinking about complex relations, but it also provides a mathematical model for assessing these relations, that is, the rela-tion of events in system A to events in system B. The unit of analysis is the transmisison of information from sender to receiver. The effect of Bob's behavior on Sue may be studied in terms of the manner in which a given type of behavior on his part limits or constrains her behavior or the extent to which his behavior increases or decreases the probability of certain types of behavior by her. For example, we may have ascertained from a frequency count and coding of her statements that she tends to be nice 50 percent of the time and nasty 50 percent of the time (her response repertoire). If we further observe the contingency relationships between husband and wife statements, we may obtain the additional information that Sue is nice 90 percent of the time and nasty 10 percent of the time after Bob has been nice to her, but nasty 90 percent of the time and nice 10 percent of the time after he has been nasty to her. The relationships are shown in Figure 2.

In the above example one can infer that Bob's antecedent acts had considerable effect on Sue's statements; that is, there is

Wife's Consequent Act

Husband's Antecedent Act	NICE	NASTY
NICE	90	10
NASTY	10	90

FIGURE 2. A contingency matrix in which there is com-munication.

communication between him and her. Two extreme examples of situations where there is no observable communication are (1) the wife is nasty or nice 50 percent of the time following either a nasty or a nice statement by the husband, and (2) the wife is nasty 90 percent of the time whether the husband is nasty or nice (see Figure 3).

	SITUATION 1 Wife Consequent Act			SITUATION 2 Wife Consequent Act	
Husband Antecedent Act	NICE	NASTY	Husband Antecedent Act	NICE	NASTY
NICE	50	50	NICE	10	90
NASTY	50	50	NASTY	10	90

FIGURE 3. Contingency matrices in which there is no communication.

The effect of each spouse's statement on the behavior of the other or the extent to which each spouse's statement increases or decreases the likelihood of certain statements by the other spouse may be quantified and assessed statistically by information analyses (Attneave, 1959; McGill, 1954; Smith, 1953). One of the main indices of communication in such analyses is the *reduction of uncertainty*. We can measure the effect of one spouse's behavior on the other in terms of the reduction of uncertainty that the sender brings to the response repertoire of the receiver. For example, if we did not take into account the behavior of the husband in the previous example, the probability of a wife's statement being nice or nasty at any point in time would be 50–50 (high uncertainty); taking into account the husband's previous statement, the probability of her statement being nice or nasty would be either 90–10 or 10–90 (lower uncertainty). Once it has been determined that communication has occurred (that the spouses' signals have reduced the uncertainty of each other's responses), we may use the qualitative aspects of those signals that seemed most effective and of those responses that seemed most affected as a means of further understanding the nature of their communication.

Variety

At its simplest level, then, when we speak of a relationship between two sets of events, X and Y, we mean that the state of X makes a difference for the state of Y. For this to be so, alternative possibilities must exist for both X and Y. If someone were to produce only one gestural act constantly, that act would not communicate to a recipient. An example might be a person in a deep coma who is breathing regularly. If no action on my part affects his breathing, then I infer that I have not communicated with him —nor does his own behavioral act communicate anything to me except that he is still alive. But if my speaking is followed by some change in his breathing, then I can infer that I have communicated. The communication is not very complex; but it is communication.

Even when there are only two possibilities at each end of the communication network—on-off, yes-no, stop-go, dot-dash—an unlimited number of messages can be sent if they are spread over time. Computer language and Morse code illustrate this principle. Where there are more than two possibilities of classification, a given amount of information can be conveyed by a shorter message; the more possibilities there are, the greater is the amount of information that can be conveyed in a given unit message length.[2] An important consideration in communication, then, is the range of event categories at sending and receiving ends, what Ashby (1961) calls the *variety* of the systems. If Bob has only two categories for perceiving a woman he is close to, for example, yielding-loving versus demanding-hating, then it will be very difficult for Sue to communicate that her desire to see her television show does not mean that she no longer loves him.

More concretely, Bob says, "If you really loved me, you would let me watch the game." Sue replies, "I do love you, Bob, but I've been looking forward to that program all day," and at the same

[2] G. A. Miller (1956) suggests that on the average the adult human is capable of keeping seven plus or minus two classes of events in mind at one time; each of the seven classes may subsume seven plus or minus two other classes; and so forth. Human communication can thus have a very high capacity for yielding information.

time she touches him gently with her hand. If Bob's categories are just the two we mentioned above, he will be affected by only one part of the message and conclude that Sue has not yielded and therefore does not love him. In other words, Sue will communicate only partially to Bob under these circumstances; the complexity of her message has no effect on him. We may now extend our earlier discussion of systemic distortion by noting that the greater the variety in system B, the greater the likelihood that system B will be able to receive event x from system A as event x.

As a consequence of the limits of Bob's receiving, or more properly, decoding channels, Sue is forced to modify her communications if the relationship is a continuing one. Unless she chooses alienation from Bob, her message options are reduced. She may prove her love by always yielding to Bob's wishes. Or she may develop complicated strategies for exercising her autonomy—seeming to yield while not yielding: "What I am demanding (doing, insisting on) is what you *really* want, even though you don't know it," or, "It's for your own good, not mine, that I'm doing this."[3] Bob, in turn, in order to feel loved and maintain a harmonious relationship with Sue, may simply "not see" Sue's autonomous acts, or he may collude with her strategy, seeing her expressions as evidence that she is yielding to what he really wants.

The limitations in Bob's capacity as a receiver of Sue's messages restrict the possibilities of their relationship and may lead to "pathologic" communication patterns in the couple's appropriate efforts to maximize the relationship given those restrictions. In continuing human relationships the restriction in variety of any part of the system limits the system as a whole. When there is little differentiation or variety there can be little playfulness or creativity. As suggested in Chapter Two, a reduction in the variety and in the probabilistic nature of contingencies in a system will limit the ability of the system to adapt to new circumstances.

The Contextual System: Control, Organization, and Temporal Chaining

The actions of another are not the sole, or even necessarily the main, determinants of a person's behavior. Neither Bob nor we

---

[3] Further illustrations of such *double-binding* messages are given in Chapter Seven.

as researchers can expect that Sue will automatically respond with, say, a y_b act each time Bob emits an x_c act. Chapter Two and Figure 1 imply that Sue's specific behaviors will derive probabilistically from multiple influences—including Bob's prior action. In this sense, other variables may *constrain* or *inform* Sue's behavior. We can easily think of a number of such influences: Sue's momentary mood; the history of her relationship with Bob; and her own prior background in relation to the subject Bob has touched upon.

In Part Three we shall examine the informational contribution of some of these variables. We shall ask to what extent a marital pair's uniqueness as a couple contributes to patterning their behavior when they are engaged in conflict. We shall examine the extent to which the nature of the conflict situation constrains behavior. We shall attempt to gauge the constraining effects of maleness and femaleness and of three early stages of marriage on behavior in conflict situations.

In a technical sense such variables may be said to communicate with behavior. That is, they select from multiple possibilities, enhancing the probabilities of some behaviors, reducing the probabilities of others. In our formal data analyses we shall examine their effects, looking on them simply as variables in the way that Bob's prior action is a variable for Sue's subsequent response and her action is a variable for his response. Such analysis is consistent with Chapter Two and Figure 1. But logically variables such as the couple, the situation, the sex, and the marital stage are of a different order than the actions of the participants. They are contextual givens. And, whereas Sue's behavior can modify Bob's and Bob's can modify Sue's, with contextual variables the communication is one way. The fact that she is married to Bob, that she is pregnant, that she is a woman may influence how Sue acts; how she acts with Bob at the moment will not reciprocally influence these contextual variables.[4]

In the interaction between Bob and Sue, contextual vari-

---

[4] Some contextual variables *are* subject to influence. For example, Sue might by her behavior change the presumed given of the situation. In Chapter Eight we shall see that couples may convert one contextual situation to another, either creatively or destructively. The extent to which there is two-way rather than one-way communication between behavior and environmental context is a measure of control over one's environment.

ables may exert their effects in either or both of two ways. One way, *control*, is through constraint on the participants' actions per se. Control may be direct (in arguments over money Sue tends to become rejecting toward Bob) or indirect (Bob tends to behave in a nagging fashion in arguments over money, and Sue tends to respond rejectingly to Bob's nagging; an argument over money, then, will exercise control over Sue's behavior indirectly through its effects on Bob's actions). Contextual variables may also exert *organizational* effects. For example, an argument over money may modify not only Bob's or Sue's behavior, but also the pattern of relation between their behaviors (Sue ordinarily tends to respond rejectingly to Bob's nagging, but in an argument over money she tends to respond by placating Bob; Bob ordinarily tends to respond reassuringly to Sue's placating gestures, but in an argument over money he is more likely to react with disparaging remarks). Fortunately, an approach via communication theory and informational analysis can examine both control and organizational effects.

Our discussion suggests that contextual variables operate as signal systems, enhancing some sets of events and patterns among events and attenuating other sets and patterns. A contextual variable thus has in effect a longer time span than the events occurring under its wing. It is in the events, the specific exchanges, of interaction that we are most aware of temporal sequence. In examining the sequence of events, we have been concerned thus far with simple contingencies, that is, that one thing leads to another. However, what enriches and complicates both our lives and our research problems is that one thing leads to another *and* that leads to something else, which in turn leads . . . . In a sequence of interactions, Bob's statement is stimulus to Sue's response, and her response becomes stimulus to his following response, and so on.

It would therefore be natural to ask about the transitional probabilities not only after a single statement but also after a series of statements. If Bob is nice in his first statement, what are the chances of Bob and Sue being nasty to each other ten statements from then? We might also ask whether there is any consistent pattern in a long series of transmissions, whether the communications between spouses consistently move in a given direction.

Analyses of such aspects of ongoing communication between

people fall under the general heading of Markovian analyses (Ashby, 1961; Kemeny and Snell, 1960; Kemeny and others, 1966; Parzen, 1962). The Markov model suggests that if we know the probabilistic contingencies between Bob's and Sue's behaviors, and if we can assume that these probabilities are stable, we can predict the outcome of a series of interactions—how the participants are likely to wind up, how long it will take them to get there, and other characteristics of their interchanges over time (Hertel, 1971; Raush, 1965, 1972).[5] Although it seems unlikely that couples would react to each other in a pattern of fixed contingencies, Hertel (1968) was able to show that the interactions of some newlywed couples could be modeled by a Markov chain generated from their responses to one another. Unfortunately, limitations of our data confined the analysis to a relatively small sample of long chains of interaction between couples, but the results suggest that, at least for some married pairs, the outcome of a series of interchanges evolves from a relatively fixed pattern of mutual contingencies.

Summary

In this chapter we have suggested a methodological and conceptual base for the study of what goes on between people. Communication theory served as our model—both for clarifying our thoughts on the nature of communication and for providing us with a mathematical mode for data analysis. We defined communication as the relation between events in one system and events in another system, and we spoke of information flow as the measurable constraint of one set of events on another. We considered some effects of variety and restriction of variety on communication, and we noted how this might influence a couple's relationship. The context in which communication takes place was seen to exert both control and organizational effects on interaction. Finally, we commented on some temporal aspects of communication.

[5] Parenthetically, the model coordinates with Sullivan's view of personality as "the relatively enduring pattern of recurrent interpersonal situations which characterize a human life" (1953, pp. 110–111). Individuality is, however, neither illusion (as Sullivan would seem to have it) nor truth, but rather a matter of what aspects one chooses to focus on. The model offers a potential, albeit a distant one, for empirical definition of core stabilities, as well as for investigating variation and change (see Raush, 1972).

Interpersonal
Conflict

CRCRCRCRCRCRCRCR

Communication theory provides us with a model that guides our thinking and enables us to explore the effects of a number of systemic properties on the interactions of our couples, but it remains a formal model that provides little if any explanation of why certain systemic properties are related to certain effects. Once we find that Bob very often insults Sue in response to her mocking remarks about his relationship to his mother—and that this interaction distinguishes Bob and Sue from other couples—then the question is why, and communication theory is no help. As noted in Chapter One and by Barry (1970), variables that correlate with marital success (or anything else about marriage for that matter) explain nothing in themselves. For example, research on marriage shows that some variables for husbands consistently correlate with marital "success" whereas there are no such consistent relationships between variables for wives and success. By themselves such results tell us little. The research findings present data in search of an explanation. An attempt to approach explanation leads us to consider the topics of conflict (in this chapter) and what we shall call *object relations schemata* (in the following chapter).

Conflict

The field of conflict research and theory is in disarray, as Fink (1968) makes plain in a review of some of its conceptual difficulties. No one theory holds sway, and this makes for conceptual and terminological confusion. Fink himself argues cogently for a general theory of social conflict in contrast to specific theories for various types of conflict. He espouses a broad definition of social conflict that includes not only overt struggle between two or more social entities, but also covert psychological antagonism. He defines social conflict "as any situation or process in which two or more social entities are linked by at least one form of antagonistic psychological relation or at least one form of antagonistic interaction" (p. 456). This definition is appealing because it takes into account the possibility of conflict between two people even though they do not engage in the usual signs of conflict, such as shouting, arguing, and fighting. All too often a relationship that seems peaceful on the surface suddenly erupts into a violent overt struggle; without the concept of covert conflict such overt behavior would be unintelligible.

Moreover, Fink's definition includes what psychologists (and other students of human behavior) consider a universal phenomenon in close relationships: ambivalence. No matter how loving Bob and Sue are, "at least one antagonistic psychological relation" will, we maintain, exist between them. Even in the closest of friendships negative affect is nestled in with the positive, since no relationship can be totally gratifying. Conflict we shall always have with us.[1]

Functional and Dysfunctional Conflict. Until fairly recent times sociologists and psychologists considered conflict to be dysfunctional (Coser, 1956). Coser, however, uses Georg Simmel's theoretical framework to argue that under certain conditions con-

---

[1] The discussion in this chapter concerns interpersonal conflict and excludes considerations of intrapsychic conflicts.

flict can be positively functional for individuals or groups. Conflict with an external enemy makes a group more cohesive; in fact it has been noted that in times of external threats even those who are prone to break down seem to function better. This aspect of Coser's argument is rather obvious. But another point he makes is less obvious and more relevant to our work on marital conflict. Coser believes that conflict within a group can also be positively functional for that group. He believes that clashes over basic principles are dysfunctional for relationships in a group, but that conflict over a matter that presupposes adherence to the same basic principles has positive value for relationships; it can be an integrating factor and an index of the group's stability. The argument here is cogent. Like Fink, Coser presumes that in any close relationship hostilities and differences are inevitable.[2] Only if Bob and Sue are secure in their relationship can they express their hostile feelings and differences freely and constructively. If they are insecure, they may suppress the hostile feelings and avoid overt conflicts, but then resentments can build up and poison the relationship. The suppression of interpersonal differences and of the feelings attached to them means that less of each person's self gets communicated, and this can lead to erosion of trust. At any rate, Coser argues, the relatively free expression of hostile feelings as they come up can be positively functional for the relationship.[3] "Conflict tends to be dysfunctional for a social structure in which there is no or insufficient toleration and institutionalization of conflict. The intensity of a conflict which threatens to 'tear apart,' which attacks the consensual basis of a social system, is related to the rigidity of the structure. What threatens the equilibrium of such a structure is not conflict as such, but the rigidity itself which permits hostilities to

[2] Coser refers to the Freudian concept of ambivalence but does not develop the idea.

[3] This, of course, is also the thesis of Bach and Wyden (1969). Coser's (1956) term "relatively free expression" means modulated expression; Bach and Wyden talk about fighting fair. An experiment by Thibaut and Coules (1952) provides some confirmation for Coser's position. They found less residual hostility in their subjects when the subjects were allowed to communicate their hostility toward the instigator of their frustration. In Chaper Thirteen we shall return to this point in our discussion of various groupings of couples.

accumulate and to be channeled along one major line of cleavage once they break out in conflict" (p. 157).

Boulding (1962), like Coser, holds that the more hostility is repressed, the more dangerous the conflict is when it breaks out. In his analysis Boulding uses the concept of *symbolic images* (1956), and in his book on conflict (1962) he speaks of the power of symbolic images to generate conflict. Symbolic images seem much the same as *values*. Their power to generate conflict is closely related to the degree of concentration the image represents and to the amount of ambivalence the person has toward what the image symbolizes. By *concentration* Boulding means the degree to which something of central value to the person is represented by the image. Take the value of manliness as an example. Suppose that for Bob Smith manliness, with concomitant ideas of behavior that is dominant, strong, aggressive, potent, unromantic, hard, and the like, is at the core of a self-image that includes a definition of women as submissive, weak, emotional, soft, and so forth. Assume that for Bob this image is very concentrated—it is a central value around which other values are integrated. If Sue were to fail to play her assigned role vis-à-vis Bob, he would be severely threatened; conflict would be inevitable, and it is very likely that such conflict would be severe and disruptive to their relationship.

Destructive and Constructive Conflict. Deutsch's (1969a, 1969b) work on conflict allows us to refine this framework. Like Coser and Boulding, Deutsch distinguishes between destructive and constructive conflict, but he goes further by trying to analyze and characterize the different processes in each. Destructive conflict is characterized by a tendency to expand and escalate so that it often becomes independent of the initial issue. In our first example of a conflict about watching television, Bob and Sue might end up fighting about in-laws and who is the most inconsiderate, forgetting all about the television program. In addition, destructive conflict shows an increasing reliance on threat, coercion, and deception— all tactics that tend to elicit reciprocation in kind. Threat, says Deutsch (1969a), leads to defensiveness and excessive tension, which in turn leads to stereotyping and the closed mind. Constructive conflict, on the other hand, is characterized by a concentration on the issue that is in conflict, use of mutual problem-solving strategies, such tactics as persuasion, openness to the other's viewpoint, and mutual enhancement with a minimum of threat and defensiveness.

Deutsch (1969a) believes that the features of constructive conflict are similar to the processes involved in creative thinking. He notes that studies of creative thinking describe seven overlapping phases:

(1) an initial period during which a problem sufficiently arousing to motivate efforts toward its solution is experienced and recognized;

(2) a period of concentrated effort to solve the problem through routine, readily available, or habitual actions;

(3) a period when, because of the failure of these customary processes, one experiences frustration, tension, and discomfort, which lead to temporary withdrawal;

(4) a stage during this period of withdrawal when the problem is perceived from a different perspective and is reformulated in a way that permits new orientations to a solution to emerge;

(5) a moment of insight in which a tentative solution appears;

(6) a period during which the solution is elaborated and tested against reality; and

(7) a stage during which the solution is communicated to relevant audiences.

These phases of creative thinking are within an intrapersonal framework. In Chapter Eight, where we examine some specific pathways of constructive conflict, we shall modify and extend the descriptions interpersonally.

The Context of Conflict

In the last chapter we spoke of contextual factors that influence communication. Conflict may be considered one such context. Certainly we would expect the interactions and communicative modes of participants to differ according to whether they are in agreement or disagreement over an issue. But conflict itself also has a context. Each person living in close relationship with another comes to learn that within the relationship there are some issues that are "cool" and others that are "hot." We learn, too, that certain times are better than others for raising conflictual issues. Each family over the course of its life together works out rules: there are certain things the members do or do not argue about; they do or do not argue in public, in front of the children, at the dinner table; and so forth. The rules are never quite perfect. Bob can never be wholly sure of Sue's response nor can she be sure of his. A minor interpersonal issue of last week can become a major conflict of this week; an issue that was latent before emerges after the baby is born; arguments over money dissipate now that income is adequate; Sue's growing commitment to a career raises a new issue. Since conflict is subject to multiple contextual influences, the degree, course, and resolution are probabilistically determined.

Although we cannot hope to examine the total contextual system that constrains the dimensions of conflict—if only because we cannot wholly know the context of another's experiences—we can consider a few aspects, here and in subsequent chapters.

The Conflict Situation. In any marriage there are many areas where the spouses have to adjust to one another. Without trying to be exhaustive we can think of sexual relations, relations with in-laws and friends, how to spend leisure time, what to eat and when, sleeping and waking patterns, allocation of responsibilities for various household tasks, finances, and how to treat and take care of children. Then there are the day-to-day desires and interests that may not match. The spouses have to *co-orient* themselves to many things, to use a term of Newcomb's (1953), and this co-orientation will require adjustment and coping with conflict. Obviously, couples differ in the extent to which a particular area is a source of conflict; for one couple disagreements over household tasks may be nonexistent and disagreements over relations with friends may be critical, whereas another couple may reverse this order. Nonetheless, we would argue that the intimate relationship of marriage predisposes to a generic salience of certain issues. Certain situations more than others touch underlying fundamental sources for interpersonal conflict.

One such core issue is that of separateness and connectedness (Hess and Handel, 1959). Under varied terms, this theme emerges in many psychological writings. Erikson (1959) presents the problem of intimacy versus isolation as the fundamental developmental issue of young adulthood, the outcome of which determines the capacity for adult love. Rank (1968) spoke in 1936 of the tension between individuation and fusion as a basic human experience. Angyal (1965) and more recently Bakan (1966) use other terms—autonomy-heteronomy, agency-communion—that refer to the same tensions. Some fifty years ago, Buber (1958) discussed the conflict between I–It and I–Thou modes of experience. Hess and Handel (1959), in a more familial context, speak of the establishment of a pattern of separateness and connectedness as an essential process of family life. Moreover, concepts related to this core issue enter increasingly into discussions of and therapeutic work with disturbed families. Wynne and others (1958) describe the pseudomutual relations of families of schizophrenic patients. Bowen (1971) speaks of the undifferentiated family ego mass in the disturbed family and develops techniques for achieving differentiation (see "Toward Differentiation," 1972); the structural family therapy of Minuchin and others (1967) involves tactics of coupling and uncoupling family subsystems. Clearly the problem—of forming a unity of two (or more) persons without losing the individuality of either—has been of recurrent concern to those who have contemplated the human condition, whether as novelists, playwrights, personality theorists, or therapists.

Although even the most trivial conflict can become a battleground for the issue of separateness-connectedness and for struggles over autonomy, some situations touch more potently than others on these matters. To return to Bob and Sue, their disagreement over a television program is less likely to impinge on the core problem of separateness-connectedness than is the situation in which Bob intends to maintain distance while Sue intends to achieve closeness. Chapter Eleven will examine how the conflict situation affects the specifics of couples' communicative processes.

The Life Stage. Themes of conflict tend to differ at different stages of the life cycle. For example, although it remains a lifelong issue and may periodically revive as a focus of intensity, the connectedness-separateness theme is likely to be particularly salient for the newlywed. With the birth of a child, latent or new issues of discord may arise, centering on the integration of a third member into an intimate two-person group or on attitudes about child-rearing. For example, preliminary work prior to our main studies involved an attempt to engage newlywed couples in a scene about which partner was going to get up in the middle of the night to respond to their (fictional) crying baby. We could not make this scene salient for newlyweds; the usual response was giggling. For couples with a new baby, there was no question about the saliency of the scene.[4]

Modes of handling conflict are also likely to differ with the stage of the life cycle and the length of marriage. Again, our preliminary work offers an illustration: teen-age newlywed partners seemed to us far less verbal and more action-oriented in dealing with conflict than older newlyweds. It might be expected that as couples go through life together they learn more compatible, more adult ways of negotiating conflict. Indeed this is not always or entirely so. In quarrels, a person may be told by the other participant or may become aware himself that he is "acting like a child," and in Chapter Eight we will see instances of "childish" interactions under the stress of conflict. But even such labeling indicates a common acceptance of a developmental aspect of the interpersonal exchanges characterizing conflict. The studies reported in Chapter Fourteen compare the same couples as newlyweds, in the course of the first pregnancy, and after the advent of the first child. They also compare couples who have children with non-child-bearing couples married an equal length of time. In a preliminary way, these studies enable us to examine the contextual influence of life stage on modes of interaction in conflict situations. They also enable us to approach questions of continuity and change in the ways couples handle conflict.

The Male-Female Context. That marriage is between man and woman provides in itself a context for conflict. Seeley and others found in their sociological analysis of a community that "the deepest cleavage in the belief system of Crestwood Heights," a cleavage that went deeper than that related to class or age or race,

---

[4] The scene was discarded from our studies for another reason: it failed to produce enough variation among couples to make analysis worthwhile.

was "created by the striking divergence in the belief systems of men and women" (1956, p. 382). Bernard (1968) also documents the differences. Certainly, differences between men and women in values, orientations, modes of thought and perception, rights, and privileges are preoccupying topics for social gatherings, psychological and sociological investigations, and literary analyses.

Both Coser (1956) and Boulding (1962) observe that conflict resolution is very difficult if the two parties are at odds on basic values. Since basic values are to a large extent shared within the same culture and social class, homogamy (like marrying like) does tend to ensure some congruence of basic values in married couples. And homogamy is the rule rather than the exception for marriage (Tharp, 1963). Indeed, the lack of basic value congruence may well be the reason for the higher incidence of divorce, separation, and marital unhappiness in cross-class marriages (Roth and Peck, 1951) and mixed-religion marriages (Landis, 1952).[5] The findings of Coombs (1966), Udry and others (1961), and other researchers indicate that, by and large, couples share basic attitudes and values. At any rate, for most couples, homogamy and attraction to those who have similar values and attitudes seem to ensure some congruence of basic values. Bernard (1964) makes the point that homogamy, by assuring a certain amount of similarity, does reduce the necessity for marital adjustments in many areas. Yet it is hard to doubt that orientations of the two sexes will differ—whether by nature, by differences in child-rearing for boys and girls, or simply by the effects of stereotyping.

As relations between men and women move toward equality, one might expect even more overt conflict than formerly, especially if it is true, as Coser (1956) says, that overt conflict is more certain when a negatively privileged group becomes aware that it is in fact negatively privileged. As to modes of handling conflict, there is the lore of masculine rages and feminine tears, of male rationality and female emotionalism. In the changing American culture the current legitimacy of this lore is open to question. Just as the feminine swoon has disappeared, we may expect that

[5] Mixed-religion marriages may become less liable to trouble as the ecumenical movement grows stronger—or as the major religions in America become more alike.

more recent tactics of managing interpersonal conflict are undergoing change. Moreover, we may hope that from these changes more creative patterns of conflict resolution may emerge. Chapter Twelve examines in detail the question of male-female differences in handling conflict.

The Individual Couple. A major context for considering marital conflict is the couple itself. The partners have exercised some choice in marrying each other, and they continue to exercise some choice in maintaining the marriage. Their conjoint mode of dealing with conflict will be affected not only by the particular situation, their stage of marriage, and their values as man and woman, but also by their particular relationship. Chapter Thirteen examines how ways of handling conflict are related to the couple's self-defined status as happy or unhappy. Chapters Seven and Eight examine in much more detail the ways in which couples constitute unique systems in their approaches to interpersonal conflict.

The Context as System. Contextual factors do not exert their effects independently. The salience of a particular conflict situation, for example, will depend in part on the couple's style of marriage, on whether the situation impinges on male-female differences, and on the particular couple. Similarly the stage of marriage helps define the particular situation, the salience of sex differences, and the relationship of the couple. Each contextual component seems to exert some limits on the others. The interdependence of the components suggests that context operates as a probabilistic system, the effects of which are other than the sum of the parts. By means of a probabilistic approach to communication we can examine the effects of the contextual system as a whole on the specific interactions of interpersonal conflict, as well as examining the effects of contextual factors individually.

Summary

The early stages of marriage bring together two people who generally share a great deal in terms of cultural values and mutual commitment and trust, but who nonetheless must learn to live with and love one another and thus provide a favorable atmosphere for their children's development. The process of adjustment to one another necessarily entails conflict if for no other reasons than that the partners are two different people of different sexes with a backlog of different relational experiences; the marital state itself presents situations that evoke conflict; and the developmental cycle of family life continually proposes new problems for resolution. The context of an intimate, continuing relationship structures both the sources of conflict and the modes of handling conflict.

We have pointed out that conflict need not be destructive—that, in fact, it can be constructive both for the individuals and for the relationship. Conflicts in marriage cannot be wholly avoided. Efforts to devise modes of handling conflict are imperative if the relationship itself is to develop, if the partners are to approach the ideal that one can love the other as the other is, without losing identity and without destroying the identity of the other. If adults can from their own ongoing experience and action convey to children—as the cycle of development moves to another generation—that communication can maintain individual integrity and mutual regard and even promote growth through the clash of opposition, that is no mean accomplishment.

V

Schemata

In discussing the argument between Bob and Sue, we commented in Chapter Three on possibilities of systemic distortion of communication, and in Chapter Four we noted how values and symbolic images—to use Boulding's (1962) term—might generate and influence conflict. We pointed to the possibility of Bob's incapacity to perceive Sue's statement of her wishes as other than a personal rejection of him, and we suggested that Bob's limitation as a receiver of her messages would in turn modify and limit Sue's capacities as a sender of messages. When Bob assigns Sue a role that defines how they are to interact, Sue's refusal to play this role can be disruptive to their relationship. Her acceptance of the assigned role, however, although perhaps less disruptive, restricts the couple's potential for growth and adaptation to changing circumstances.

But let us not foreclose too readily the possibility that Bob will be receptive and open to change. When Bob states his wish to watch a particular television program, and Sue confronts him with a wish that is incompatible, what were simple statements of intention are transformed into conflict. Bob (and Sue) may accept the conflict for what it is: a simple matter of differences over a television program, which needs to be examined and worked out. Even if Bob initially perceives Sue's opposing wish as a personal rejection, continued communication may shift the conflict out of the frame of reference of rejection. For example, if Sue can remain unthreatened by Bob's image of her as one who is rejecting, she might say, "It's not a question of caring for you; I do love you, Bob, but I've been looking forward to that program all day." If Bob is capable of "hearing" this message, the conflict might then move from the issue of rejection to the simpler issue of the television program. In theory, within continued human communication, it is always possible to clarify meaning by a further remark (see Cherry, 1966, pp. 267–268).

In our daily lives with those with whom we share intimacy there are many issues that are easily amenable to clarification and change through continued discussion. Yet we come to recognize other issues where, despite theory, further communication fails to clarify or offer hope of change. These are the touchy issues, the "hot" topics in which the encoding and decoding of messages in a mutual interchange become subject to massive distortion. On such issues, Henry comments, "the run-in becomes a savage encounter in which not only our self but everything we have ever dreamed or feared becomes the enemy, embodied now in the antagonist before us. The ability to fight a thousand demons hidden inside the visible adversary often gives an angry encounter a nightmare quality" (1971, p. 7). Within an intimate relationship such issues are recurrent. The battle is joined over and over again; or the couple learns the topics, gestures, and comments to be avoided—the Pandora's box that is not to be opened. If the issues are important enough and the relationship is valued, the psychotherapist is called in.

We shall have more to say about these matters in Chapters Seven and Eight in our descriptions of couples' modes of avoidance and engagement of conflict. In the present chapter we wish to examine how interpersonal conflicts and the communications they involve come to have diverse meanings. Given a situation of conflict, what determines whether a message will be sent distortedly or clearly, whether it will be received distortedly or clearly? What determines whether communications will move toward constructive or destructive outcomes, toward stasis or creativity? To consider these questions, and to bridge the gap between the form of communication theory and the content of conflict theory, we turn to the concept of object relations schemata.

Object Relations Schemata

By a *schema* (plural *schemata*) we mean a structure for organizing experience. A schema gives meaning to events. The meanings need not be conscious, but they define the thoughts, feelings, and behaviors that are probabilistically contingent on particular events and their contexts. Schemata are organized structures. To quote Piaget, "contacts with experience . . . do not become stabilized until and unless assimilated to structures; these structures need not be innate, nor are they necessarily immutable, but they must be more settled and coherent than the mere groupings with which empirical knowledge begins" (1970, p. 51). Schemata, as Piaget indicates, assimilate experience. "Psychologically (behaviorally) considered, assimilation is the process whereby a function, once exercised, presses toward repetition, and in 'reproducing' its own activity produces a schema into which the objects propitious to its exercise, whether familiar . . . or new . . . become incorporated. Some assimilation, the process or activity common to all forms of life, is the source of that continual relating, setting up of correspondences, establishing of functional connections, and so on. . . . Assimilation is the functional aspect of structure-formation, intervening in each particular case of constructive activity, but sooner or later leading to the mutual assimilation of structures to one another, and so establishing even more intimate interstructural connections" (pp. 71–72).

Schemata are modified by experience through the process of accommodation. A schema may either assimilate a new experience into a familiar structure, or the structure may be modified in accommodating to the experience. In an earlier work, Piaget (1926) suggests that the development in childhood from an egocentric to a socialized use of language is related to a shift from assimilation to accommodation, and he implies that conflicts between children play a major part in establishing a balance between assimilative and accommodative modes.

Object relations schemata are organized structures of images of the self and others, together with the needs and affects characterizing the relationships between the images; the schemata evolve out of contact with varying psychosocial contexts, and they influence the individual's actual and fantasied interpersonal interactions.[1] Put more concretely, this definition says that Bob's specific interactions with Sue are determined by his images of himself and others along with the positive and negative affects that characterize the schema under which these images are organized (see Boszormenyi-Nagy, 1965). In other words, no new relationship arises like Venus full blown without any antecedents. A new person one meets is assimilated to an object relations schema. There should also be an accommodation of the schema to the reality of the new person— and indeed this is one of the hinges on which our theory about constructive and destructive marital conflict hangs.

Differentiation

The schemata that influence our thoughts, feelings, and actions in relation to others, including the communications we send and receive, may be more or less differentiated. The development of differentiated substructures is part of the accommodative process by which new experiences come to modify an object relations schema.

The question and the degree of differentiation depends in part on the availability of new experiences and in part on their nature. Consider the matter of availability. Bob may have had few experiences with women. His schemata defining relations between men and women may have derived mostly from his own family, and his limited extrafamilial relationships with women may not have disconfirmed these schemata. Bob's mother, for example, may

[1] We have modified a definition elaborated by Anita Lohman (in a personal communication to the authors in 1968) in collaboration with Martin Mayman.

never have directly expressed wishes opposing Bob's father, and Bob's concepts of women do not include the notion of direct confrontation. It may then come as a bit of a shock that Sue states her wishes directly in opposition to him. Bob might first think, "She doesn't love me," or "That's not the way a wife is supposed to be." But if his schemata about women have not been burdened with severe anxiety, he can recognize Sue's reply, "I do love you, Bob, but I really want to watch that program," for what it is. He can learn that all women are not or need not be like his mother. His schemata may come to include a concept of masculine-feminine relations that comprehends open direct conflict and joint resolution. He may even take pleasure in this growth. Sue's schemata about men and husbands may also change through her experiences with Bob. Each partner thus may serve to enhance the development of the other and this too may be gratifying for each of them.

New experiences need to be available for differentiation to occur. But the nature of the experience can inhibit or enhance the possibilities for differentiation. Consider the simple example of the infant who has developed a schema that differentiates out of his world a "what makes me feel really good" on the basis of a few facial features. "What makes me feel really good" is imaged as round with two little circles inside. Whenever anything resembling this image hoves into view (and it can be a simple drawing, as experimenters have shown), the baby coos, gurgles, and smiles. One day, when something that fits this image comes into view, all of a sudden baby does not feel good; in fact, he feels hurt (for example, he gets slapped). To make sense of this experience the schema has to accommodate, become more differentiated. Some round things with two little circles inside do not make him feel really good; what's the distinction? If the baby is not too traumatized by the experience and has more experiences that are good than bad, his schema will accommodate, and he will be able to differentiate expressions on the round thing with two circles. One expression is then associated with "what makes me feel really good" while another is associated with "what makes me feel really bad." If, however, the experience of the infant is terrifying, then he will learn avoidance of "what makes me feel really bad" and anything else that is associated with it or can be assimilated to it. The approach of anyone who triggers that schema leads to avoidance behavior—and the child never learns that he need not be so afraid.[2] The schema thus fails to become differentiated.

Schemata that are differentiated into substructures will assimilate information into the substructures that are most isomorphic with the information. For example, if Bob and Sue have come to differentiate conflicts over minor situations, such as choice of a television program, from conflicts that concern core values, different substructures will come into play depending on the nature of the conflict. We may expect that not only will their communications differ, but also messages that are the same objectively will have different meanings in the two situations. In other words, the substructure selects what is transmitted, what is received, and how messages are encoded and decoded. Substructures may become further refined. Bob and Sue may come to recognize their own and one another's moods so well that they can predict reasonably well the substructures that will be called into play at particular times and places. Where there is failure of differentiation, nuances are lost. Bob reads any and all of Sue's messages as rejection of him or as unfeminine behavior. Usually, undifferentiated schemata read "threat" into a number of sources that may not be threatening in reality and indeed may be benign. The opposite, however, is also possible: a schema may assimilate to benignity events that are objectively threatening.

Permeability

In order for a schema to differentiate, its boundaries must be permeable to new experience. A schema with rigid boundaries cannot form substructures. In the resolution of conflict, Deutsch (1969a) notes three key psychological elements: the arousal of an appropriate level of motivation, the development of conditions that permit reformulation of the problem once an impasse is reached,

[2] Sullivan (1953) makes a similar observation. The experimental paradigm is avoidance conditioning, which does not die easily when the conditional stimulus no longer operates.

and the concurrent availability of diverse ideas that can be flexibly combined into novel and varied patterns. In a conflict situation in marriage, for example, to reach the appropriate level of motivation both parties must see the issue as important enough to need working at but not so threatening as to lead to grossly defensive behavior. The conditions that permit reformulation of the problem once an impasse is reached are that each of the partners becomes aware of the reality of the other's needs and desires and acknowledges them as real while maintaining an awareness of his own feelings. The availability of diverse ideas seems to us to depend on the flexibility of the partners under the stress of conflict.

Each of these aspects—seeing the issue as important, recognizing the other's as well as one's own needs and feelings, and being open to new ideas—depends on the permeability of one's object relations schemata and their substructures. A rigid, impermeable structure prevents learning. Boulding (1962) contrasts the *authoritarian,* who is characterized by too rigid a set of core values or images, with what he calls the *reconciling personality,* one who has identified himself not with a rigid set of values but with the learning process itself.

It may even be that many of those couples who do not share basic values fail to find this out in courtship because one or both parties have too rigid object relations schemata, so that they tend to see each other in terms of past relationships instead of as real contemporary people. We are tempted to think along these lines by the work of Newcomb (1965) on interpersonal attractions in a college sample of housemates. Nonauthoritarians in his sample judged rather accurately who agreed with their attitudes and values and let their attractions be determined accordingly. Authoritarian personalities, however, tended to perceive more agreement in attitudes than actually existed in those to whom they were attracted. Interestingly enough, Dymond (1954), in a study of a small group of couples who were asked to answer Minnesota Multiphasic Personality Inventory items for both themselves and their spouses, found that the unhappy spouses made significantly more errors in assuming similarities between mates, when in fact they were dissimilar, than in assuming difference where similarity actually existed. Such data are compatible with the theory that a rigid object relations schema will assimilate even contradictory events to its own structure.

Anxiety, Object Relations Schemata, and Marital Conflict

A rigid marital structure that cannot tolerate conflict results, we believe, from the presence in one or both parties of rigid and relatively undifferentiated object relations schemata into whose Procrustean bed all must fit. The circumstances for such developments are insufficiently known. Considerable clinical evidence suggests, however, that rigid schemata are closely associated with severe anxiety and signals of severe anxiety. The state of severe anxiety or the threat of its arousal seems to institute an inhibition in recognizing, responding to, and learning from new experiences (Sullivan, 1953). Under the threat of anxiety, events become assimilated to schemata associated with the earlier anxieties with which the person was unable to cope as a child. In these conditions it is an old (and now inappropriate) battle that is being fought or avoided.

One might well expect that of all human relationships marriage has greatest potential for redintegrating the schemata associated with anxieties of childhood—schemata concerned with trust, giving and receiving love, autonomy, expression and inhibition of anger and other feelings, concepts of maleness and femaleness, closeness and distance. To return to our earlier example, if Bob's childhood relations with his mother were such that all conflicts in wishes between his mother and himself became transformed into questions of total love versus total hate, and if young Bob was unable to achieve any sense of mastery over these recurrent scenes, then we need not be surprised at his failure to be attuned to Sue's "I do love you, Bob, but I really want to watch that program." Sue's expression of a wish contrary to Bob's has touched off in him an earlier and frightening schema. Bob can, of course, avoid this sort of thing by denying that he has any wishes of his own that are contrary to Sue's and indeed coming to believe that this is true. A seeming equanimity might be achieved, but such a solution takes a severe toll—most obviously on Bob, whose relations with Sue become extremely inhibited, but also on Sue who must come to feel the unreality and falseness of their relationship. Over time we may expect that the mask of Bob's agreeableness will be periodically shattered by his mounting resentment. Since there has been no overt issue of conflict, Sue will find it difficult to understand these outbursts of feeling.

The sketch from the position of Bob's schemata is one-sided. Sue has her own developmental history. Bob's accusations about love may touch off a schema associated with *her* earlier anxieties— for example, "a girl is not aggressive," or "a girl does not express her wishes directly," or "you are an unloving (or ungiving or selfish) child." Sue then may respond to Bob as though his accusations had a hidden reality. She may come to avoid any expression of her own desires, not simply as a matter of discretion, but because she believes fundamentally that she is unloving, or selfish, or unfeminine. We might expect that she too will break periodically and disruptively from the boundaries of guilt.

The object relations schemata we have been discussing are those associated with overwhelming anxieties of childhood. These are especially sensitive to arousal, and their arousal revives the reactions of the immature child. Once they are aroused, ordinary rational discourse or action has little or no effect on the outcome. There are, of course, other object relations schemata that are not associated with anxiety. Our responses to new events are interpreted in terms of our former experiences—schemata derived from recurrent similar experiences in the past. But when severe anxiety does not impose its distorting lens, the schemata can be progressively modified. There is then, optimally, a continual dialectic and balance between the assimilation of new events to existing schemata and the accommodation of schemata to new events.

Interpersonal conflict can be thought of as both a test of a schema and an opportunity for its development. A conflict that presents something new, requiring assimilation or accommodation, tests the capacities of the schema—its permeability to new information, the rigidity of its boundaries, the differentiation of substructures. The more flexible and differentiated the system is, the more able the person is to accommodate to the reality of another, to learn new things about others and himself, and thus to change. To put the matter another way, the more flexible and differentiated the system, the less threatening is newness in the other, the more appropriate is the affect, and the more able the person is to learn from the interaction. On the other hand, the more rigid and undifferentiated the system, the more necessary it is that the other conform to it, the more likely it is that rigid pigeonholing will occur, the more threatening otherness or newness is, and therefore the less likely it is that learning and creative resolution of interpersonal conflict will take place.

Summary

This chapter presents the concept of schemata as organizing structures for experiential events. Schemata determine the meanings of events and the contingencies they have for thoughts, feelings, and actions. Object relations schemata develop from experiences with others; they organize images of oneself and others and the relations between oneself and others. New events become assimilated to these schemata or the schemata may change to accommodate to experience.

What is communicated between interacting partners depends on object relations schemata. Should a schema relevant to a particular situation be relatively undifferentiated for either partner, nuances will not be communicated. To the extent that the boundaries of a schema are relatively impermeable, the possibilities for modification and learning are reduced. Anxiety inhibits differentiation and rigidifies structural boundaries.

The theory presented here mitigates the controversy between intrapersonal and interpersonal theories of personality (see Miller, 1963). The structures we are talking about (object relations schemata) are personality structures (intrapersonal), but they need others to become operative. Indeed, which schema will be activated depends on the other as much as on oneself. A person's schemata, in other words, need to be "informed" in order to initiate reaction —and the input not only activates a schema but can also lead to its transformation or change if the person is sufficiently impressed by the information and flexible enough to use it. Interpersonal conflict thus presents a test of a schema and an opportunity for further differentiation. The processes of constructive and destructive conflict between people can be understood on the basis of an understanding of the relative flexibility, differentiation, and integration of schemata of the participants.

The concept of object relations schemata forms a bridge between communication and conflict theories. It also helps avoid the twin dangers of a monadistic view of personality and a purely role-playing or stimulus-control view.

VI

Couples, Stages,
and Scenes

◈◈◈◈◈◈◈◈◈◈◈◈◈◈

With the present chapter we turn from the broad outlines of theory to the specific examination of the interactions of intimates as they face interpersonal conflict.

Couples

Investigators at the Child Research Branch of the National Institute of Mental Health in Bethesda, Maryland, a suburb of Washington, D.C., began in 1961 to obtain the names of newly married couples from local marriage license records. Since there is a general trend for marriages of young couples to take place in the community of residence of the wife's parents, selection through marriage license records predisposes toward a more residentially stable sample than is likely to be found in a highly transient urban area. Furthermore, because the couples were required to spend some

evenings at the research offices, their addresses needed to be within
about a half hour's driving radius of the research center. In the
interests of obtaining a relatively homogeneous sample a number of
other criteria were used. Only couples in which neither partner had
previously been married were considered. Since preliminary investigations had suggested that both teen-age couples and older couples
were likely to present atypical patterns, the age range was restricted;
husbands selected were between twenty and twenty-seven, wives
between eighteen and twenty-six. Both full-time students and full-
time military personnel were eliminated from the design, again with
the purpose of predisposing toward a less transient population.
Educational limits were also set; all subjects had to have completed
high school, but none was to have achieved a degree beyond the
baccalaureate (although a number of the subjects were undertaking
part-time postgraduate education). All couples were white. A final
criterion, established before the couple entered the study, was that
wives not be knowingly pregnant as of three months after marriage.
Couples were initially approached by a letter explaining the general
purpose of the study and offering a modest fee for their voluntary
participation. About 70 percent of those who were approached and
who fit the screening criteria agreed to participate.

The study started with forty-eight newlywed couples. Loss of
data due to inadequate tape recording led to a final sample of forty-
six. Mean and median age for the husbands was twenty-four, for
the wives twenty-two. Median education was between two and three
years of college for both sexes. In all cases wives were working.
Although it was not planned that way, couples divided into approximately equal thirds of Protestants, Catholics, and Jews. It was a
relatively homogeneous, urban, middle-class, stable sample of young
married couples.

Stages

The study was designed to follow young couples through
selected periods of their early marital lives. Given a practical need
for selecting among possible points of time for a developmentally
oriented study, the investigator chooses the points of transition
between one stage and another. D. W. Goodrich (1961) suggests

that the transactions peculiar to a developmental stage are often introduced by a specific *transition event*. For example, the wedding is a transition event between the stage of mutual commitment and the stage of initial marriage; the birth of the child is similarly a transition event toward early stages of parenthood. "As each new stage is ushered in by a transition event, new demands are placed on the family members and new developmental issues assume critical importance, becoming the foci for growth during subsequent developmental transactions" (Raush and others, 1963, p. 369). An investigative spotlight centering on the transition event is particularly appropriate for a focus on the crisis associated with developmental change. Because the data it spotlights may primarily reflect transitional phenomena, however, such a focus may miss the characteristic aspects of particular developmental stages themselves.

On the other hand, a developmental investigation may choose to focus on time periods that are likely to reflect maximum stability. In that case, the investigator gains power to achieve characteristic stage descriptions, although his data may fail to provide information about the sources that led to stage changes. The choice made by the NIMH investigations was a compromise between these alternatives.

Newlyweds. Couples were initially seen during the fourth month following marriage. The investigators hoped that by the time the partners would have worked out some of the salient roles and relations that would characterize their lives together. At the same time the couples would not be too removed in time from the developmental issues posed by the new stage, and their modes of working through stage-related problems would not be too retrospectively distant. By the fourth month of marriage our newlywed couples had settled on a place to live and had established some regularities in their day-to-day living with one another.

Pregnant and Nonpregnant Couples. The second stage of investigation was during pregnancy. For reasons similar to those stated above, the seventh month of pregnancy was chosen. By the seventh month of pregnancy the early physical symptoms, such as morning sickness, have disappeared, and the focus of concern has shifted to the reality of the coming child. The wife's protruding abdomen and signals of fetal movement emphasizes this reality. At about the seventh month wives often quit work to spend their time buying the layette and furnishing the nursery.

For each couple for whom pregnancy occurred a matched couple who had been married approximately the same length of time was chosen. On the average, pregnant and matched couples had been married eighteen months by the second period of data collection, and there was less than a month's difference between first and second data collection periods for a pregnant couple and its matched couple.

The obvious difference between pregnant and matched couples is in the occurrence or nonoccurrence of pregnancy within the approximately three years set by the investigators for data collection. Any couple who did not become pregnant in that time was excluded from the pregnancy sample. The selection of matched couples obviously depended on which of the couples became pregnant. From the start, then, the selection was not random. Most of the matched wives (nine out of thirteen) at the second data collection period said "no" to the question, "Do you wish you were pregnant right now?" whereas only two of the pregnant wives answered "yes" to the question, "Did you become pregnant while you were practicing contraception?" One of the latter wives admitted she "forgot" on that occasion; the other said that the couple had agreed to practice contraception but that it was too much trouble. Other systematic differences between pregnant and matched couples, even at the newlywed stage, when pregnancy had not occurred for any, are suggested by Raush and others (1970). Couples who became pregnant tended to use more "I" related words than matched couples, who used relatively more "we" words. The interpretation of these authors contrasts a *task orientation*, predisposing couples toward having children earlier in marriage, with a *relationship orientation,* emphasizing the interpersonal aspects of the marriage. Undoubtedly, a number of other unknown factors influence one couple and not another to begin a family, and these factors bias the results of our studies.

Parenthood. The third stage of investigation followed the birth of the child. Couples were again seen in the fourth month after childbirth. By this time most new parents have overcome their fears of handling the baby. The digestive disturbances and generalized fretfulness that often characterize newborns have generally faded (Spock, 1957), and both parents and child have adjusted to some predictable routines.

The Final Sample. Mobility was a factor that kept some couples from longitudinal participation in the study. Nevertheless, overall continued participation was very high. Only six couples failed to respond to a follow-up by mail conducted in the early months of 1969. It seems safe to assume that the majority of couples who do not appear in either the pregnancy-childbirth or the pregnancy-matched sample were not lost to the study by reason of lack of cooperation.

Of the forty-six couples for whom there were full sets of Improvisations at the newlywed stage, thirteen completed all three phases—newlywed, pregnancy, and childbirth—with sets of codable Improvisations at all three phases. The data of the following chapters are thus based on forty-six newlywed couples (ninety-two people), thirteen couples who became pregnant and thirteen matched couples who did not, and finally thirteen pairs of parents. The first couple included in the study was seen in January 1961; the last newlywed couple was studied beginning in June 1963. Data collection for all stages was completed by December 1964.

Procedures

At the newlywed stage, four evenings were spent with each couple, two in the home and two at NIMH. The first meeting was a joint interview at home that focused primarily on the general background of the spouses and how they came to be married. The second evening was at NIMH where each partner was interviewed separately. The content focused on the individual's past history, in this case including childhood experience with his or her own family and adolescent sexual experiences. While one partner was being interviewed, the other filled out questionnaires. The evening concluded with administration of the Color Matching Test (Goodrich and Boomer, 1963) to the couple. The third evening was also spent at the institute. Again each spouse was interviewed separately, this time with the focus on current relationships with his or her own family of origin, sexual behavior in marriage, and the prospective view of becoming parents. Again questionnaires were administered, and the evening concluded with the Improvisations. The final meeting was a joint interview in the home.[1]

Investigations at the later phases were somewhat briefer. Data collection for the pregnancy and nonpregnancy groups consisted of questionnaires and experimental conflict situations, a single joint interview followed by individual interviews for each spouse, and the Improvisations. These procedures were repeated for the stage following the birth of the first child.

The Improvisation Scenes

The Improvisations, developed by Paul Blank and Wells Goodrich, were designed to engage couples in quasi-experimental, quasi-naturalistic situations of interaction where because of the separate instructions given to each partner a conflict of interest was created. Four basic scenes were used.[2] In each, efforts were made to get the couples personally involved in the situations so that they would be themselves as much as possible rather than play stylized roles. To attain this end, no standardized set of instructions was read to each person. Instead, although the general form was the same, the instructor was free to vary the instructions to make them maximally relevant to the individual. For example, in the first scene the wife was told that she had spent the whole afternoon preparing a special dinner for their anniversary; then she was asked about her husband's favorite foods, what she prepared really well, how she would prepare the table, etc. Instructors spent time with each person before each scene trying to establish personal involvement in

[1] Specific procedures and the results of some analyses of data are discussed more extensively in Goodrich and Boomer (1963); Goodrich and others (1968); Raush and others (1963); Ryder (1966, 1970); Ryder and Goodrich (1966); and Ryder and others (1971).

[2] A fifth scene was added in the later phases: the spouses are told they are parents of a newborn baby. It is suggested to each partner that he or she is extremely tired this night and is resolved to get a good night's sleep. The partners are placed on cots alongside one another, the lights are turned off, and they are presumably asleep when a recording of distressed infant cries is played from an adjoining room. The scene, though vivid, produces little variance in the verbal interactions of couples, and it has thus far not been analyzed.

the mood of the scene. Emphasis was placed not on role-playing but rather on the couple being themselves when they got together for the scene.

The setting was arranged to look as much as possible like a living room. In fact, the room used had been a large living room in what had formerly been a children's treatment residence. The room was furnished with a comfortable sofa, some lamps, and other accessories. On one side of the room, visible but obscured by semi-darkness, were chairs and recording equipment for the observers. From another side of the room a door led to a kitchen; from the opposite side a door led to a bank of offices; the fourth side contained a large picture window. The kitchen and an office were used for individual instructions to each spouse and for the entrances and exits of the scenes. Couples were encouraged to ignore the observers and to concentrate on one another. It would, of course, be naive in the extreme to believe that the presence of observers had no effect on the interaction, but listening to the tapes and comparing the results of our analyses to independently obtained material from the couples convinced us that the data from the Improvisations were not determined primarily by observer effects. Moreover, only once did a couple break the scene to ask a question of the observers. The setting was designed to create the atmosphere of a couple alone in their living room.

Scene One: Anniversary.   Husband and wife are jointly informed that it is their first wedding anniversary. The wife then goes to the kitchen with her instructor, the husband to an office with his. The husband is told that this ought to be a very special celebration and that he has planned to surprise his wife by taking her to their favorite restaurant that evening. He is asked what restaurant he would choose. He is told that he has already made the arrangements and ordered the dinner and is asked to specify what he would order for his wife and himself. After the meal has been planned, the husband is told that he has already paid in advance for everything. The wife separately is told that she wishes to make this a very special ocasion and has taken a half-day off work to prepare a very special dinner at home. She is asked to plan the meal and to imagine the setting (candles, china, wine, etc.), the instructor gauging his remarks to the orientation of the couple. The dinner is cooking and almost ready as her husband comes home from work. The husband and wife enter the living room from different doors, she from the "kitchen," he from the "front door." They enter at a signal.

As can be seen, this is a fairly innocuous conflict. Both parties have done something for the other to celebrate a happy occasion; the only real problem, it would seem, is that, because they wanted to surprise one another, money will be lost and time expended that need not have been. This scene takes the least amount of time to bring to a conclusion of any of the four. It is, indeed, not atypical for one of the spouses to give up his or her intention rather quickly with a statement like: "Well, I prefer a home-cooked [or restaurant] meal anytime."

Let us speculate on how the participants experience these situations. It must soon become obvious to each spouse that the experimenters have set up a conflict between the two of them, but they have no indication of what the experimenters want. Do they want each one to hold out to the bitter end for his or her intention? Do they want them to agree quickly? Each spouse might also wonder what the experimenters will think if he or she gives in. While these concerns about the experimenters are in their minds, the newlywed couples also must be thinking of one another and their relationship: "If I hold out adamantly for my position, how will he [or she] take it? What will he [or she] feel?" On the one hand, there is the press from the experimental situation to hold out, to continue the conflict; on the other hand, there is the press from the relationship—and perhaps from the presence of observers—to find some solution.

Scene Two: Television. Together the couple is told that the wife is pregnant and will soon (in a couple of months) deliver. Separately the husband is told that there is a special television program that evening at nine o'clock that he would like to watch, and he is asked what such a program might be. If the husband refers to a program that is part of a weekly series, it is suggested that this is much more special. Choices made by husbands range from sports programs such as the World Series to presidential news conferences. The wife is told that there is a special panel show on at nine o'clock, in which psychological and psychiatric authorities will discuss the naming of babies and the implications of various names for the psychological health of the child. She is told that, since they have not settled on names for the baby, she especially wants them both to watch this program. After the individual instructions the couple is brought into the "living room." They sit down on the sofa in front of an imaginary TV set. Before starting they are told that it is a few minutes to nine.

Here the aim of the researchers is to set up a situation where each person wants something that is incompatible with what the other wants. With regard to the objects desired both cannot be satisfied at the same time. Moreover, unlike the first scene in which even the loser may gain from the outcome, here the loser gets no positive compensation. The situation is a common one in any relationship, though the content, of course, will vary.

Scene Three: Husband Distant; Scene Four: Wife Distant. These scenes are reciprocals of one another and are designed to be more emotionally involving than the first two scenes. For scene three the instructor asks the husband whether he has ever experienced the feeling of not wanting someone next to him, of wanting nothing whatsoever to do with that person, of being unable to tolerate that person's presence, and of wishing to be left alone. The instructor supports these feelings by acknowledging that everyone has felt this way at one time or another. The husband is then instructed that this is precisely the way he feels about his wife tonight. To reinforce this mood, the instructor asks the husband whether anything about his wife or anything she has ever done had made him feel this way about her. If the husband denies having felt so intensely alienated from his wife—and almost all husbands at the newlywed stage deny having felt this way—the instructor asks the husband to imagine an incident or quality about his wife that would disturb him that intensely and makes further attempts to induce the proper mood. Meanwhile, the wife is asked to imagine that her husband has become like a total stranger to her, very unlike the man she married. He has been cold, distant, and irritable. This has gone on for several days, and she feels it is disruptive of their marriage. Tonight she has decided she must try to overcome the barrier and reestablish closeness. The scene begins with the husband staring out the window as the wife enters the room.

Scene four is the reciprocal of scene three. In this case it is the wife who is distant and the husband who wants to reestablish closeness. This scene begins with the wife in an armchair, reading a magazine as her husband returns from an errand.[3]

These scenes were obviously much more threatening than the first two to the couples, especially at the newlywed stage. Most couples became heavily involved in the later scenes. The reasons for distance varied from real grievances against the spouse ("You don't talk to me any more"; "You spend too much money"; "You bring the boys over here and ignore me"; "You're sloppy around the house"; "You don't let me see my parents enough") to imagined grievances ("If she showed interest in another guy, I'd feel that way"; "If he saw his old girl friend, I'd feel that way"; and the like) to things outside the marriage (trouble at work, for example) that would make one spouse feel like not talking to the other. Unlike the anniversary and television scenes, in which the confrontation between opposing desires is specific and in a sense simple, the issue of the third and fourth scenes is more complex. It is the relationship itself that is at the center of the conflict. The problem here is an integrative one—the relationship rather than a specific decision is at stake. The partner who succeeds in maintaining distance against his partner's attempts to establish closeness may win the battle but must lose in the relationship.

It is not surprising, then, that the latter two scenes were often threatening to the couples. In Chapter Five we discussed object relations schemata that were associated with issues of closeness and distance and the further associations of these schemata with earlier anxieties. The scenes seemed to evoke schemata (or parts of schemata) that perhaps had not surfaced previously. A number of newlywed partners expressed surprise and consternation, commenting in discussions after the Improvisation that they never knew their spouses could be so cold and distant. On occasion subjects even expressed surprise at their own anger. The partner or the subject

---

[3] We may comment retrospectively that the consistent ordering of the last two scenes makes it impossible to estimate the effect on wives of having seen their husbands play the distance role. This is unfortunate methodologically. Wives in scene four could be motivated to get even and could have learned about playing the role from the previous scene.

did not match previous images, and this often produced a sense of shock and threat. Postsession discussions, in which examiners often took an active part in attenuating affective residues, were essential, and these sometimes continued over into the following meeting with the couple.

In these scenes the spouse with the distance set must have strongly felt the dilemma of being pressured by the experimental setting to refuse communication while being pressured by the relationship and the partner to communicate. The partner who was trying to reestablish closeness, caught in a situation he or she had not experienced before with the spouse, had the problem of trying to break the barrier. The question was how flexible and varied he or she could be in these efforts. Depending on the couple and how the threats and problems of these scenes affected them, the conflicts could be handled relatively easily or with great difficulty. The greatest difficulty occurred when the scene became a power struggle between the two parties and both remained inflexible.

At no time did the instructions for the scenes ask the couples to reach agreement. Indeed, the fact of discrepancy between the sets of intentions given to husband and wife was unstated and was left to emerge only as the scene gradually unfolded, although some subjects guessed it. In this respect, the Improvisations differ from techniques such as Strodtbeck's (1951) "revealed differences" and Goodrich and Boomer's (1963) Color Matching Test (see also Ryder, 1966), which explicitly call for the joint settlement of rather explicit differences.[4] The Improvisations thus broaden the range of possibilities open to the couples.

Summary

Our studies of marital interaction in situations of conflict began with forty-six young recently married couples. Thirteen of these were studied again in late pregnancy and shortly after they became parents. Another thirteen couples for whom pregnancy did not occur served as a comparison sample for the pregnancy stage.

[4] Ravich's (1969) Interpersonal Game-Test presents couples with an experimental bargaining situation closer in form to the Improvisations but content-free.

In order to study the interactions of couples in dealing with interpersonal conflict, four scenes were developed. Two of these dealt with specific issues; the other two concerned the relationship itself. Conflict was evoked by presenting the two partners with contrasting intentions. All enactments were recorded.

In the following two chapters we present an overview of what transpired between husbands and wives as they went about coping with the conflicts created for them. The overview results from clinical examination of the protocols and tapes in their raw form. This examination suggests some of the nuances of interaction and points to some patterns by which two people meet problems and attempt to establish a life together. Moreover, study of the protocols in their raw form can help us concretize some of the rather abstract notions of the earlier theoretical chapters. More formal analyses and further concretization are reserved for Part Three (Chapters Nine through Fifteen).

VII

Coping with Conflict: Avoidance

Consider the dilemma faced by the subject in each of the scenes. Very early in the scene he is likely to become aware of the discrepancy in goals between himself and his partner. If he continues to follow his instructor's directives, he may win the point but he thereby risks disrupting the bond between himself and his partner. Each partner is thus faced with a tension between individual wishes and the requirements of the relationship.

In the sense that all the scenes impinge on a dialectic between individual autonomy and mutuality, they reflect one lasting ongoing concern of marriage (see Hess and Handel, 1959, 1967). As Bach and Wyden (1969) note, in such conflicts between intimates, to win—to get one's way—is often to lose, and to lose is often to win. For this reason our studies gave little or no attention to the issues of many conflict experiments, which seek to identify who wins and who loses, who dominates and who submits, and the conditions for such outcomes. Indeed, as we shall see, even resolution or failure of resolution of a particular conflict says little about a particular marriage. Some easy resolutions seem little more than evasions; some failures of resolution seem to set a frame for constructive recognition of the other.

In this and the following chapter we consider some of the modes employed by couples in their attempts to cope with interpersonal conflict. We describe styles of interpersonal communication, their intermeshing, and their continuity over time. We begin here to relate specific interactions to the concepts of communication and conflict in the earlier chapters and to examine in detail constructive and destructive approaches to conflict in intimate relationships. The course of our descriptions also provides an opportunity to convey qualitative aspects of the Improvisations.

Coping by Avoidance

The instructions to the couples instigate conflict. If we can assume that couples understand the instructions and are motivated to cooperate, then conflict is present. The distinction needs to be made between avoiding interpersonal conflict in relationships and dealing with interpersonal conflict by avoidance. It is the latter that we discuss here.

A way out of interpersonal conflict is to deny the problem, that is, to distort the instructions and pretend that no conflict exists. In about 15 percent of the scenes over the three phases, couples avoided direct confrontation with one another. For example, Mrs. Greene[1] in the anniversary scene discusses the dinner she has cooked; only after twenty-five "acts" (interchanges) does Mr. Greene at last indicate that he has made tentative arrangements for eating out, but he simultaneously offers to call these off and himself suggests eating at home. In the husband distant scene, Mr. Greene continues to maintain distance but avoids any direct confrontation with his wife—there is something he wants to take care of, he suggests; it is only that he doesn't want to be disturbed; it has to do

_____

[1] In this and following chapters the names of the couples are changed and minor additional changes are made in descriptions and quotations so as to preclude identification.

with his work; he will tell her about it tomorrow. Fourteen months later, Mr. Greene chooses the same form of externalizing and of avoiding responsibility—either his own or his wife's—for distancing. He is not unique in externalizing the issue of distancing. One-fourth of the husbands in the sample chose a similar way out. Most often they said it was their jobs that were to blame; sometimes it was a headache or other physical symptoms.

Avoidance and Limited Involvement. Although avoidance suggests some degree of inhibition, it is not by itself necessarily an indication of disturbed communication. At times for some of our couples we had the impression that the issue was simply not that important. This was particularly true for the first scene. Thus, Mr. Morris and Mr. Vreeland never get to the point of starting their plans for taking their wives out to dinner; in each case there is playful, positive-toned discussion about the wives' menus and arrangements, and in each case the husbands propose going out *after* dinner. Similarly, Mrs. Everett accepts her husband's plans immediately, suggesting that they can save her dinner for the next evening; she gives the impression that, despite the instructions, she really wants to go out to dinner. Even for the closeness-distance scenes it is not always easy to judge whether avoidance represents less than full involvement in the issue, reasonable discretion, or a defense against real or imagined dangers.

Avoidance and Defense—the Double Bind. Although some potential interpersonal conflicts seem to be avoided because the issues are relatively unimportant, this is clearly not true of all instances of avoidance. In most cases avoidance of the conflict suggests defense against confrontation with the partner. The cues for avoidance as defense are not that the schemata touched on by the instructions are insufficiently relevant to evoke conflict, but rather that the schemata associated with confrontation of the issue or the partner are in a sense too important and too anxiety-provoking.

Sometimes avoidance as a defense lies fairly close to the surface. One partner may signal the other that it is advisable to close off or to defer communication. Mr. Arthur, for example, suggests that his failure to state the basis for his distancing is, "I'm liable to get mad—really mad." Mrs. Arthur is skeptical: *"You* get mad?" Mr. Arthur retreats: "No. But I might hurt your feelings, and I

don't want to do that." Interview material suggests that as a couple
the Arthurs are highly pragmatic people, rather lacking in imagination, who show little evidence of intimacy or concern with each
other's inner experiences, while they are much concerned with maintaining an appearance of agreement. The data do not tell us why,
but it is clear that Mr. Arthur sees a direct confrontation with his
wife as dangerous. One has an impression that his concern is less
with his wife's sensitivities than with ruffling his own rather tightly
controlled equanimity. But even with couples who are engrossed
in efforts at mutual understanding, one sees on occasion an overt
statement about the dangers of confrontation. Mrs. Gorman, for
example, says: "If I do sit down and talk about it, I will get angry
with you, and I will be very vicious and nasty, so I want you to
leave me alone." Or Mrs. Harman states: "I'm not going to tell
you, because it hurts my feelings."

Usually the defensive aspects of avoidance are less overt and
probably less conscious. As noted above, blaming the job or a
physical symptom is a common way of divorcing onself from the
interpersonal implications of distancing. The partner says in essence:
"It may look like I'm rejecting you, but really it's entirely something
else." Even this avoidance of threat is at times underlined by inter-
posing words or acts of endearment or by implicit promises of future
communication. Mr. Morris, for example, uses a preoccupation with
the office as an excuse for distancing; to his wife's offer of help he
says, "I don't think so, *honey* [italics ours], I appreciate it, but I
don't think you can do much to help me right now." Mrs. Morris
in scene four claims that she is just tired, but later implies a promise
that they will discuss things in the near future. Mr. Birne also
denies any personal element in rejection of his wife; he underlines
this by kissing her good-night. Words or gestures of endearment
reinforce the denial of interpersonal conflict.

Such avoidance sometimes edges on a "double bind," a
communication situation initially defined by Bateson and others
(1956),[2] that involves the simultaneous communication of two
initially exclusive messages in the context of an important relationship. In a true double bind, the recipient is unable, because of

---

[2] See also Bateson and others (1963); Watzlawick and others (1967).

threat, to comment on the fact that one message denies the other. Moreover, he is unable to escape the field. In the development of patterns of pathological communication, it is assumed that such messages are persistently repeated. When a distancing partner says, in effect, "there is no problem between us," but implies anger toward his spouse by gesture and expression, and moreover suggests that he would be even more angry were the other to take his words at face value, then he is inducing a double bind. Some of our couples approach this, saying something like, "There is no issue between us, and besides the issue is too hot right now, so let's talk about it later." The saving grace is in the latter phrase—the inference of future, more direct communication. The message is mixed, but if the spouse accepts it the scene is likely to end relatively benignly— though unresolved. Less benign are scenes that evoke what might be called an escalation of avoidance.

Escalation of Avoidance

Externalization, Denial, Disqualification. When conflict-avoidance scenes escalate they often assume a truly double-binding character. That is, in the context of an important relationship, repeated contradictory messages are sent that can be neither escaped nor commented on. One technique for escalating avoidance is to pile on extraneous denials. The Cranes provide a clear illustration. In the anniversary scene Mr. Crane avoids giving any indication of his plans for going out, and in the television scene he yields almost immediately to his wife's wishes. The persistence of defensive avoidance becomes particularly striking in his distancing scene, however:

3W: Why don't you, uh, come sit down?
4H: I don't feel too good right now.
5W: Well, how are things at work?
6H: Oh, [ten-second pause], all right, I guess. Well, fair to middling.

. . .

9W: Is something bothering you?
10H: Well, yes and no. I don't feel too well, and things are on my mind.

. . .

13W: Are you sick?

14H: Well, I don't feel too good. I have a little bit of a headache, little upset feeling.

• • •

19W: Is something at work bothering you?

20H: [Pause for six seconds] Yeah. Well, not really bothering
me. I'm naturally concerned with anything at work.

We may note here, along with the denial, Mr. Crane's constant disqualifications of his own statements ("I don't feel *too* good,"
"well, yes and no," "not really bothering me") contradicted by "I'm
naturally concerned."[3] By her emphasis on work and on Mr. Crane's
physical condition, Mrs. Crane cooperates in externalizing the issue
of their relationship. Nonetheless, she is confused by Mr. Crane's
not-quite-made statements and retractions; her question about work
in 5W is repeated in 19 W. The static, cyclical quality of the interchange continues with nothing ever quite getting said. Mrs. Crane
attempts to break from the pattern, but without success:

31W: Well, is it something I've done, or . . . ?

32H: Oh, no, no, no.

33W: Are you sure?

34H: Uh huh.

Mr. Crane cannot, however, allow even his own denial to
stand unqualified. He goes on to say that whatever it is that is bothering him is complicated and hard to explain. There is a double-binding quality to this: one message says there is nothing for Mrs. Crane
to be concerned about; the other message is a seduction toward
increasing her concern. Mrs. Crane continues to probe, but no
clarification ensues:

43W: Well, what is that you were thinking about that's bothering you?

44H: It's just a minor problem. More a series of problems—all
things. I don't feel too well, I have a headache, and a

[3] For a discussion of disqualification see Watzlawick and others
(1967).

little upset . . . stomach feels a little upset, I was thinking about the job and social problems and so on.

To this Mr. Crane later adds that he might have the flu and also
may be overworking. The scene ends with a pseudoresolution: he
will see a doctor.

At the newlywed stage, Mrs. Crane was far more direct than
her husband. As her reason for distancing in scene four, she accuses
him of playing poker with the boys when he is presumably working
late. Two years later there appears to be a slight shift in their
patterns of interaction. Mr. Crane continues his disqualifications,
and the double-binding aspects of his communications remain prominent; he is, however, a bit more direct:

4H: I don't feel well.
5W: Are you sick?

· · ·

8H: Well, not sick—that type of thing. I am just, you know,
      kind of fed up.

· · ·

11W: Is something the matter?
12H: Well, you have been getting under my skin lately. A little
      bit.
13W: How?
14H: Just bothering me. Nothing serious. You just, you bitch
      too much.

Although disqualified by "nothing serious," an interpersonal
complaint is stated. Mr. Crane also later adds that he is tired, but
there is no multiplication of the avoidance issues as in the earlier
scene. Another double bind is posed, however: not only is a serious
complaint, calculated to provoke discussion, presented with the
counterstatement of "nothing serious," but also when Mrs. Crane
attempts to discuss the issue, Mr. Crane accuses her of bitching at
him again.

Mrs. Crane, two years later, is less direct. Although she
eventually does state an issue, her initial approach is to deny that
there is anything important going on, while at the same time implying that there is a matter of concern: "It wouldn't do any good to

tell you about it anyway." The couple's unawareness of their patterns of communication is indicated by the fact that Mr. Crane,
despite his own constant evasions, says to his wife: "I mean if there
is something bothering you, then you [should] just come right out
with it."

The Rogerses play conjoint supportive roles in piling up
denials. In the husband distant scene Mr. Rogers initially denies
that anything is bothering him, yet remains distant. After sixty-four
acts he claims a hard day at the office and some difficulty with his
boss. Mrs. Rogers's initial attempts at closeness are externalized
denials of the possibility of a serious issue between them: "I'm going
to tickle you"; "It's a nice night"; "Let's go for a walk." Mr. Rogers
mentions the office difficulty only after Mrs. Rogers shifts to say:
"Honey, you know what we said: if anything was bothering you,
you'd tell me." But even then, he later goes back to generalized
complaints of tiredness and nervousness. The scene, as might be
expected, gets no place.

In the wife distant scene, there is a wild, hysterical quality
to Mrs. Rogers's piling up of denials: she wants to call a friend; she
wants to work on her sewing; she has to do the dishes; she wants
to wash the floor; she is preoccupied with a magazine article; she
wants to go for a walk; she is tired. Mr. Rogers at one point asks,
"Anything I've done [that's bothering you]?" Her response is,
"No, no. You've been fine, honey. No, nothing you've done." Again,
there is no progressive development in the couple's communications.
The scene ends in a peculiarly hysterical statement by Mrs. Rogers:
"Why don't you sit down? Why don't you—why don't you come?
Why don't you sit down, read a—read a magazine? Nothing to do.
I'm not mad at you, you're not mad at me, I just want to, I just
want to—OK? Please."

Things have not changed much when the Rogerses are seen
again more than a year and a half later. Mr. Rogers's proclivities
for avoidance are fostered by Mrs. Rogers's flighty externalizations.
Her attempts at reducing his distance are directed toward external
distraction: inviting friends over; asking for help with dishes; suggesting visiting friends; claiming a phone call her husband needs to
respond to; and the like. It is she who offers him excuses—he is
tired or he is sick—while he continues to claim through some 270

acts that there is nothing wrong, that he is just tired. There is much
laughter by the wife throughout the scene, but there is no humor.
The entire scene is static. The early statements could well be interposed with later statements, and vice versa, with little or no difference. There is little communication in the sense discussed in
Chapter Three. The investigators finally end the scene.

The externalization and piling up of denials continue in
scene four: she has to cook something; something needs fixing; she
is trying to read a magazine; she is thinking about going for a walk.
Later, to his insistent probing, she just says that it is all his fault,
and he should know. Still later, she protests:

459W: There isn't any problem. I just want to go for a walk.
514W: There is nothing wrong. There's nothing wrong.

The scene goes on for 528 acts, when it is finally interrupted by the
investigators. In neither scene is there a tangible issue or any change
or development of interaction. There is no way for the scene to end
except through exhaustion.

Not all couples who defend against interpersonal involvement by externalization and denial become so locked in. Although
as newlyweds the Abramses locked in on mutual avoidance and
continued over a long series of interchanges without resolution, six
months later they have an easier time. A cue to the change is given
in their postscene comments at the newlywed stage, in which each
partner suggests that he sees the other as a helper in "snapping out
of bad moods." In the later husband distant scene, Mrs. Abrams
does this effectively. Mr. Abrams begins with multiple complaints:
his work, the boss, his mother, his wife's cooking, coming home on
a hot bus. She takes up these issues directly, explicitly, and pa-
tiently. He offers her a consolation via denial: "Doesn't it help to
know it's not your fault?" She doesn't buy this: "No, it doesn't
help to know." He asks: "What do you want me to do?" She replies: "Snap out of it." And he does. The modes have not changed;
both externalize. Yet the fact that Mrs. Abrams can comment on
the absurdity of her husband's position breaks the potential double
bind, albeit arbitrarily. The pattern continues again six months later
when the couple is seen for the third time. Despite the externaliza-

tion both deal more directly with one another. Moods are seen as somewhat impersonal, and the other's role is to help one "snap out of it."

Avoidance Manipulation—the Tangential Reply. Another form of externalization that presents a particularly destructive double bind should be noted. In this, avoidance is used for what seems fairly conscious manipulation.[4] The tenor is, "You know what's wrong, and I won't tell you," but, in addition, a tangential remark is used to disqualify the other's concern. The Joneses employed the tangential reply dramatically in the husband distant scene:

> 1W: Bob, would you like something to drink or some ice cream? [Pause] Bob? [Pause] Look, honey, I know you well enough to know that when something is wrong you often withdraw, you don't talk about it, I can't get anything out of you. I'm not the kind of person who can go on like that. I've got to explode and get it off my chest and talk about it. Now, something has been wrong for several days. Bob, is anything wrong at work? Have I done anything? We can't go on avoiding the situation. Please listen. Stop pouting, and tell me what's wrong.
>
> 2H: Did you feed the cat?
>
> 3W: Yes, but that has nothing to do with what we're talking about. Please talk to me. Tell me anything that's wrong. What is the matter with you?
>
> 4H: [Sighs] You know what's wrong.

Mrs. Jones replies again at length, denying that she knows what's wrong, pointing out that they can't continue marriage ignoring one another, claiming that she loves him very much. To all this, he replies: "Did you let the cat out?" The scene continues with her lengthy appeals to him countered by either his insistence that she knows what's wrong or his cool extraneous remarks ("Do you want a coke?" "Did you cash the check?") The scene ends with no resolution and the wife distraught. The partners reverse the tables in the following scene: it is now Mrs. Jones who requires her hus-

---

[4] Ruesch (1957) refers to this as the *tangential reply* and notes its manipulative function.

band to guess what's wrong, and it is she who comments to his probes: "The flowers need straightening." Such statements disqualify the other. They say, in essence, "Nothing you have just said makes any difference; neither you nor your attempt to communicate exists for me."

Avoidance as Conjoint Defensive Contract

The avoidance of intimacy and the approach to conflict via externalization and denial seem often a conjoint, mutually agreed on defensive contract. One tends, of course, to believe that among white, middle-class, college-educated American adults, such inhibitions always represent disturbances of individual development continuing from earlier psychogenetic stages. Although there are suggestions that the Allens' avoidance of engagement with one another is related to the individual anxieties of each partner, as a couple they seem to have worked out nonescalating conjoint modes of avoidance and denial. In none of the scenes over three phases and two years is there any direct interpersonal confrontation. Issues for distancing are unstated or externalized. Attempts at resolution consist of offering the other a present. Each accepts the other's distancing without much overt concern. In interviews the Allens speak of themselves in terms of "we" less than any other couple in the sample.[5] Their marriage seems oriented toward the accomplishment of specific marital tasks rather than toward aspects of their relationship. The conjoint defensive avoidance in this case, so far as we can see, fosters a stable and tenable marriage, although an observer might well find it dull.

The Millers, on the other hand, although they, too, externalize and deny interpersonal involvement, demand much more of one another than do the Allens. Avoidance here is clearly distrust of the partner. The distrust is played out communicatively in symmetrical, competitive guilt-induction, against a background of passive resentment at the partner's intrusive manipulations. The newlywed anniversary scene foretells the tenor of the couple's relations throughout the Improvisations.

[5] See Raush and others (1970), in which the Allens are discussed in greater detail.

4W: . . . What's today?
5H: Today. What's today? Oh, I can't remember.
6W: You better—after all I did today.

• • •

12W: Bob, I'm waiting for you to tell me.
13H: What? I don't remember.

Among our couples the initial teasing interplay in this scene is not unusual. The wife's tone of demand and the husband's tone of passive hostility is, however. When he does state his intention, Mr. Miller avoids any direct expression of his own wish:

21H: Well, we're supposed to go out.

• • •

23H: Well, we had somebody come in from out of town at the office.

• • •

25H: . . . and we are kind of obligated to go.

Mr. Miller then denies (despite instructions) remembering the anniversary at all:

27H: I was so busy, I couldn't remember it. Really.

Mrs. Miller responds with a series of guilt-inducing maneuvers:

28W: And I have an anniversary card and a present [for you].

• • •

32W: I worked so hard and made everything for you.

Mr. Miller's resentment is suggested by a slip:

33H: Well, I'm sorry, I didn't forget [sic]—or remember.

The guilt-induction continues:

44W: I'm really disappointed, dear.

• • •

46W: . . . Now you will have to get me an extra present.

The television scene opens with an intrusive, distrustful, steamroller attack by Mrs. Miller:

1W: At nine o'clock we're going to watch this show, and it's going to help us decide about a name for the baby. So, you can look at it with an open mind, without being stubborn, without giving no good reason for any of the answers. Any of the names that I give you, you say "no" to.

2H: What show—what show?

3W: A show about naming babies. Because this is the season when there are a lot of babies born. And they have so many doctors, and they are all authorities, and they know a lot more about it than you do.

The attack continues until Mr. Miller yields. Mrs. Miller, victorious, says, "You change the channel. Go on."

His distancing scene offers an arena for Mr. Miller's resentment. Again, he cannot face her directly. The issue is denied; instead he says there is an appointment he must keep. She threatens to be gone when he returns. He leaves as she says, "You're taking a big chance." She winds up shouting: "Come back here."

Mrs. Miller's pattern of guilt-induction continues when it is her turn to be distant:

11H: Is there any reason for it? Anything I've done?

12W: No, nothing really. Nothing you can put your finger on right this second.

            •   •   •

14W: Nothing, nothing. I'll get over it.

            •   •   •

16W: . . . Let's just forget it. What did you do in the day's work?

Three years later and four months after the birth of their baby, nothing much seems to have changed. The denials, and a pattern in which passive resentment and guilt-induction reinforce one another, continue. In the husband distant scene:

16H: There's nothing that you can do. Let's just forget about it.

In the wife distant scene:

25H: What brought on the mood?
26W: You should know. If you don't there's no point in me telling you. It wouldn't do any good anyhow.
27H: Well, why don't you try it and see?
28W: I did it once before. You ignored my requests. So forget it, that's all.

For each partner there is a discrepancy between overt communication and covert metacommunication. Mr. Miller overtly insists that there is nothing wrong between them; on a covert level he manages to imply that something is very wrong and that there is something his wife can do about it that she is not doing. The communications and metacommunications of Mrs. Miller are also mutually contradictory. She is, however, somewhat more variable. At times her overt communication says, in effect, "I'm very much concerned about you, but you don't care about me," while the metacommunication is, "Whatever you say and feel is unimportant." At other times communication and metacommunication reverse. The relationship between the Millers, as enacted in the Improvisation scenes, is an interplay between conjoint double binds.

Neither the Improvisations nor the interview data tell us much, unfortunately, about the individual concerns from which the above patterns evolve. One might speculate that for each partner some specific psychosocial core issue touches off a primary affect that, because of earlier dangers, arouses anxiety. Defense against anxiety, in conjunction with the primary affect, leads to the characteristic behavior. Figure 4 suggests a hypothetical relation between schemata for the Millers. On an interactive level Mr. Miller's passively aggressive behavior arouses potentials for depression over loss of love in Mrs. Miller. Her response of active aggression and guilt-induction arouse potentials of anger in Mr. Miller along with anxieties over the expression of his own aggression, thus leading back to passive aggression. Each partner thus feeds into a cyclic interchange with the other.

MRS. MILLER   MR. MILLER

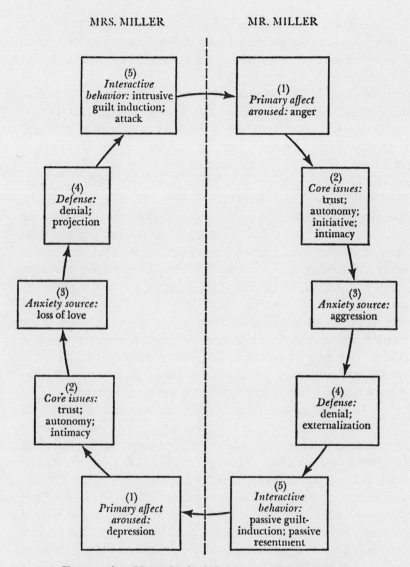

FIGURE 4. Hypothetical Schemata Interrelations

The Improvisations might lead us to expect a marriage of considerable strain. In fact, there is no evidence that this is so. So far as one can judge from several sets of interviews, the Millers are astonishingly well matched. Individual developmental problems, such as those implied in the hypothetically dynamic description above, might well be inferred if only from the facts that Mr. Miller is the younger of two brothers by nine years, and that Mrs. Miller is the older of two sisters by eight years. But repression and denial pervade each of the Millers' individually presented background descriptions: neither admits to awareness of any childhood problems; according to their reports neither set of parents ever fought or showed signs of marital strain. The Millers' descriptions of their own lives and of the interactions between the two of them are entirely bland. Despite the interviewer's perplexity, probings, cajolings, enticements, and skepticism, there is never a break in the bland denial of difficulties. Their values and tastes are exactly the same, their marriage is entirely happy; when either one might be upset, the other simply leaves him or her alone. They "try not to worry each other with complaints"; they "never have hurt one another." Mrs. Miller places consistent emphasis on her easygoing nature, Mr. Miller on his responsible self-control. According to them they have no disagreements, they understand each other, their relationship has not changed at all in almost four years, and it is exactly as they expected it to be. Neither partner is at all introspective about his own or the other's feelings. Both are involved in many social activities, sometimes jointly but often separately.

In a sense, the Improvisations are characteristic. In fact, the spouses describe them as reflecting what would happen in real life. Massive denial and avoidance of the interpersonal typify their Improvisations, individual self-descriptions, and joint self-descriptions. But the Improvisations are misleading in that they bind the couple into a field of conflict, whereas in their daily lives the Millers offer one another ready escapes from the possibilities of confrontation. In real life the precise intermeshing of the Millers' denials is supported by their clear role definitions and by their coordinate values. Moreover, avoidance as an interpersonal mode is wholly syntonic with each of their individual ego-modes of denial. The syntonicity between individual and interpersonal styles enables a coalition in which each partner is both protected from and protector against potential intrusions of anxiety from his own or his partner's wishes. That the Millers might come to want something more of one another, as is hinted in the confines of the Improvisation scenes, is of course possible. In that case one might expect the marriage to become severely strained, since neither can cope with his own or the other's feelings. But so far the marriage is a perfect match—entirely stable and, indeed, static. The present and probable future of the Millers' relationship is that of the passive-congenial, utilitarian marriage described by Cuber and Harroff (1965) as a life-style that asks for nothing more of marriage than convenience and comfort.

Summary

Avoidance, Communication, and Marriage. In some Improvisations, avoidance seemed to represent a nearly conscious decision to disavow the instructions—either because the relationship weighed more strongly in the balance or because the issue itself was not particularly salient. The line between distortion and discretion, although theoretically discernible, is not always easy to draw in a particular interaction. And the fact that a couple handled a particular scene by avoidance tells us, by itself, very little.

Avoidance as an approach to coping with existent interpersonal conflict can be readily inferred when, despite rejection of interpersonal implications by the participants, the intensity of conflict escalates and this is a repeated pattern of relation. The piling up of successive denials, externalizations, and disqualifications, the presentation of contradictions between communicative and metacommunicative levels of discourse, and the sending of double-binding messages all serve as indications of conflict and defense against confronting interpersonal issues. An obvious avoidance technique that predisposes toward escalation is the manipulative use of extraneous, distracting, and irrelevant remarks while maintaining a stance of rejecting the other.

Most often we found that partners colluded with one another in avoiding interpersonal issues. Couples form a system in which the husband's externalizations and denials will often be supported by parallel externalizations and denials by his wife, and vice versa. The conjoint defensive contract nevertheless usually fails when avoidance is used for coping with an existent conflict. That is, when each partner denies any interpersonal implications of his own or his partner's behavior, yet by his actions implies fault in the other, the interpersonal tension mounts. And since the underlying interpersonal issue is avoided, there can be no genuine mutually satisfactory resolution. Resolution fails, or is arbitrarily one-sided, or has a spurious quality.

From a communicative perspective, escalation of avoidance through a multiplicity of denials is analogous to channel overloading. The recipient presented with too many discrete messages within a short interval of time is faced with decoding difficulties. Receipt is apt to be garbled, with the result that no information is conveyed in the messages themselves. What may be conveyed to the sensitive recipient is the sender's metacommunication: his anxiety; his effort to overwhelm the receiver; his garbled, sometimes contradictory messages; the quality of "protesting too much." If the recipient is attuned to the metacommunicative level, information is transmitted. By shifting his own response to the metacommunicative issues ("Whoa, let's take one thing at a time"), the recipient can sometimes intervene to modify the sender's pattern. Occasionally, we have seen at least hints of such shifts—such as between the Abramses. More often the situation remains static with little or no information exchange. A collusive joint pattern of avoidance seems particularly likely to foreclose the possibility of shift to a metacommunicative level.

The double-binding avoidance poses a different communicational problem: a message A is sent, and an appropriate response might be B or C, but simultaneously message A' is sent, to which the appropriate response is non-B or non-C. A common example from the closeness-distance scenes is: "Nothing is bothering me, and it wouldn't do any good to tell you anyway." The most favorable intervention for clarifying two pieces of information that are mutually contradictory is again a metacommunicative comment using the contradiction as the primary information and pointing out this very fact. Were such a comment possible, by definition the situation would not be double-binding. In fact, the data yield no illustrations of metacommunicative attempts to break double-binding avoidance messages. Either one aspect of the message is responded to, provoking reemphasis on the other aspect, or the response is a reciprocal double-binding statement.

In the manipulative use of distraction, the recipient denies that any information has been received. An example noted above is the response, "Do you want a coke?" to the statement, "Please tell me what's bothering you." Here the contrast between communication ("Do you want a coke?") and metacommunication ("I am ignoring what you say") is particularly sharp.

Whatever the specific pattern, where avoidance predominates as a mode for dealing with interpersonal conflict, one is struck by the static quality of the interchange. The same remarks and actions are apt to be repeated early and late in the sequence, and even when they differ, early and late could well be interposed with little appreciable loss. Scenes do not develop, although they may end with arbitrary pseudoresolutions. There is no sense of movement or growth. That is—as suggested in Chapter Three—if what one partner says makes absolutely no difference to what the other says and vice versa, then successive interchanges over time can neither bring the two people to a common point nor even give increasing precision to their respective positions. The progressive development of form and differentiation that informational exchange is capable of yielding through a succession of events is absent.

On the other hand, a static quality can derive from a rigidly deterministic informational exchange system: wife's A statement always evokes husband's B statement, which in turn always evokes wife's A statement, and so on. Both informational patterns are suggested by the data. The former seems more typical when one partner escalates denials or uses avoidance as a conscious manipulative technique. The latter seems more typical when the data suggest a conjoint defensive contract in the service of avoidance. Because the avoidance mechanism encompasses little variety, exchanges move readily, as we have seen, into recurrent cyclic patterns.

From the standpoint of information and communication, avoidance conveys little to the recipient. From a longer range view, changes over time in the marital relation where avoidance is predominant cannot evolve from what goes on between the partners. Changes in the relationship might, of course, derive from the press of external events—social and economic changes, the birth and growth of children, or the occurrence of crises. But the relationship itself would not be a primary medium for learning, and the forces supporting avoidance as a mode of interpersonal coping serve to promote a static equilibrium with inertia working against change.

Avoidance, Conflict, and Marriage.   When we find some seven couples who, against all reasonable statistical odds, avoid interpersonal implications in some three to six scenes, the suspicion seems warranted that a characteristic mode is being presented. The discussion in Chapter Five suggests that avoidance as a characteristic mode of coping with interpersonal conflict is related to schemata in which interpersonal confrontations signal anxieties that cannot be faced openly. The schemata become impermeable. External events are excluded, denied, distorted. The tenor of this discussion suggests that avoidance as a characteristic mode of handling interpersonal conflict is pathological. The suggestion is warranted if by pathological we mean a condition that inhibits growth and development of a relationship. Avoidance of interpersonal involvement bars the possibility of learning and differentiating aspects of the other and so of modifying one's own relations with the other. When patterns of avoidance are conjoint between two partners, possibilities of change intrinsic to the relationship are precluded.

Avoidance as a pattern of communication in dealing with interpersonal conflict is from the above point of view unsuccessful. Even so, the evidence from our studies clearly refutes the idea that avoidance as a technique for dealing with marital conflict signifies a disruptive, unstable marital situation.

On a pragmatic level, ignoring such criteria as growth, development, learning, and potential for change in a relationship, the word *pathological* can be misleading. The marriages of those who avoid and deny interpersonal involvement are, so far as we can see, no less stable, no less compatible, no less comfortable than other marriages. Indeed, it would be coordinate with a mode of avoidance and denial that partners would report and perceive themselves as happy in their marriages. The constricted patterns of communication and the inefficacy of joint problem-solving, do not, within our limited findings, preclude relationships that are subjectively satisfying to the participants.

Some couples appear able to maintain consistent patterns of avoidance through at least the early years of their marriage without undue strain. Such couples in their real lives avoid interpersonal involvement. Avoidance as a mode of coping with interpersonal issues seldom comes into play, then, since interpersonal issues seldom arise for them. As an interpersonal mode, avoidance seems pragmatically benign (1) when, as is likely, it is syntonic with individual intrapsychic styles—repression and denial, deemphasis of feeling, lack of introspection; (2) when the participants have and accept clearly differentiated roles; and (3) when it is in the context of a bond of mutual affection. Given all three of these conditions, avoidance does not escalate interpersonal tension or does so only momentarily. Spouses whose relations satisfy the conditions are perhaps even more apt to describe their marriages as happy and more predisposed to have stable marriages than are those who are more involved with one another.

VIII

Coping with Conflict: Engagement

When an interpersonal conflict exists, avoidance of the issue precludes immediate constructive resolution. Yet avoidance can have a constructive function when used consciously to defer an issue that does not demand immediate resolution. As such it is a metacommunication that says, "Let's hold off until a more propitious moment or until we've had some time for thought or until momentary passions have cooled a bit." The Improvisations attempt to create nondeferrable issues of conflict in intentions. Even so, some participants on some occasions did try to attentuate conflict by giving a temporal perspective to avoidance—a "not now, but later" statement. When avoidance is clearly a recurrent defense against interpersonal involvement, however, there is little hope for resolution of interpersonal issues, although some couples seem to find this condition a satisfactory modus vivendi.

Facing up to issues of conflict obviously offers greater hope for constructive outcomes; yet ordinary experience tells us that this hope can come to ruin. Our purpose in this section is to examine some modes by which marital partners engage in conflict.

Variety versus Constriction

As indicated in Chapter Three, the greater the variety in a system, the greater its potential for information transmission. That is, the more categories there are that are distinguishable, the greater the information that may be conveyed; for example, the letters of the alphabet convey more information than does a binary on-off system. As we noted, however, the decoding capacity of the receiver must contain variety at least equal to that of the sender or information will be lost. For example, a mother may be capable of expressing any of a large number of states, but if her child can only distinguish between pleasurable and unpleasurable messages, the subtleties of the mother's communications are irrelevant from the point of view of the information transmitted to the child.

So, too, with our couples. If each partner, for example, communicates only, "Do this and I will love you; do that and I will hate you," or if one partner decodes diverse messages from the other as solely, "I love you," or "I hate you," information will be sharply restricted. Each may come to learn exactly what to expect from the other, but each knows or comes to learn only a small amount about the other. The potentials for new learning and for change are meager.

Constricted Repertoires. Like avoidance, a constricted repertoire for dealing with interpersonal conflict produces a static quality in a sequence of interactions. And like avoidance a limited repertoire does not necessarily evolve into high conflict. Some couples with very limited response ranges show no signs of emotional escalation. However, in contrast to avoidance, the restricted repertoire does not in itself preclude easy and mutually satisfactory joint resolutions to conflict.

A case in point is the Friedmans. In each scene, each partner states his or her position quickly and directly. There are no embellishments or elaborations. In the anniversary scene, he yields to her in eighteen acts; in the television scene she yields to him in five.

In the third scene he avoids interpersonal implications by claiming not to feel well. She, however, is persistent in pointing out that his lack of affectionate behavior has gone on for several days. Her tone is one of concern, and although her statements are repetitive, as are his, we got no sense of nagging. The scene ends with his promising to talk about it tomorrow. Despite his not yielding verbally, he has moved to sit beside her on the couch. Her final comment, "Men!" accepts his stand good-humoredly. In the last scene she complains that he repeatedly invited some neighbors she doesn't like. He offers to invite them less often, and finally accepts without apparent strain her unwillingness to discuss the matter further. Their actions and postsession comments give the impression that both Friedmans are fully involved in the scenes. It is their approach that is circumscribed. In their case, there is no evidence that the circumscription is defensive. Variation is slight, there is repetition, and there is little sense of development; but, although there are no frills, there are also no complications. Neither partner ever threatens the other, and there is no sense of covert hostilities. One observer of the scenes commented that a "solid meat and potato sort of affect" passed between them and that in the scenes the pragmatic spouses were "like two work horses being comfortable with each other rather than [like] lovers."

For the Friedmans, the restricted response range seems to represent a compatible intermeshing of individually characteristic styles lacking in current defensive overtones. A contrasting situation is presented by the Harrises. Like the Friedmans, they show a very limited repertoire of behaviors in dealing with interpersonal conflict. They too are direct in confronting one another with their aims, and their dealings with one another are devoid of ornamentation. Unlike the Friedmans, however, the Harrises begin and end conflicts in an undifferentiated battle of wills. Conflict is joined immediately, and each responds to the other with coercion, threat, and mockery, even when the task is to establish closeness. Although there is escalation in tonality, insult tending to move toward physical coercion, no new information is conveyed by any act. Mrs. Harris suggested the latter herself at one point. Following the wife distant scene during late pregnancy, in which Mr. Harris, although presumably trying to reestablish closeness, ends by threatening to throw her out, Mrs.

Harris commented: "I couldn't figure out what he was trying to do." The limited repertoire, the lack of development, the joint attacks, the failure to reach mutually accepted resolutions continued without change in the three sessions and two years of marriage over which the couple were seen. The Harrises are not unique. Other couples show similar patterns of repetitive, undifferentiated attack and counterattack and repeated failure in resolution, and, as far as we can see, within the first several years of marriage the patterns may remain stable.

From indications outside of the Improvisations, the Harrises are both bright and capable people. Yet their interactions with one another have a startlingly primitive quality. One is reminded of nothing so much as a battle between three- or four-year olds consisting of repeated interchanges between "Yes, I will," and "No, you won't." The newlywed television scene, for example, went:

24H: . . . You just sit back.
25W: Oh, I don't want to.
26H: Now, sit there, there you go.
27W: No, I want to watch that.
28H: Just sit back.
29W: It's my TV.
30H: Tough. I'll break it.

Even the language is that of the three-year old, resembling the egocentric speech described by Piaget (1926).

The restricted repertoire of the Harrises seems less a matter of style and cognitive limitations than first a matter of defense against interpersonal commitment and then regression when the defense is threatened. Closer investigation suggests that their toughness with one another is mostly surface and illusion, a way of allowing a covert intimacy that each must deny overtly. The interviewers were struck by the discrepancy between what they expressed verbally and what they actually did. Each partner avoids expressing any feeling or affection for the other; each sees himself and the other as tough and independent. She wants a baby only so she can quit work; he doesn't care—having a baby is entirely up to her, and she'll have to take care of it. But surprisingly, in action they share many things. They shop together, he helps her make curtains, and, despite his verbalized rejection of their infant, he knows quite a bit about babies, and she tells about his playing with the baby and making toys for it. She, in turn, seems a surprisingly effective mother, warm and nurturant in her observed handling of the baby. Each of the Harrises seems to be rather fragile, fearful of his or her own needs for closeness and nurturance, superficially insistent on toughness and autonomy. The intermeshing of their relationship supports and protects the defensive front, yet allows each partner covert affectional gratifications.

For the Harrises restriction of range seems a conjoint defense that is part of a marital style expressed in high overt conflict, while the marriage is sustained by covert mutual support. To use Cuber and Harroff's (1965) terms, the marriage seems "conflict-habituated." For another couple, the Gallers, covert support is missing. The Gallers are young newlyweds who, like the Harrises, engage in intense conflict with a restricted range of responses. In the anniversary scene, for example, Mrs. Galler insists that her husband eat her fried chicken or choke, against his persistent stand that they are going out. In the television scene she threatens to smash the set. In the final scene, she bases her distance on the complaint that Mr. Galler never talks to her, while his efforts at achieving closeness consist of physical coercions and some seven repetitions of "come here." The restriction of range and primitiveness are intensified by the conflict, but unlike the Harrises, the Gallers do not seem specifically defensive about the current interpersonal conflict. Rather, they seem to reflect limited cognitive capacities enacted in a context of high conflict. Interviews show overt dissatisfaction and much undercutting of one spouse by the other while giving little indication of hidden sources of satisfaction in the relationship. We had the impression that the marriage was a joining of two impulsive, narcissistic people, each an only child, whose decision to get married after two dates was based primarily on good looks. The couple separated and divorced shortly after they were seen as newlyweds.

Restriction of variety in response to interpersonal conflict limits growth and creativity. The restriction itself need not predispose toward intense conflict or preclude mutually satisfactory resolution, if it occurs in the context of open awareness of joint affection, as in the case of the Friedmans. When conflict is high, however, or when restriction is either defensive against interpersonal involvement or a regressive response to the threat of involvement, then a limited repertoire tends to foreclose resolution. In either case the situation is likely to remain relatively static.

Varied Repertoires. Couples who are capable of a variety of responses in conflict situations enact interesting scenes. One often gets a sense of process in these scenes: exploration (sometimes highly elaborate) is followed by resolution (sometimes unique and creative), and that is followed by a working-through not only of the practical ramifications of the resolution but also of the feelings of each partner. Moreover, one has the impression at times that for the couple it is less the solution that counts—and, indeed, the issues are not always resolved—than the process itself. The primary concern seems not so much with the solution as with searching out the hidden dimensions of the situation. Thus, for example, when Mrs. Bradley in the television scene yields to her husband's wishes, he refuses to accept an easy victory, saying jokingly, "Don't think you're going to win that way," and the scene continues with a mutual exploration of feelings.[1] Similarly, other couples may spend considerable time exploring the implications of various possibilities before reaching a decision—or failing to reach one. The implications, moreover, are not simply practical, but often have to do with each partner's feelings: "Well, does it really mean that much to you?" "You're really set on this, aren't you?" "Is it a big thing for you?" Practical issues may be similarly explored: "Well, [if we eat out] will the dinner keep?" "Could we switch the reservation to tomorrow night?" "How about giving the dinner to the Thomases, next door?" "How long does your program last?" "Will there be a rerun?" "Could you watch it at the neighbors?" The Harmiks, for example, develop a unique resolution to the anniversary scene:

87H: Well, first I'm going to eat your dinner.
88W: OK.
89H: And apparently you're not going to be eating very much.
90W: No. I don't usually eat a lot when I cook.
91H: Then we're going out to dinner so you can eat.

[1] See Raush and others (1970) for a further discussion of this couple.

Variety and Constructive Conflict. As suggested above, exploration often continues after the specific acts that signify joint acceptance of a resolution of the conflict. Concern about the relationship extends beyond the scene itself. Indeed some 10 percent of the acts at the newlywed stage are composed of postresolution comments, and many couples devote considerable effort to reestablishing a sense of mutuality. Most often this occurs in the first two scenes as a "cooling out" by the winner, an attempt to ameliorate hurt feelings. For example, Mr. Moran, after his wife has agreed to go out to dinner, expresses concern about the home-cooked meal spoiling. Even following his wife's reassurance about this, he asks, "Are you sure?" and a moment later, "You won't be hurt?" On occasion the interplay involved in salving the real or potential injuries to the partner goes so far as to reverse the initial intentions. For example, after she has won her case for eating at home, Mrs. Berner begins to shift to arguing for going out, if that is what her husband wishes; he meanwhile insists that he is perfectly happy with his agreement to stay home. More commonly one spouse attempts to make some compensatory gesture—suggesting that they go dancing after dinner, celebrate twice, or eat out but have dessert at home.

In the more intense distancing scenes, reconciliation, if it occurs, is more apt to be at a physical level, the partners moving to sit beside each other or kissing and making up. The impression is that, despite resolution, the tension is yet too high to permit an exploratory working-through. A general process is, however, suggested by two couples who are each so direct that they may very well capture within the space of a single scene a process that requires much more time for most couples. Mrs. Birne comes to the point quickly about her reason for distancing, and the spouses reach a rapid resolution:

20W: You're always nagging me about the dust on the floor and stuff like that.

21H: Could be. Do you think it would fix it if I quit nagging about dust on the floor?

22W: Well, could you try?

23H: Yeah. I'm not very good about checking myself, but I'll give it a try.

24W: Well, I'll try to be better dusting, [pause] but I don't want you to say anything [about it].

Note the prospective orientation, which is lacking in many scenes. Both partners presume that the relationship is a continuing one; the assumption underlies and indeed is the foundation for their plan, though it is not stated overtly. The scene does not end here, however. The resolution is followed by talk about plans for going away for the weekend, extending the affirmation of the couple's relationship.

The Binghams take the process a step further. In the husband distant scene he is angry with her for nagging him about hunting trips. Both husband and wife stay with the issue, each expressing his own wants clearly and strongly. The solution is a compromise—he will continue hunting but go less often—and neither partner seems fully satisfied. In a simple, easy way, however—like the Birnes—they shift to talking about plans to visit friends for the weekend. The consolidation then seems to enable a return to the issue of improving their relationship:

43H: Would you like to do that [go with Tom and Mary to the mountains]?
44W: Yes.
45H: OK. Let's go to the mountains with them then.
46W: Yeah, but you have to quit being fussy toward me.

The scene continues with a brief discussion eventuating in agreement not to let issues pile up before bringing them in the open:

54W: . . . If I start nagging at you, why don't you just start telling me?
55H: OK. I have told you.
56W: Yes, but only after two or three days, and I finally have to say, "What is wrong with you?"

If one can generalize, such data suggest that in a continuing, emotionally invested relationship the process by which conflict is resolved continues beyond the resolution of a specific issue. Beyond resolution three steps are suggested: emotional reconciliation with regard to the issue, consolidation and reaffirmation of the relationship, working-through of future directions.

Variety, Adaptive Probabilism, and Growth. Variety in response suggests the use of diverse approaches in dealing with conflict. Enactments that show high variety illustrate the range of the coding scheme (see the Manual at the end of this book) with which later chapters will be concerned. The point to be made here is that such enactments show a sense of movement. They are more than exchanges of rational arguments, or of appeals and counterappeals, or of coercion and countercoercion, or of threat and counterthreat. A sense of movement also requires more than a simple repetitive cross-exchange between, let us say, rational argument and appeal, or coercion and threat. That is, to the extent that the same modal exchange is repeated over and over again, growth is limited. High variety requires flexibility on the part of the communicators. While theoretically such flexibility could be arbitrary—partner A always varying his response no matter what partner B does—in practice we found that this does not occur. Typically, communicants shift from unsuccessful to what they hope will be more successful tactics in a somewhat orderly sequence, going from rational arguments and suggestions to emotional appeals to coercive comments and gestures. One might guess that the sequence would break at the earliest successful step with a stated resolution, followed by emotional reconciliation in the pattern discussed above. Often this is so. With some couples we have the impression that conflict is so easily resolved, or so readily (albeit perhaps defensively) avoided, or so quickly locked into unnegotiable positions that capacities for individual flexibility are never quite tested. Extremes of uninvolvement, defensiveness, or anxiety all reduce flexibility. But for other couples, such as the Bradleys above, resolution has only secondary value and exploration itself seems to be primary. Such couples seem to reflect what Cuber and Harroff (1965) have called, "intrinsic" in contrast to "utilitarian" marriages and what Raush and others (1970) referred to as relationship orientation rather than task orientation. As suggested in Chapter Two, the variety in response ranges among couples who emphasize exploration may have an adaptive function. The exploration of one another's capacities that is undertaken in noncritical situations can be useful in terms of testing oneself and one's partner for future developmental changes and life crises or for redefining roles of relationship—much as Moore and Anderson (1962) describe processes of children's play.

Unfortunately, flexibility, exploration, and wide response range ensure neither tranquility nor successful outcomes in marital conflicts or in marriage itself. They do, however, provide a *possibility* for growth. The Vreelands at the newlywed stage are spontaneous and playful in the first two scenes. Along with humor, there is much mutual support. In the wife distant scene, Mrs. Vreeland complains that her husband brings home friends to work on cars and that she feels left out of the picture. (The issue of neglect and lack of attention is a common one among wives in our sample.) Mr. Vreeland does not argue with this:

42H: Well, I wasn't really aware that—that I was ignoring you that much.
43W: Well, it's probably my imagination, but I don't know . . .
44H: No, I don't think it's necessarily your imagination either.

Mrs. Vreeland then admits that it does bother her, and together they work out a better arrangement, followed by a brief discussion about why she had not told him her concerns earlier and by planning for the following week. What are particularly interesting, however, are Mrs. Vreeland's comments following the Improvisations. She speaks of the problem as having been one they had discussed at home: "We had discussed it, and it wasn't the real problem at all. . . . Because I wasn't annoyed at his having his friends out, . . . I was annoyed because I was doing housework, and he was more or less doing things he wanted to do—that's what was really making me mad. . . . I don't think I would have gotten to the problem—what I was really annoyed with—if he hadn't worked around it and practically said it for me, and I realized what—what I was so annoyed about."

When the couple is seen again more than a year later the range of responsiveness is still evident. There is an increased directness in their approach to one another, something less of caution and delicacy, yet there is a sense of development and movement. Again,

we may turn to the wife distant scene. Mr. Vreeland's opening remark is a direct confrontation: "Are you happy? Is this your idea of
life?" His wife initially hesitates and finally says:

9W: What do you want me to say?
10H: I want you to say whatever is in your mind. I want to
      know what's going on. You're certainly aware that this is
      not the most ideal form of life.

Mrs. Vreeland continues to be evasive:

11W: Oh, I don't know. I sort of put it down under conflict.
12H: Conflict with what? Like what?
13W: Oh, I . . .
14H: What do you feel? You love me greatly, you hate me
      madly, uh, what? Yeah. Yeah, what?
15W: Oh, I don't know. I would sort of like to have a drink,
      you know. Get your mind off—
16H: And then what?
17W: If you don't smile, I'll stay drunk.
18H: Why?
19W: Oh, that's just the way I feel . . .

The scene moves to a direct confrontation:

20H: If that's the way you want to feel. Look, this can't go on
      forever. So we get a divorce and get it over with.
21W: All right, that sounds like a good idea.
22H: Why? Do you want to quit? Give up? End it? That's it?
23W: If you feel that way. Are you sure you feel that way? Do
      you want to carry it that far?
24H: No.

The confrontation and commitment seem to enable a new step:

25W: . . . You should feel that way sometimes. Because when
      you don't and I do, then I feel guilty.

Mrs. Vreeland goes on to talk about her feelings of hating him and especially of hating herself at times. She speaks of being bored with her work and with the continual round of housekeeping. Mr. Vreeland is sympathetic, talks about getting household help. The scene could very well end here, but by his probing Mr. Vreeland suggests that there is something more to the situation:

72H: I don't think this is the problem. You enjoy this? I mean is this your idea, uh, of happiness?

73W: What do you mean, do I enjoy it?

74H: Well, you, you seem unconcerned—like you couldn't care less.

Mrs. Vreeland indicates that at times she doesn't know what she cares about. She is obviously depressed, though it is not clear what she is depressed about. Mr. Vreeland attentuates the situation by the interjection of a playful interlude, yet still keeping to the point:

78H: . . . care about us? Care about me? Care about you? Care about Oscar?

79W: Why should I care about Oscar?

80H: Why?

81W: 'Cause he's a cat. 'Cause he's an idiot sometimes. Sometimes he's pretty funny.

With Mrs. Vreeland's admission of caring, she is able then to go on to talk about her impulses to be mean at times, her feelings of sometimes being exploited by her husband, her disappointments with him, her feeling of being overburdened with responsibilities, her occasional wishes of wanting out, and her feelings of guilt for such thoughts. No specific solution is achieved but there is evident clarification and increased mutual understanding.[2]

The Vreelands fight hard, and theirs may not be a tranquil marriage. But their flexibility provides a capacity for growth. It is important to note, however, that the Vreelands' wide repertoires are set in a context of mutual affection and concern. Without this con-

[2] Some further comments about this couple are presented in Raush and others (1963).

text variety can serve ends other than individual and mutual development.

Issue Expansion

Temporal Expansion. As Deutsch (1969a) suggests, issue expansion escalates conflict. Expansion may take any of a number of directions, one of which is temporal. That is, the issue is generalized over time, and the expression is usually total—key words being *always* and *never:* "You always get what you want"; "I always do what you want to do"; "I know you—you always say, 'I'll do this, I'll do that' "; "You never want to . . ."; "All you ever think about . . ." Sometimes the temporal dimension is only exaggerated: "This has been going on for three or four months now." The temporal mode of expansion is a disguised signal that the issue at stake is not the ostensible one. The phrases "you never" and "you always" imply that it is not the present instance that is critical but rather the core issue of individual autonomy and mutuality. In such remarks the partner is projected as an external force trampling, neglecting, controlling the speaker's individual rights and autonomy. The disguise suggests that the schema touched on recapitulates earlier painful struggles in defining self-other relations. The only appropriate responses to this mode of expansion seem to be metacommunicative ones, either statements suggesting refocus on the present instance or—if, as is likely, emotions are strong—statements suggesting focus on the core autonomy issue. In fact, our data yield no such examples. Temporal expansion by one partner is perceived by the other as an attack—in line with the projective aspect. The quarrel escalates, and the "you always" or "you never" tends to become a prophecy that is jointly fulfilled.

Disparaging the Other. Other core issues may be invoked to expand a conflict. Most common are attacks on the identity or self-image of the other, such as simple depreciative remarks: "That garbage [the television program] you can look at any time"; "You're so stupid you don't know what to do with [the baby]"; "You look like an idiot when you're dancing"; "You're spoiled"; "You only think of yourself." Such direct attacks—on the person rather than the issue—tend obviously to escalation. Yet here the metacommunicative aspect must be taken into account. A few couples are able to trade strong direct insults in an atmosphere of good feeling. The Harmiks, for example, pull no punches with one another, but there is no escalation, and they stay with the issue:

109W: I can't help it if you're too stupid to know I'm hinting.
110H: Well, you should know me well enough to—
111W: [Interrupting] Know that you're stupid. Yeah.
112H: Absolutely. But right now the last thing—
113W: [Interrupting] What are you going to do if it's triplets? Twins run in your family.
114H: If it's triplets, I'll drown the first two.

The direct insults are modulated by humor and good feeling; the partners seem to enjoy the battle, and the relationship seems strong enough to sustain strong momentary personal attacks. Such a situation is, however, relatively rare in our sample.

Generational Expansion. A common mode of attack on the identity of the other expands the focus to his or her family of origin. Most often it is mothers who are referred to, sometimes the generalized family, rarely siblings, and never in our sample specifically fathers. "Your mother" are fighting words for most of our couples, particularly though not exclusively at the newlywed stage, and they seldom fail to expand and escalate the original issue of conflict:

143W: . . . Look who you were named after.
144H: That wasn't my fault. And, I'm not my mother and neither are you.
145W: You're a lot like her.
146H: No, I'm not; you're a lot like her.
147W: [Shouting] Like your mother? You know that isn't true. I'm not like your mother.

Other examples leading to expansion include, "You, you're worse than your mother," and "All you care about is your family." In this form of issue expansion, the husband generally deprecates the wife's mother or the wife's family, implying a failure of separation; the wife attacks the husband's mother implying spoiling. Rarely does the partner fail to respond to the gambit. Occasionally, though, this does happen:

178W: . . . You got raised by the book. Your mother said so.
179H: And look how I turned out.
180W: Well, I want my children to be just like you, dear.
181H: You're crazier than I thought you were.

An even clearer example of control on this form of issue expansion is:

61H: You've never been so stubborn before. I don't know what's gotten into you all of a sudden.
62W: I've been talking to my mother [laugh].
63H: I won't discuss *that* at this time.

Crucializing.   Expansion into a core issue is often achieved by "crucializing" the specific issue—that is, the focus shifts from the particular problem to a generalized test of power or love, the specific issue serving as representative. For example: "Would you be willing if that's the only thing that would make our anniversary happy?" A common form, especially for wives, is: "If you really loved me, you would . . ." Such issues touch on core schemata, and the focus can readily expand. Often, however, one has the impression that such statements are not quite as serious as they appear. That is, they are tactics of appeal or coercion, used and recognized by the partner as such. They lead to expansion less often than one might expect.

Steamrolling.   A simple mode of issue expansion that does not necessarily impinge on core issues resembles the piling up of denials discussed under avoidance. The attempt seems to be to overwhelm or confuse the partner. Although issues are obviously expanded in these circumstances, the result is more likely to be a lack of movement than an escalation.

The Hidden Issue.   In some scenes the real issue seems to be hidden. Under such circumstances the conflict can easily expand and escalate. The ostensible issue presented in the relationship scenes may mask another problem that neither partner may be willing or able to face openly—at least in the experimental context. To the observer such scenes have a peculiar quality. The tonality or the intensity seems inappropriate to what is overtly at stake, and the observer finds himself wondering, "Just what are they talking about?" Yet neither partner seems aware of anything strange about their argument or its escalation. One has the impression that at either a conscious or an unconscious level there is a mutual understanding that they are talking about a topic that has little to do with the overt issue. The hidden issue that suggests itself in the rare protocols of this type is sex. None of the couples makes sex an overt issue in distance scenes. But for a few it seems to be implied in the tonality and metaphors of the argument. In those cases the overtly stated issues and the conflict seem to expand in a way that strikes the external observer as arbitrary and causeless.

Issue Focus

We have already noted that the issue specificity of the anniversary and television scenes makes them easier to resolve than the husband and wife distant scenes. The function of issue specificity in mitigating conflict is even more apparent in the latter two scenes. There each partner has the option of stating or failing to state the issue upon which his distancing from the other is premised. Most often—in 79 percent of the scenes—the conflict takes a specific focus around a stated issue. In such cases, the distant partner is likely to break his set, and there is a resolution in favor of reestablishing closeness. Of the 192 scenes in which the issue is stated, 66 percent are so resolved. In contrast, when the issue remains unstated, resolution is unlikely; the scene ends with the distant partner most often maintaining his or her stance. Only 18 percent of the 51 scenes in which no specific issue is presented achieve resolution.

Specificity and directness optimize informational exchange. When each partner knows what the other is talking about and how the other feels about it, each has the possibility of modulating his own reactions toward the other. The goal may be attainment of his own wishes, achievement of a joint solution, or simply increased differentiation and refinement of information about the issue. It would be wrong, however, to think of the informational exchange solely in terms of rational problem-solving. The exchange may consist of intense expressions of affect about a specific issue. Moreover, each partner may maintain his stance, and the conflict may remain unresolved. But when the issue is stated specifically and directly there is a control on escalation. Even the failure to find a resolution to the issue may reflect a progression toward an acceptance of one another and augur more favorably for the relationship than arbitrary pseudoresolutions do.

For example, the Binghams, quoted above as illustrating the resolution process in a continuing affective relationship, are very direct with one another. They do not always resolve the experimental conflicts, but neither do they expand or escalate them. After about two years of marriage, Mr. Bingham in the husband distant scene presents an issue intensely and directly:

> 36H: You bug me about your parents: "Say thank you. Be nice to Mother. Don't say those bad things about Mother. I can say them but you can't." You know—yakkity, yak, yak. I'm just getting fed up with it, that's all. I just want to be alone. Leave me alone for a little while.

Although, as noted, "mother" for most couples is a fighting word, Mrs. Bingham responds directly in terms of her goals of resolving the issue and reestablishing closeness. She does not succeed. Mr. Bingham leaves:

> 40H: I'm going to the drugstore to get a pack of cigarettes; I'll talk about this tomorow night.

The affect is strong, but there is no evidence of hidden hostility. The scene is short (forty acts), and, although Mr. Bingham walks out, it is with a promise of future discussion. There are no threats by either partner in the scene. In the wife distant scene, Mrs. Bingham expresses directly her annoyance about her husband's "cuteness" at parties. She maintains her distance until he promises to try to change, and then she yields her position.

Mrs. Roberts is angry about a chair given the couple by Mr. Roberts's mother. She dislikes the chair greatly and feels that she has been pressured to accept it by her husband out of courtesy to his mother. Again this is a situation fraught with escalation potential. But note the control (as well as the temptation):

> 31H: The chair is just the chair.
> 32W: It's not this chair, it's your mother.

33H: So I'll be mad at my mother.
34W: Well, that'll cause in-law problems.
35H: . . . You won't have in-law problems unless you think of in-law problems.

Mr. Roberts then brings the issue specifically back to the chair and offers to support his wife in returning it to his mother.

Focus and Conflict. In a summary of his own extensive experiments, Deutsch (1969b) refers to a discussion by Fisher (1964) on international conflict. Fisher suggests that smaller, substantive conflicts are easier to resolve than larger conflicts over general principles and that participants may have a degree of choice in defining a conflict as large or small. Deutsch's own work suggests that issues bearing on self-esteem or on change in power or status are likely to enhance conflict. Moreover, in an experimental manipulation of conflict size with college student subjects, Deutsch finds that, as the size of the conflict grows, cooperative behavior deteriorates and joint outcomes are poorer. Our own data confirm these directions. A limited substantive issue seems, furthermore, to allow sensitivity to the relationship itself, whereas, when the relationship is threatened, sensitivity easily retreats to individual core issues of loss of love, power, or self-esteem. The formal analyses of Chapter Thirteen explore this matter further, particularly as it relates to differences between two groups of couples.

Directness, Vagueness, and Communication

Closely allied to the directions of issue expansion versus issue focus are modalities of directness and specificity in contrast to tangentiality and vagueness. Vagueness and tangentiality were illustrated in discussions of avoidance. But even when an issue is not ostensibly avoided, the flow of information may be impeded, as in the following example. Mr. Gore in the anniversary scene at the newlywed stage seems to be offering to yield to his wife:

68H: I'll sort of take them [tickets to a dinner-dance] back— you went to this much trouble with me—even though I do like to stay home and have a nice home-cooked meal.

Note the tangentiality and disqualification: he will "sort of" take the tickets back; trouble "with" him rather than "for" him; he is offering to stay home and eat her dinner "even though" he likes to stay home.[3] Mrs. Gore's reply suggests that she has received no information from what Mr. Gore must consciously presume is his effort to meet her wishes:

> 69W: Well, I don't want to start an argument, but I think you should appreciate what I've done today and stay home and have dinner and take me some other time.

The order of the two statements could well be reversed. In the husband distant scene, in response to Mr. Gore's criticism that she dismantled and wrecked the toaster, it is Mrs. Gore who says:

> 97W: Well, if you hadn't been so bitchy about it, it wouldn't have happened, and besides I didn't do anything to it.

In the wife distant scene, Mrs. Gore presents multiple issues:

> 84W: And then when you come home and say, "The meat's not cooked enough," or "The carrots are this," or "Why aren't the potatoes mashed?" or "Why are they boiled?" "Where's the sugar? And how come the dishes aren't done? Look you haven't made the bed yet," and you sit on your rear end and look at the paper. And you expect me to run all over, and I never get a chance to look at the paper or enjoy it or anything.

Obviously, the only appropriate reply to this flood of complaint would be at a metacommunicative level. Mr. Gore's comment is to agree that things are bad, but "I don't think we're going to solve a thing by not talking to each other, do you?"—a comment that is irrelevant at this point. Two years later and after their baby is born, their interchanges in the conflict situations consist of multiple complaints, trades of insult, and direct win-lose confrontations. Neither seems to listen to the other. Nonetheless the highly segregated roles

---

[3] See Watzlawick and others (1967) for other examples.

they adopt may preserve the stability of the marriage in its utilitarian conflict-habituated form.

Most often, as implied in much of the above discussion, the styles of the two partners seem to match. That is, they share styles of avoidance or constriction or engagement. So, too, with directness versus vagueness. Two couples in the sample are, however, discrepant. In both cases, the wife is direct and the husband evasive. It is interesting that this discrepancy itself becomes an issue. Mr. Carter, for example, is critical in the husband distant scene of what he considers his wife's rudeness to her parents. She defends her style of directness with her parents (reflecting her style toward him as well). In relation to the scene itself she asks why he didn't tell her sooner about his concern. He says:

35H: You should have asked me what was bothering me.
36W: Why can't you come home and say I'm mad at you?
37H: Because I don't do that.

Over time both discrepant couples developed a pattern in which the wives's directness becomes transformed into a steam rolling intrusive tactic, and in which the husbands' evasiveness becomes transformed into a style of denied, indirect hostile acts.

Other Engagement Modes

One may readily think of other broad modes that characterize couples' engagement in interpersonal conflict. To a great extent these modes are incorporated in the above discussions on variety versus constriction and issue expansion versus issue focus. For example, the humor, playfulness, and spontaneity that typify the interactions of some couples are forms of variety. Humor and playfulness can, as some cited examples suggest, attenuate the intensity of conflict, enhancing the prospect of constructive resolution. On the other hand, humor can serve defensive ends, and some protocols suggest a merely manipulative use—in a sense, a "humoring" of the partner. Moreover, some protocols show a degradation of humor and playfulness into biting sarcasm and sadomasochistic interplay. One bright couple, divorced after the birth of their first child, illustrate this progressive transformation of wit in the course of the three years of their marriage. A literary example is given in Edward Albee's *Who's Afraid of Virginia Woolf?*

Temporal perspective versus temporal encapsulation has also been referred to peripherally in discussions of variety and of issue expansion. Intense conflict tends to lead to a tunnel vision whereby the present moment absorbs the entire relationship, negating both past and future. The "you always" argument illustrates this. Yet, as suggested, some couples can maintain a temporal perspective despite intense conflict. Even when a problem remains unresolved, a future hope of resolution is projected.

Throughout the above discussion there is implied a modality of intimacy versus isolation and distantiation (Erikson, 1959, 1963). This is perhaps the clearest dimension emerging from our clinical perspective. For some couples the essentials of the conflict situations are the mutual recognition and awareness of one another. At the opposite extreme, for other couples the conflict situations are total win-lose confrontations and tests of individual identity in the assertion of power. For most couples the weight is balanced in one direction or the other but the balance can shift with the nature of the scene—with the issue it poses and with the threat or support of the partner's actions.

Summary

Destructive Engagement. In contrast to avoidance, engagement of an existent interpersonal conflict offers hope for constructive mutual resolution. This is so even when the partners show constricted ranges of response. A limited repertoire of interactions may reflect cognitive limitations or characteristic interpersonal styles; though it may limit the possible outcomes of interpersonal conflict, it does not preclude constructive, jointly satisfactory outcomes. If, however, a constricted repertoire derives from a view of interpersonal commitment as threatening, or if it is a regressive reaction to interpersonal confrontation, then the chances of a constructive outcome are markedly reduced. The conflict is likely to escalate in intensity and, as in the case of avoidance, there will be little information exchange and little development.

In the heat of interpersonal conflict, issues can easily spread. The conflict can absorb the entire temporal perspective of the relationship; it can spread to attacks on and defenses of personal identity; or it can seek out special areas of vulnerability, such as parental relationships. Other modes of expansion are "crucializing" an issue or piling up diverse issues so as to overwhelm the partner. Whatever the specific mode, expansion of the issue suggests that the interpersonal conflict has impinged on other problems and that something more than the immediate issue is at stake. We may guess that the current conflict is being assimilated to a schema that arouses anxiety. The schemata associated with anxiety are most often those connected with core issues of trust, autonomy, power, and love, and some couples give the impression that almost any interpersonal disagreement is capable of impinging on these schemata.

Anxiety is reflected in deterioration and inappropriateness of communication. Messages are garbled in their sending and in their receiving. They are crude and undifferentiated; they are not coordinated with the capabilities of the partners in the exchange. There are discrepancies between verbal and nonverbal aspects of communication, between communication and metacommunication: agreement is stated in the tonality of disagreement; intentions toward closeness are conveyed in the tonality of rejection.

As was suggested in Chapter Four and by Deutsch (1969a), threat and anxiety lead to defensiveness and the closed mind. Defenses against anxiety appear in denials, disqualifications, and most often impermeability of schemata to new information. Input becomes assimilated only into the preexisting schema. Nothing new is heard, nothing new is said. There is a static, cyclic quality to the sequence of successive interactions. Contingencies become absolute— "Yes, you will," followed inevitably by "No, I won't," followed inevitably by "Yes, you will"—rather than probabilistic. As noted in Chapters Three and Five, under such circumstances further communication fails to clarify or offer hope of change.

Constructive Engagement. Modes of engaging interpersonal conflict may involve humor, playfulness, and spontaneity; they may lack these; or they may involve bitter sarcasm and sadomasochistic interplay. Couples differ in the extent to which their approaches to one another imply temporal perspective or temporal encapsulation. A general modality is suggested in Erikson's conceptualization of intimacy versus isolation and "distantiation" as the major developmental issue of this stage of life. All couples must deal with this issue one way or another. For some, communication with marital partners seems to play a major role in a process of enhancing and redefining intimacy; for others—and we cannot really say that they are lacking in intimacy—communication is simply a sometimes necessary means to a practical end. Studies of marriage repeatedly come up with similar dimensions under different rubrics: traditional versus companionate marriages, utilitarian versus intrinsic marriages, shared versus segregated roles, individual versus mutual orientation, task- versus relationship-oriented couples. The dimensions differ somewhat but all touch on a core human issue in the relation between the personal and the interpersonal—from the joining strivings of Freud's eros and the dissolution strivings of his death instinct through Rank's (1968) tension between separation and unity to Angyal's (1965) autonomy and heteronomy to Bakan's (1966) agency and communion.

Interpersonal modes of avoidance and engagement reflect these poles. Clinical perusal suggests—despite our initial prejudices —that both directions are tenable for stable marriages and that neither makes per se "happier" marriages than the other—*given the context of continuing positive affection.* Love does not conquer all, but it goes a long way. Both avoidance and engagement provide pathways to escalation or attenuation of conflict. Engagement does offer a greater prospect for growth, but it may, as suggested elsewhere (Raush and others, 1963), place greater burdens on both the individuals and the dyad.

Couples who share a bond of mutual affection and who, in facing the particular conflict presented them, are capable of variety and of avoiding issue expansion as a mode of attack, produce scenes that have a sense of development. Such couples tend to emphasize the process of interacting with one another rather than the specific outcome of their interchange. Within the seriousness of their engagement in the conflict and the intensity of their interchanges, there is a probabilistic playfulness, a concerned emphasis on exploration of self and other. In Chapter Two we spoke of such adaptive probabilism in connection with systems where change is required.

In this optimal context, outcomes, despite their deemphasis, are more likely to be jointly satisfactory and are sometimes specially creative. Cases like this provide us with an idealized sketch of the sequential steps in conflict resolution in a relationship that has positive emotional investment and that is projected as continuing in the future:

(1) introduction and specification of the interpersonal issue;

(2) exploration of alternative solutions in terms of their practical, individually affective, and interpersonal implications;

(3) resolution;

(4) practical planning in terms of resolution;

(5) emotional reconciliation in relation to the conflict ("cooling off");

(6) consolidation and reaffirmation of the relationship—talking about other joint plans and activities; and

(7) return to the conflict but in a general sense—working out suggestions for future coping with interpersonal issues.

In actual cases not all the steps are negotiated and the order is not precise. The sequence is an idealized version. But what is interesting and what we do see in the data is that in an ongoing invested relationship an interpersonal conflict does not end with a simple resolution but rather progresses under optimal circumstances to reconciliation, consolidation, and generalized learning for the future.

The Couple as a System.   Emerging from clinical analysis is an overwhelming impression of the intermeshing of couples as a unit. Generally, though not always, the *couple* can be said to have a style. Although we have not explored the matter, and although there are exceptions (like the mesh between steamrolling and evasive partners) couples seems to share even the formal aspects of communication styles. That is, in some couples both partners speak in short bursts, in others both speak in paragraphs; there are partners who use complete sentences and those who do not.

Apart from such unexplored intermeshing of formal styles, we have seen that when the relationship itself is highly salient, interpersonal defensiveness of one partner is likely to result in communications that touch on core issues for the other. Anxiety and defensiveness thus tend to become mutual. The escalation of conflict or its static cycling is conjoint. Conjoint also are exploration and constructive conflict. In interaction the couple constitutes a unit.

In the statistical analyses of Part Three where individual couples are distinguished, the couple dimension emerges as the most powerful source of information. That is, if one wants to predict what actions will take place in a given scene, one does better by knowing the particular couple than by knowing the sex of the actor, the stage of marriage, or even the immediately preceding actions. Only the nature of the scene will sometimes tell more. Moreover, the interaction protocols suggest that couples maintain characteristic styles of interaction across the several phases of marriage, averaging two years, of the study. Clinical impressions of couple consistency are again confirmed by statistical data—there is no loss in information from the couple variable across the three phases of study.

This is not to say that the couples do not change at all. Some systematic general changes over time are discussed in Chapter Fourteen. Clinical impressions suggest several categories for specific couples. Some couples change not at all or only very slightly over the three phases; some seem to learn how to deal better—more efficiently, with less strain—with one another *as each person is;* a few relationships move toward more communicative disruption; and in a few each partner seems to have grown. In general, though, the couple as a unit seems remarkably consistent. Couples with conjoint styles of coping with interpersonal conflict by escalation and defense, like those with conjoint styles of avoidance (again, somewhat to our surprise), can have tenable, presumably "happy," and seemingly stable marriages. In such cases the defensive styles of the partners intermesh, and there are sustaining elements of mutual affection or covert mutual gratifications. Growth in the relationship, however, seems to require more adaptive communication modes.

IX

A Coding Scheme for Interpersonal Conflict

We have paused often in our theoretical and clinical treatments of communication, conflict, and marriage to ask contextual questions: what are the effects of one partner's acts on the other partner's acts; of the presenting conflict; of the sex of the actor; of length and stage of marriage; of each couple's definition of its marriage as "happy" or "unhappy"? We have questioned how each of these influences communication and coping with conflict.

Clinical perusal and appraisal, powerful in defining quality, revealing patterns, and suggesting rules of interaction, cannot abstract and weigh contextual influences most effectively. To do this requires methods that are both cruder and more refined. We have chosen to use methods of coding and counting, which will be discussed in this chapter, and the chapters that follow apply the quantitative methods of informational analysis (suggested in Chapter Three) to some contextual dimensions of interpersonal conflict.

The Data

All Improvisation scenes were tape-recorded with the knowledge of the couples. Transcripts were later made from the tapes. Given the technical problems of recording free interactions, the data are remarkably good. Only a minor fraction of the remarks, and these usually interjections, were indecipherable. For coding purposes both the tape and the transcript were used. Transcripts helped the coders' to know exactly what was said, while the use of the tape enhanced interpretation of the act by use of the tone of voice, inflection, and manner of speaking. While undoubtedly a film recording would give an even clearer picture of the meaning of certain remarks in the transcript, the tape does allow a judgment of the meaning from the tone of voice with some accuracy. Gestures and expressions that might be available from film recording are, of course, lost.

In the transcripts, acts of husband and wife were numbered sequentially for each scene. An act was any remark or statement by one spouse between decipherable statements by the other spouse. Thus, it could be a single word or a few sentences. In the process of coding and after repeated listening, the coders were able to decipher remarks not deciphered by the original transcribers, and they added these to the transcripts. Also, in the course of independent coding and arriving at a consensus, the coders made a relatively small number of judgments that silences on the part of one spouse in response to questions or pleas in the husband distant and wife distant scenes should be coded as acts of rejection by the silent spouse. Where, for instance, the wife pleaded with her husband to say what was wrong and was met by a measurable period of silence by him before she resumed, the coders considered his silence an act and so numbered it in the sequence.

The Coding Scheme

Any investigator who tries to cope with the problems of analyzing interaction faces problems for which there are no simple solutions. The dimensions by which we as human beings judge and respond to other human beings are as yet unclear, and there are no absolute scales for anchoring the events of human interchange. The problems are simpler when the investigator binds himself to the test of specific hypotheses. These set limits on what he is to look for. But, when an investigation is mostly exploratory, seeking to describe and order what people do with each other and how they go about it, the limits are obscure.

Problems of coding observations have received considerable attention. Heyns and Lippitt surveyed the issues in 1954, and a more recent chapter by Weick (1968) brings the discussion relatively up to date. Yet, despite the proliferation of observational studies and commentaries in recent years, some fundamental questions are unresolved, and each investigator tends, unfortunately, to develop his own methods.

Our initial wish was to avoid adding yet another scheme to those that already exist for describing interaction. Some early efforts were devoted to an attempt to fit what went on between our husbands and wives into the well-developed systems of Bales (1950) and Leary and his colleagues (Leary, 1957; Freedman and others, 1951). Both systems try to code interaction exhaustively—that is, all relevant behavior between people can presumably be classified into the categories of each system. In theory, every action of one person toward another is codable. We found that the task of coding per se was not difficult but rather that the methods that had been developed for small groups were not wholly appropriate for describing the interactions of intimate dyads. Particularly, it seemed that modes of affiliation and coercion expressed by our young couples were of greater range and more differentiated than either of the two schemes accommodated. A fit could be made, but we feared that too much would be forced.

It is not surprising that different situations and different relationships are conducive to different coding schemes. The interactions between parents and children, in peer discussion groups, and between marital partners trying to resolve conflict share common sets of behaviors, but each partakes of a somewhat different range and each has emphases and differentiations that the others lack. The Coding Scheme for Interpersonal Conflict grew out of our attempts to encompass the range and refinements in the events produced by our young couples faced with conflict-provoking issues. We tried to define the categories of the scheme so that they would be applicable to any interpersonal conflict situation.

The manual for the scheme is reproduced at the back of the book. The thirty-six categories of acts encompass, presumably, all the interactive events that occurred. In our studies the categories are considered as discrete rather than continuous, although the manual does suggest possibilities for considering successive steps in intensity of coercion and rejection. Besides the act categories we divided each scene into three phases: (1) introductory, (2) conflict, and (3) resolution and postresolution. These are described in the Manual. Thus, each act received a phase code and a category code. Not every scene has all three phases, of course, since in some cases the conflict began without introduction, in other cases no resolution was achieved, and in one or two instances no conflict was generated (for instance, one husband immediately agreed with his wife's suggestion that they eat their anniversary dinner at home).[1]

Coding Procedures and Reliability

Using the thirty-six categories, each protocol was coded at least three times. A minimum of two and most often three coders worked independently using both tape recording and transcripts. Each act was coded as it occurred sequentially in the scene; the coders avoided as much as possible listening or reading ahead. In addition to the independent coding, each protocol was coded conjointly by two coders who had available not only the tapes and transcripts but also all the independent codings. The coders working conjointly reached a consensus, which became the standard code. It was, of course, preferable that the consensus judgment be done by coders other than those who did the independent codings; this was not always possible, and in the earlier phases of the work one of the independent coders participated in the consensus procedure. The multiple coding process requires considerable time and energy. Nevertheless, this careful consideration and reconsideration of the

[1] Codings from the introductory phase were dropped from analysis, since they were stereotypical and produced little or no variance; a typical example is, "Hi." "Hi." "How are you?" "Fine. How are you?"

protocols justifies a measure of confidence in the standard codes as representations of the quality and flow of a couple's interactions.

The final scheme, as presented in the Manual, was the result of a number of revisions, which included eliminating some categories, combining others, refining definitions, establishing some coding conventions, and finding adequate illustrative examples. Some revisions came about in the practice of coding. Others derived from more formal reliability studies. It is to these latter we now turn.

Although reliability is often a shibboleth of empirical investigation, there is no magical single index that defines the adequacy of an instrument. Like validity, reliability must be evaluated in terms of the uses to which the instrument is put. Early studies with forty categories suggested fair agreement among three independent coders who coded protocols for four couples. All three coders agreed 36 percent of the time, two out of three agreed 40 percent of the time, and there was total disagreement 24 percent of the time. Thus, there was partial or total agreement 76 percent of the time among independent coders. Preliminary work also indicated that, by lumping the categories into six groups, complete agreement could be increased to 50 percent and partial or complete agreement to 90 percent. Moreover, an analysis of variance, in which three judges coded five couples using the forty categories, indicated that, although judges differed in their use of the categories, couples were clearly differentiated from one another. That is, one judge as compared to another might favor the use of a particular category, but all judges agreed on the characteristic distribution of codings for the specific couples. For adequate reliability, the variance attributable to couple differences should be far greater than that attributable to coder differences, and it was. For these five couples either two out of three or three out of three judges agreed on codings 76 percent of the time.

These preliminary checks were encouraging. The next step was to develop a computer program that would enable a comparison among three sets of independent codings and the consensus standard codings for twenty-one couples. The comparison suggested that some of the forty categories needed to be eliminated, revised, or combined with others in order to achieve reliable judgment. On the basis of these findings the scheme of thirty-six categories that is presented in the Manual was developed. In the revised scheme the overall agreement of the independent coders with the standard was 65 percent, which means that on the average two out of three coders agreed with the standard on all acts and categories. Some weak points remained. Seven categories, which fortunately were among the least frequently used, showed less than 40 percent agreement between independent codings and the consensus standard.

As we realized that for purposes of statistical treatment we would have to reduce the number of categories to a more manageable level, we began to think of lumping schemes that would maintain psychological meaningfulness and capture the flavor of the interaction. Our first reduction was to twelve categories, and from this we later derived the final six-category scheme (see the Manual). We compared coder agreement with the standard with the thirty-six categories lumped into twelve, again using the same twenty-one couples. The agreement of coders with the standard ranged from 45 percent to 85 percent among the categories, and total agreement with the standard increased to 70 percent.

The final reduction was to the six categories used in the formal data analyses (Table 1). Coder agreement with the standard ranged from 58 percent to 88 percent, but five of the six categories ranged between 58 percent and 65 percent. There was 77 percent total agreement between independent and standard codings.

Additional reliability studies were undertaken using the revised scheme. One aspect of reliability is reproducibility, or test-retest reliability. Couples were divided by length of protocol into long, medium, and short; one couple was selected randomly from each of these groups. Two of the original coders independently recoded the twelve scenes (four scenes per couple times three couples) approximately one year later; a consensus coding was also redone by the original consensus judges. Between new and old consensus ratings for the thirty-six categories there was 70 percent absolute agreement. Newly trained coders independently coded the same three couples, and new consensus ratings were derived. Absolute agreement of the newly trained coders with the original consensus codings was 67 percent, and with codings repeated a year later it was again 67 percent. Lumping the thirty-six categories into twelve, reliability went from 70 percent absolute agreement to about 75 percent for

Table 1

SIX-CATEGORY CODING SCHEME FOR INTERPERSONAL CONFLICT

Category[a]	Description
1	*Cognitive acts:* neutral acts, suggestions, and rational arguments
2	*Resolving acts:* acts aimed at cooling the conflict or resolving the conflict issue
3	*Reconciling acts:* acts aimed at reconciling the two partners emotionally
4	*Appealing acts:* acts appealing to the other to grant one's wish
5	*Rejecting acts:* acts showing a cold or nasty rejection of the other's argument or person
6	*Coercive acts or personal attacks:* acts aimed at forcing compliance by power plays, guilt induction, or disparagement of the other

[a] The individual coding categories lumped here are indicated in the Manual at the back of the book under "Six-Category Lumping Scheme."

more experienced coders and from 67 percent to about 72 percent for less experienced coders. Lumping into six categories (see Table 1), reliability goes to 77 percent absolute agreement for both old and new coders. Again we conclude that the coding, while not ideal, does produce fairly reliable results on an act-by-act basis—the most difficult test of reliability, since it is akin to single-item reliability on a paper-and-pencil test. Another analysis, which compared how the three coders ranked the newlyweds in the use of the six categories, showed substantial agreements between coders; this analysis, equivalent to a test-retest reliability, produced rank-order correlations for each category that ranged from .64 to .80.

Summary

Tapes and transcripts were made of the couples' enactments of the Improvisation conflict situations, and a Coding Scheme for

Interpersonal Conflict was developed. The scheme enabled the classification of interpersonal acts into either thirty-six or twelve or six categories. Using multiple coders, categorization was shown to be reasonably reliable.

Research tools offer no easy compromise between the aim of capturing the nuances and richness of human interchange and the aim of drawing legitimate general conclusions about human interchange. The first aim risks entanglement in subtlety, misdirection by one's own biases, and misconstruing a specific case for a general principle. The second risks overdependence on method as a substitute for thoughtful examination, canceling findings through misguided abstractions, and drawing an overview so broad that only clichés can emerge.

Thus, while the coding scheme attempts to articulate interaction with some fair degree of refinement, in order to examine some general relationships we were forced to reduce the original thirty-six to a final six categories. Further, statistical requirements at times demanded grouping subjects or Improvisation scenes as well as specific acts. We gain something through this, but something is lost, too. Our attempt to manage the dilemma is reflected in a shuttling between "zooming in" and "zooming out" on our data. The analyses of the preceding two chapters zoomed in on the qualitative nuances of interactions and modes of coping with interpersonal conflict. In the following chapters we zoom out to examine some quantitative findings relating to the broader context of conflict.

X

The Contextual
Dimensions—
An Overview

In Chapter Three we spoke of communication as essentially the relationship set up between events in two or more systems. That relationship has been characterized as one where an occurence of event X in system A constrains the response Y in system B. In other words, knowing that event X has occurred in system A reduces our uncertainty about what will happen in system B. The occurrence of X yields information precisely because X "selects" or "gives shape to" a limited number of possibilities with varying probabilities from among a more extensive set of possibilities.

A major question, then, concerns dependencies among acts: to what extent does the message a person receives lessen our uncertainty about his reply? Such antecedent-to-consequent contingency is basic to all communication. But acts, whether antecedent or consequent, do not occur in a vacuum. In our particular studies the act is directed by a particular husband or wife to his or her specific marital partner in a particular situation (an Improvisation scene) at a particular stage of their married life. What this means, to return once again to the abstract, is that acts occur between systems and, indeed, within a larger system (the relationship). The systemic properties we try to examine statistically are such things as the particular couple, the sex of the person who responds to an antecedent act, the instructions given to this respondent, and the stage of the marriage. As discussed in Chapters Three and Four, we view these dimensions as contextual properties inherent in the system from which specific interactions emanate.

Our questions have to do with the relative importance of these systemic properties and their interrelations in determining responses. For example, Sue says to Bob in a pleading tone, "Please, tell me what's the matter!" We assume that Bob's response to this act is influenced by the set he has in the Improvisation scene (for example, to remain distant), by the fact that he is a man, not a woman, by his ongoing relationship with Sue, and by the fact that she is now pregnant, as well as by what she says and how she says it. Statistically we try to tease out the influence of these factors separately and in combination.[1]

The Analytic Approach

At the newlywed stage forty-six couples completed each of the four Improvisation scenes yielding a total of 15,132 acts, even excluding introductory comments. The analyses of this and the following chapters examine how these acts are distributed in relation to the dimensions described above and in relation to the theoretical concepts of earlier chapters. Before turning to more abstract analysis, however, a concrete illustration of the nature of the data may help.

Two Couple Matrices.   In Chapter Eight we described, among others, two couples, the Harrises and the Vreelands, who

---

[1] We are, of course, aware that Bob's response is influenced by the presence of observers and the whole experimental situation, but we see no way of assessing these effects.

both became deeply involved in the conflict situations. The Harrises entered into a destructive escalating battle of wills in which their interactions showed little variation or differentiation. In contrast, the Vreelands were characterized by flexibility and exploration of each other's communications, and their mode of coping with conflict, though intense, was seen as constructive. Let us examine how each of the two couples interact in terms of the Coding Scheme for Interpersonal Conflict presented in Chapter Nine.

Table 2 includes all the Harrises' interactions in the four newlywed Improvisation scenes. There are two matrices. The one on the left shows Mrs. Harris's responses to her husband's acts; the one on the right shows his responses to her acts. Reading across the first row of the left side of the table, we see that in response to the twenty-one cognitively oriented acts produced by Mr. Harris, Mrs. Harris returned cognitive responses fourteen times; in the first row on the right, we note that Mr. Harris returned twelve cognitive responses to the thirty-five cognitive acts of his wife, but that he also responded with acts of rejection ten times to Mrs. Harris's cognitive antecedent acts. Looking at row (4) on the left, we see that to her husband's appeals Mrs. Harris responds predominately with rejection; in row (5) on the right we find that to his wife's rejecting acts Mr. Harris responds predominantly with appeals. Each partner behaves differently, but in their interaction they tend to produce a tight and destructive communicative cycle: Mr. Harris's appeals to his wife "select" rejections from her repertoire; Mrs. Harris' rejections "select" appeals from his repertoire. The cycling could be interminable, but we may note that even for the Harrises there are variations within the pattern: there is some probabilistic possibility of her responding with something other than rejection to his appeals, and of his responding with something other than appeals to her rejecting acts.

Table 2 shows that the Vreelands' interactions differ strikingly from the Harrises'. The marginal totals indicate that in contrast to the Harrises the Vreelands very rarely reject one another and are often engaged in efforts at emotional reconciliation—row (3). But the difference between the Vreelands and the Harrises is not only in their acts but also in the pattern of their interactions. For example, to his wife's appeals (row (4) right) Mr. Vreeland—

Table 2.
Interaction Matrices (Response Frequencies) for Four Newlywed Scenes

I. HARRIS

			Wife's Response				
Code	(1)	(2)	(3)	(4)	(5)	(6)	T
(1)	14	3	0	0	3	1	21
(2)	6	3	1	1	2	2	15
(3)	0	0	0	0	1	0	1
(4)	1	0	0	0	10	2	13
(5)	12	2	1	2	3	2	22
(6)	2	0	0	2	4	3	11
T	35	8	2	5	23	10	83

Husband's Antecedent Act

			Husband's Response				
Code	(1)	(2)	(3)	(4)	(5)	(6)	T
(1)	12	8	0	1	10	4	35
(2)	2	2	0	0	2	1	7
(3)	0	0	0	0	2	0	2
(4)	2	1	0	0	4	0	7
(5)	3	1	1	10	3	6	24
(6)	2	2	0	1	4	1	10
T	21	14	1	12	25	12	85

Wife's Antecedent Act

II. VREELAND

			Wife's Response				
Code	(1)	(2)	(3)	(4)	(5)	(6)	T
(1)	35	7	1	9	0	2	54
(2)	4	1	0	2	0	0	7
(3)	11	3	5	8	0	0	27
(4)	2	1	0	1	1	0	4
(5)	1	0	1	1	0	0	3
(6)	0	0	0	0	0	0	0
T	53	12	7	21	0	2	95

Husband's Antecedent Act

			Husband's Response				
Code	(1)	(2)	(3)	(4)	(5)	(6)	T
(1)	35	5	12	3	1	0	56
(2)	6	1	1	0	0	1	9
(3)	3	0	5	0	0	0	8
(4)	10	1	6	0	1	0	18
(5)	0	0	0	0	0	0	0
(6)	1	0	1	0	0	0	2
T	55	7	25	3	2	1	93

Wife's Antecedent Act

CODES:
(1) Cognitive acts
(2) Resolving acts
(3) Reconciling acts
(4) Appeals
(5) Rejecting acts
(6) Coercive acts

unlike Mr. Harris—responds more than half the time with cognitive acts, and one-third of the time with attemps at emotional reconciliation. Communicative cycling for the Vreelands tends to occur in the interchange of cognitive acts. There are no indications of the destructive cycling noted for the Harrises. At the end of Chapter Eight we commented on the intermeshing of partners into a couple unit with a particular style. Although we shall discuss this later, even casual perusal of Table 2 suggests that, despite differences between the individuals within the marital pairs, each couple shares a style of interaction.

Organization of Matrices. Table 2 combines the four newlywed Improvisation scenes. Similar matrices exist for each of the scenes separately. Thus, at the newlywed stage alone there are 368 basic interaction matrices—four conflict situations for each of the ninety-two persons in the forty-six couples. In order to zoom out to examine different contextual dimensions of communication and conflict and to explore theory more concretely, we combine these matrices in different ways. For example, when we consider the contingency relations between antecedent and consequent acts, we combine all couples; in considering the effect of the conflict situation we combine antecedent and consequent acts.

Before examining each contextual dimension in detail, however, a broad overall analysis will help us in ordering our findings. For this general level, and consonant with the discussion of communication theory in Chapter Three, we chose multivariate informational analysis.[2]

Multivariate Informational Analysis. Multivariate informational analysis has a formal or logical equivalence to variance analysis (Garner and McGill, 1956) in that it makes possible the partitioning of total variability into component parts (predictor and error components). Informational analysis, unlike variance analysis,

---

[2] Even with thousands of acts, we were not able to assess all the variables simultaneously. Ensuring an adequate number of entries in the cells of the matrices required two separate uncertainty analyses of the newlywed data. The first analysis uses scene (or Improvisation) (I), sex (S), and antecedent act (A) as predictors of the consequent act (C); the second uses couple (or pair) (P), sex (S), and antecedent act (A) as predictors.

makes no assumptions about the metric of the criterion variable and is thus appropriate for nominal data and for frequencies in discrete categories, as in the present instance. More concretely, Bob's actions toward his wife are identified by being placed in a category in terms of the Coding Scheme for Interpersonal Conflict. Sue's responses to these actions become in a sense a criterion variable. These responses are also identified by category. Because the data are not described in terms of degrees of quantity, but rather are labeled qualitatively, variance analysis is impossible, but informational analysis, which flows from information theory, fits the bill perfectly. For an excellent and thorough presentation the reader is referred to Attneave (1959).

The logic of multivariate informational analysis is straightforward. It allows one to answer the following questions: (1) How much does knowing one variable reduce our uncertainty about possible outcomes—that is, increase our power to predict the occurrence of another variable? Does knowing that the speaker is male, for example, provide any information about the manner in which he will act? (2) To what extent does knowing the joint effects of two variables reduce our uncertainty about a third? For example, men and women may communicate differently in different situations; by knowing the sex of the respondent and the situation, our prediction of the response is enhanced. (3) How is the information given by one variable about another affected by holding a third variable constant? For example, asking people to enact specific instructions may mask the true effects of antecedent messages on consequent replies; partialing out the confounding variable may enhance our information about existing sequential dependencies in the communication process.[3]

[3] The analyses treat populations of acts rather than populations of couples. One may legitimately argue that the statistical requirements of independence have been violated. Unfortunately, there is no way around the problem; it is germane to all studies where one repeatedly samples the behavior of individuals and then combines the frequencies obtained from one individual with those obtained from another. Since the condition of non-independence tends to inflate the chi-square values, one must interpret the resulting significance levels with caution. Because of the large number of acts involved, chi-square tests of significance tend to yield significance levels beyond the .001 level. The more important statistic, as Hays (1963) points out, is the measure of strength of association between two variables or the

Informational Analyses

The analyses, which are abridged in Table 3, set the task of this and the following three chapters: to examine the effects of marital partners' acts on each other and to examine how these interactions are affected by the scene, the sex, and the couple. Let us first look at some general findings. The conflict situation (Improvisation scene) accounts for 3.6 percent of the uncertainty of responses $(I;C)$, male-female differences for 0.2 percent $(S;C)$, the immediately preceding act for 4.2 percent $(A;C)$, and differences among couples for 4.7 percent $(P;C)$. Not unexpectedly, the more one knows about the specific situation and the participants involved, the more predictive power one gains about how they will behave. Knowing the sex of the respondent together with the immediately preceding message and the nature of the conflict situation reduces uncertainty about his reply by 10.8 percent $(I,S,A;C)$. This figure is roughly equivalent to a multiple correlation coefficient of .33. Still more information is conveyed by knowing exactly which couple is engaged in the interaction: even omitting the nature of the conflict scene from consideration, we can reduce our uncertainty about responses by 16.4 percent, a figure roughly equivalent to a multiple correlation coefficient of .40 $(P,S,A;C)$.

An important point to grasp about Table 3 is that knowing the joint effect of variables increases our information about what is communicated beyond what might be expected from independent effects. For example, the information gain from knowing both couple and immediate antecedent act is greater than would be expected were these variables additive—11.8 percent as compared to 8.9 percent. As suggested in our earlier comments about the Harrises and the Vreelands, Bob and Sue differ from Tom and Mary not only in the distribution of their responses—such as the frequency of using complaints versus appeals—but also in the pattern of their interactive exchanges. For instance, given a complaint from their wives, Bob and Tom respond differently $(P_A;C = 7.6$ percent as compared to $P;C = 4.7$ percent). Similarly, the predictive power

amount of variance in one variable accounted for by knowledge of another variable. In our case, this measure is the $\%sU(C)$, the amount by which the uncertainty of the consequent response—$U(C)$—is reduced by knowledge or control of the other variables.

Table 3.
TWO UNCERTAINTY ANALYSES OF NEWLYWED DATA

Source	$\%sU(C)^a$	Source	$\%sU(C)$
I;C	3.64	I_S;C	7.36
S;C	0.18	I_A;C	6.30
A;C	4.24	S_I;C	3.89
P;C	4.71	S_A;C	0.32
I,S;C	7.54	A_I;C	6.90
I,A;C	10.54	A_S;C	4.38
S,A;C	4.56	P_S;C	6.62
P,S;C	6.80	P_A;C	7.56
P,A;C	11.79	S_P;C	2.09
I,S,A;C	10.81	A_P;C	7.08
P,S,A;C	16.37	P,S_A;C	9.15
		P,A_S;C	14.15
		S,A_P;C	6.91
		A_{PS};C	9.57
		P_{SA};C	11.81
		S_{PA};C	4.58

[a] All results are significant beyond the .001 level.
$N = 15,132$ acts for forty-six couples.

I	Scene or improvisation		consequent act within
S	Sex		each of the sexes (or
A	Antecedent		with sex held statisti-
P	Couple or pair		cally constant)
I,S;C	Joint effects of scene	A_{PS};C	Effects of antecedent
	and sex on consequent		on consequent act
	act		with couple and sex
I_S;C	Effects of scene on		held constant

of the antecedent act is enhanced beyond additive expectations when we include consideration of the particular conflict scene. Contextual dimensions, then, do not operate independently of one another. In at least some cases they enhance each other, amplifying the information conveyed between participants more than might be expected. As suggested in Chapter Three, the context for interaction may not only influence behavior directly (control) but also affect its patterning (organization).

Summary

We have tried to show how communication theory and its mathematical translation (multivariate informational analysis) can be used to provide answers to questions about human interaction. This chapter describes how, using the Coding Scheme for Interpersonal Conflict, we organized the data to provide matrices of interaction. Illustrative matrices for two couples suggested some aspects of destructive and constructive communication and coping styles. By subjecting the matrices to multivariate informational analyses we achieve an overview of some contextual dimensions of communication and conflict. In a preliminary way we note that the conflict situation, the couple, and the nature of the other partner's immediately antecedent act all affect the course of interaction; male-female differences have comparatively minor effects. The contextual dimensions are not independent of one another, and they may exert organizational as well as control effects on communication. We find that at least in some cases they work conjunctively to amplify communicative yield beyond simply additive expectations.

XI

The Situational
Context and
the Other's Act

The Situational Context

The preliminary sketch of findings in Chapter Ten shows that people respond not solely to stimuli but also in terms of their definitions of the situation and their relationships with each other. The findings are in the tradition of Charles Cooley and George Herbert Mead and are consistent with other studies that have found improvements in prediction by systematically assessing behavior within defined settings (Block and Bennett, 1955; Cottrell, 1942; Moos, 1968; Raush and others, 1959, 1960). Much of social learning involves coming to distinguish between different situations.

A closer look at the effects of the different situations provided by the scenes is in order.

Scene. Even apart from the informational analyses, prior data indicate that the situation makes a difference to our couples. The fairly innocuous anniversary scene produces the smallest average number of acts; the more conflictual television scene involves significantly more interactions; and the even more intense closeness-distance scenes yield significantly more acts than the television scene. Moreover, whereas only two couples fail to achieve a satisfactory resolution in the anniversary scene and four fail to do so in the television scene, fourteen and thirteen couples, respectively, fail to resolve the two closeness-distance scenes (see Doehrman, 1968). If we consider the first two scenes as issue-oriented and specific and the latter two scenes as relationship-oriented and unspecific, it is clear—as suggested in Chapters Four and Eight—that conflict is far easier to cope with given a specific issue.

We also expected that people would respond differently in different situations. The informational analysis reported in Chapter Ten confirmed this expectation. A detailed picture of the differences in responses generated by the four scenes is given by Table 4.

The relative benignity of the anniversary scene is reflected in the distribution of responses. Couples engage in predominantly cognitive exchanges or acts designed to resolve or reconcile their differences. There is little tendency to resort to rejection or coercion of the other.

A more heated exchange develops in the television scene, a competitive conflict of interest. There is still a heavy reliance on cognitive exploration of the problem, but the more conflictual quality of the exchange can be seen in the increased frequency of rejecting and coercive acts and in the correspondingly reduced number of resolving and reconciling acts.

As noted, both the anniversary and television scenes concern a specific issue and are, thus, markedly different phenomenologically from the relationship-oriented closeness-distance scenes. The difference is strikingly reflected in Table 4. In the closeness-distance conflicts, couples engage in far fewer cognitive explorations and resort to far more rejection and coercion.

Table 4.
Percentages of Acts Used in Each Category by Scene

Scene	Categories of Acts						
	Cognitive	Resolving	Reconciling	Appealing	Rejecting	Coercive	N
Anniversary	54.1	15.6	12.2	13.5	1.1	3.4	2437
Television	57.0	10.8	4.2	9.8	6.1	12.1	3312
Husband							
Distant	38.5	5.4	9.6	12.2	16.1	18.1	4347
Wife Distant	35.6	7.3	11.4	10.1	16.7	18.9	5036

Issue-oriented and Relationship-oriented Conflicts. The effect of the situation on response distributions is seen even more clearly when we combine the relationship scenes in terms of the roles given by the instructions. Table 5 compares response distributions when the instructions are to maintain distance with those when the instructions are to achieve closeness. As might be expected, the partner who is attempting to maintain distance is far more rejecting than his mate; rejection is part of the role. What is less expected is that to maintain distance the person in this role apparently moves toward coercion and personal attack—that is, guilt-induction, disparagement, and threat. The partner whose role is to achieve closeness quite expectedly attempts to modify the conflict situation by means of appeals and efforts at reconciliation. But given that almost half of the distancing partners' responses are rejecting or coercive acts, it is not surprising that conflict escalates, as suggested by the relatively high proportion of unresolved scenes and the length of the protocols. Obviously the relationship-oriented scenes, as compared to the issue-oriented scenes, come closer to Deutsch's description of destructive conflicts where "there is an increasing reliance upon a strategy of power and upon the tactics of threat, coercion, and deception. Correspondingly, there is a shift away from a strategy of persuasion and from the tactics of conciliation, minimizing differences, and enhancing mutual understanding and good will" (1969a, p. 11). This is not to say that relationship issues inevitably eventuate in destructive conflicts; some constructive outcomes were illustrated in Chapter Eight. In Chapter Thirteen we shall return to this issue when we discuss a group of troubled couples and their interactions.

The Antecedent Message

The communication process is predicted on the assumption that individuals share definitions of situations and expectations about appropriate behavior. Man is born into a social structure that presents meanings, values, and expectations. His development hinges on his learning those meanings and sharing in a common use of language and messages. The above discussion of scene effects demonstrates the power of specific situations to constrain behavior

Table 5.

Percentages of Acts Used in Distance and Closeness Roles

Role[a]	Categories						
	Cognitive	Resolving	Reconciling	Appealing	Rejecting	Coercive	N
To maintain distance	35.0	5.8	7.1	2.6	26.9	22.4	4700
To achieve closeness	38.6	7.0	14.1	19.5	6.0	14.6	4683

[a] Combines husband data from husband distant scenes with wife data from wife distant scenes and similarly combines data on closeness.

and affect communication. That discussion might be thought of as descriptive of stimuli effects at a macro level; couples placed in the same situations tend to respond in a similar fashion to a considerable degree. (That they also tend to respond differently from one another we shall see later, particularly in Chapter Thirteen.) We now turn to the micro level and examine the effects of the specific stimulus, the message that immediately precedes a response.

That there are regularities in the communication process at the level of specific stimuli is very clear. The antecedent act reduced by 4.2 percent the uncertainty of the consequent act (see Table 3, source A;C). Evidently the antecedent act (what Bob says to Sue) does constrain the consequent act (how Sue responds). The constraining effect of the antecedent message is, however, stronger than this simple relationship might indicate; it is masked by the effects of other variables. The analysis of scene effects might suggest that the same antecedent message could elicit different responses depending on the situation. In fact, this is so. When scene effects are held constant statistically, the antecedent message accounts for a higher proportion of response variation (see Table 3, source A_I;C), 6.9 percent. We see that the nature of the conflict is a determinant not only of outcomes but also of the patterning of interaction. A particularly clear example appears in the closeness-distance scenes where, because of the instruction to maintain distance, appeals meet with rejection far more often than in the issue-oriented scenes.[1]

Because the instructions in the closeness-distance scenes have such a powerful effect on the response distributions, we felt that these scenes would hinder our search for ordinary regularities in communication between spouses in conflict. Hence, we decided to use the issue-oriented scenes for our examination of antecedent-to-consequent relationships. The information values for each of these first two scenes are approximately equal, and inspection of the patterns of interaction within each reveals marked similarities. Table 6 presents the results of combining the antecedent-to-conse-

---

[1] We may note here that other variables similarly mask the constraining effect of the immediately antecedent act; these will be discussed in later chapters.

quent matrices of husbands and wives in the anniversary and television scenes.

As in Chapter Ten, the row totals indicate the number of times each category was used as an antecedent act, the column totals the number of times each was used as a consequent act. The cell entries are percentages, the frequency of the cell divided by the row total. Thus, in the first row, 65.0 percent of the responses to the 3236 cognitive antecedent messages were also cognitive in nature. The percentage figures beneath the column totals represent the proportion of total responses accounted for by each category. The percentage figures for average category usage further represent the proportion of times a given message is likely to be sent (E). Thus, one would expect 11.4 percent of all communications to be appeals; but knowing that the previous antecedent message was a rejecting one increases one's expectation (to 18.2 percent) of an appeal as a reply. To simplify things for the reader, contingent replies that occur more frequently than would be expected by 5 percent or more are highlighted by a plus sign and those that occur less often by 5 percent or more are preceded by a minus sign.

The Communication Process. The entries in Table 6 reflect what is assumed to be the general nature of the communication process. Most of the interactions between people are of a cognitive nature. We give each other information, ask questions, offer suggestions, and argue positions and issues. Even in the intense closeness-distance scenes the predominant response was cognitive.

The table illustrates some of the theoretical notions of Part One. As might be expected, what one partner does affects the following act of the other. The pluses and minuses in the cell entries indicate communication. The acts of one partner "select" responses from the repertoire of the other. A glance at the diagonal of the table suggests that communication is likely to be symmetrically reciprocal in nature. That is, a cognitive act will most probably induce a cognitive reply, an attempt at resolution will most probably be reciprocated by a similar attempt, and so on. Cognitive messages receive the highest reciprocation; knowing that the preceding message had been cognitive makes guessing a cognitive reply a fairly safe bet. We may note, moreover, that when one spouse moves to more emotional communications the interaction as

Table 6.
PERCENTAGES OF CONSEQUENT ACTS FOR EACH ANTECEDENT ACT IN ISSUE-ORIENTED SCENES

Antecedent Categories	Consequent Categories						
	Cognitive	Resolving	Reconciling	Appealing	Rejecting	Coercive	N
Cognitive	+65.0	11.6	4.2	10.2	2.2	6.7	3236
Resolving	−47.2	+22.1	11.4	10.2	3.5	5.5	763
Reconciling	−32.5	11.6	+31.8	+16.4	2.2	5.5	415
Appealing	54.3	11.1	7.8	14.9	4.7	7.2	639
Rejecting	−28.2	11.8	4.1	+18.2	7.3	+30.5	220
Coercive	−41.6	10.5	4.4	9.2	+15.8	+18.5	476
N	3207	738	436	655	229	484	5749
E (percent)	55.8	12.7	7.4	11.4	4.0	8.4	

NOTE: Plus (+) = contingencies that are greater than column expectations (E) by 5 or more percent; minus (−) = contingencies 5 or more percent less than expectations.

a whole moves in that direction; except for appeals, responses to emotional messages are less often cognitive in nature than would be expected. Offers to resolve the conflict, attempts to reconcile the relationship, and coercive messages are returned in kind more frequently than would be expected. Data from the later stages of marriage indicate that these tendencies to reciprocation are stable over time.

Positive and Negative Messages.   Newlywed couples engage in mutual exchanges designed to resolve or reconcile their differences. Without such reciprocity, it is difficult to see how conflict could end satisfactorily. This reciprocity indicates a commitment to maintain the relationship, and the commitment seems to remain stable through a period of years. It is not surprising that couples who stayed married and who were seen again during the wife's first pregnancy and following the birth of that child continued such mutually gratifying interactions (see Chapter Fourteen).

Negatively affective messages (rejection and coercion) also tend to elicit reciprocation in kind. Deutsch (1969a) too found such tendencies and pointed out that negatively affective tactics lead to prolonged and destructive conflict. Our data corroborate Deutsch's remarks about such tactics. Heavy use of rejection and coercion was significantly associated with inability to resolve the closeness-distance scenes (Doehrman, 1968). Further evidence will be presented in Chapter Thirteen suggesting that prolonged use of acts in these categories is also associated with deterioration of the marital relationship itself.

Not all categories are symmetrically reciprocal. For example, an act of rejection leads more often to appeal and coercion than to reciprocal rejection. The heightened use of appeals and coercion as responses to rejection makes intuitive sense. Rejection in this study is most generally a cold refusal to become engaged with the other. "Leave me alone!" is its paradigm. Such a rejection, especially when it continues in spite of efforts to find out what is wrong, leaves the partner no handle for argument or reconciliation. Hence, when the relationship itself is highly valued, one spouse tries to appeal to the other or to coerce the other in order to break the impasse. Were rejection by one partner to lead to rejection by the other, the conflict would end in mutual separation. Appeals and coercion (plus arguments) at the least keep open the lines of communication.[2]

The Probabilistic Nature of Communication. Fortunately, reciprocation of negatively affective messages is neither absolutely deterministic nor accomplished at the expense of resolving and reconciling acts; note that in the response distributions to rejection and coercion there is a decrease of cognitive responses but no noticeable decrease of resolving and reconciling responses. It appears that these newlywed couples can cycle out of the negative tit-for-tat and into resolution and reconciliation.

Indeed, there are no one-to-one antecedent-to-consequent relationships in our data. Each antecedent message can receive any of the six categories as a reply with each response category having a probability of occurrence greater than zero. The probabilistic nature of the communicative process allows for shifts into another mode or category even though there is a tendency to reciprocation in kind. It is true that if Bob argues unemotionally for his position, Sue tends to take the same tack. If he makes an attempt to resolve the issue or to bring about reconciliation, she reciprocates. If he gets nasty, so does she. But all of these statements are to be understood probabilistically, not absolutely. Though there are tendencies to reciprocation, the amount of uncertainty that remains is still very high. Even when the nature of the scene and the instructions bias responses in a certain direction, such as toward rejection no matter what the spouse says, such a bias only increases the probability of a rejection, it does not absolutely determine it.

Summary

The situational context was examined in detail. The data argue strongly that the determinants of human behavior range beyond the immediate stimulus conditions and include the total situation, social roles, and the expectations of others. We have

[2] As an aside, we may note that an appeal—a composite of appeals to fairness, to the other's motives, to the love of the other, and pleading, coaxing, or the offer of a bribe—has little or no special effect on the respondent. We may also note that coercion induces rejection; the best way to get rejected is to be coercive. See Table 6.

shown specifically that the set given to participants has a definite impact on the nature of their communication—that different categories of acts are used under varying instructions and that the same messages elicit different replies in different circumstances.

Issue-oriented conflict scenes produce higher levels of cognitive exchanges and lower levels of rejection and coercion than do relationship-oriented conflicts. The differences in frequency of category usage make both intuitive and theoretical sense. Under instruction to remain distant, spouses concentrate their messages in the rejecting and coercive categories; under instruction to reestablish closeness, they make more appeals to the other and show more attempts at reconciliation of the relationship. Moreover, when the conflict is issue-oriented, efforts at resolving the issue are paramount; when the conflict is relationship-oriented, efforts at interpersonal reconciliation assume more importance. As indicated, the shifts from resolving and reconciling messages to threatening communications could have been predicted from theories on the nature of destructive conflicts.

We have offered the barest beginning of the attempt to learn the nature of the relationship between messages received and replies made. We examined the effects of the immediately antecedent act on the recipient's immediately consequent response.[3] What one partner does clearly influences how the other responds. But similar acts will to some extent induce different patterns of response depending on the situation. Again, as implied in Chapter Three, we see that experience is influenced not only directly, but also in its patterning, by the context in which it occurs. In later chapters, we shall examine some further contextual connections between antecedent and consequent acts.

We noted the probabilistic nature of constraint in interpersonal messages. Within a probabilistic framework, messages tend to receive symmetrically reciprocal responses. Thus, cognitive mes-

[3] Further possibilities for research concern the chaining of communications as discussed in Chapter Three. Here the question would be not what effect the immediately preceding statement had on the response, but what effect(s) the statements two or three or ten steps previously had on the response. Certainly there are some crucial events, say an especially hostile exchange, that may permeate the whole sequence to follow so that every subsequent act is really a response to that crucial exchange.

sages tend especially to induce cognitive replies and emotional messages emotional replies. But such reciprocation is not invariable. Rejection, for example, did not, among our newlywed couples, lead to rejecting reactions. We can infer that a commitment to continuation of their relationship and to further communication often enables participants to escape what would otherwise become a mutually destructive cycle. We may note, also, that the findings suggest a basis for credence in the validity of the data generated by our procedures.

XII

The Male-Female
Context:
Husbands and Wives

Several times in earlier chapters (especially Chapters Four and Seven) we have discussed the tensions between separation and connectedness as a fundamental dilemma of human relationships. An ideal shared by diverse authors (for example, Bowen, 1971; Buber, 1957; Erikson, 1959) and many American couples is that one can love another precisely as the other is, establishing unity without losing identity or destroying the identity of the other. In terms of this ideal a sound mutual commitment to the marital relationship means that each partner shares responsibility for maintaining and enhancing unity, yet each is able to tolerate separation and independence of action. Interpersonal conflict puts this ideal to test.

In the not too distant past there was considerable lore about sex differences in terms of separateness and connectedness. Old jokes about the wife's resentment of the husband's night out with the boys or about independent male golf, hunting, or gambling expeditions pointed to an assumed central difference in the way men and women looked at intimacy. Men were supposed to fear absorption and loss of individuality while women were supposed to fear separation and loss of intimacy. The old western movie exemplified the theme—the male struggling to be free and the female struggling to tie him down.

The culture fostered these images. Males were taught the values of an individualistic, instrumental, rational, achievement-oriented style, while females were expected to develop an emotional, romantic, interpersonal, dependent style. Traditionally, wives complained about the paucity of their husbands' attentions, and husbands complained of being trapped and suffocated by marriage. Women had a greater stake in the continuity and cohesiveness of the marriage, men a greater stake in their own individuality and external pursuits.

Such traditional differences may be changing. Whether and for what proportion of the population they are changing in the actions of daily life (as compared to talk about such actions) we do not know. Nor do we know the degree of change. Women are, however, more and more educated in a system based on traditionally male notions of achievement and competition. Men, on the other hand, are beginning to recognize in themselves a softer side, a human need for dependable and attentive others. It may well be that we are in the midst of a cultural revolution in which sex roles are being questioned and may be radically altered. The couples in our study grew up in the forties and fifties when the distinction between sex roles was perhaps less clear-cut than it was in an earlier era but more than it is at present. In a sense they may be a transition group.

One might expect that couples at very early stages of an intimate relationship would be less conscious of the need for distance and separation. But we expect also that the honeymoon period of fusion (which lasts longer than the one-week wedding trip) will be characterized by relatively more violent eruptions of the need for separation because the pattern of intimacy has yet to be established and precisely because the need for separation is less conscious. We may expect the first months of marriage to be rather volatile. By the fourth month some patterns should have emerged, although we do not expect that the work of this stage has been completed. With these thoughts in mind let us look at how our sample men and women corresponded and differed in their handling of the conflicts presented to them in the Improvisation scenes.

Husband-Wife Differences in Handling Conflict

Any supposition that men and women differ greatly in how they communicate and deal with conflict is clearly refuted by the data. The informational analysis of Chapter Ten (Table 3) showed that sex differences accounted for an extremely small, though statistically significant, amount of the uncertainty of the responses— 0.18 percent. The analysis also showed that controlling for antecedent responses did not appreciably increase predictive power ($S_A;C$ was 0.32 percent). In other words, the matrix of antecedent-to-consequent relationships for all wives over all scenes was very similar to the corresponding matrix for all husbands. Unlike the situational context in Chapter Eleven, the male-female context did not organize the patterning of interaction. In general, then, husbands and wives tend to respond in the same way to each other's acts, and knowing only that the respondent is male or female does not afford much differential predictive power about how he or she will respond.

Furthermore, the data yield no evidence for the theory offered by Parsons and Bales (1955) about sex-role differentiation in marriage—that men are more instrumental (concerned with tasks) and women are more expressive (concerned with emotions). These husbands and wives appear to share responsibility for both instrumental and expressive acts. The findings agree with those of Heiss (1962), Leik (1963), and Levinger (1964), who found no real sex-role differentiation in interaction in intimate dyads. Moreover, certain trends in the data are surprising. It is generally assumed that wives are the more supportive members within families, but our results contradict this assumption. Husbands made more attempts to resolve the conflict and to restore harmony to the relationship. Furthermore, wives used more of the negatively toned categories, rejection and coercion or personal attack, than did husbands.

A first glance, then, suggests that husbands and wives differ only slightly (despite statistical significance) in their communicative approaches to interpersonal conflict. Some trends do, however, appear. These trends emerge more clearly when we eliminate the masking effects induced by the Improvisation scenes. A separate informational analysis suggested that the closeness-distance scenes, which demand contrasting reciprocal roles for the two partners, exercised such a masking effect.[1]

Unlike the closeness-distance scenes in which partners are given opposing role sets, the issue-oriented anniversary and television scenes do not, prima facie, bias the responses of either partner in any direction. Analysis of these scenes can give us a better idea of whether the sexes respond differently in conflict. Sex differences are still small (0.67 percent reduction in response uncertainty), although greater than in the overall analysis. After examining these two issue-oriented scenes, we will turn briefly to the final two scenes.

The combined matrices for the first two scenes suggest that husbands engaged in more acts directed toward resolving the conflict and reconciling their partners than did wives; the wives, on the other hand, engaged in more appeals and more acts of coercion or personal attack (see Table 7, bottom two rows). These directions are even more apparent when we examine the differences between husbands and wives in their responses to the same antecedent acts. We see that husbands were more likely to use the resolving and reconciling categories, no matter what their wives said or did in the

---

[1] It may be noted that the informational gain suggested by controlling for scene $(S_I; C)$ in Table 3 is deceptive. Within each closeness-distance scene husbands and wives may be expected to differ in their interactions because they are instructed to take contrasting roles—getting close versus staying distant. Because roles are confounded with sex differences, it would be spurious to interpret the informational gain that is obtained by controlling for scene as representing a truer picture of sex differences.

immediately preceding moment; wives were more likely to respond with appeals and coercion, irrespective of their husbands' preceding actions.

Given the prevalent assumption that wives are the socioemotional experts in the family and more supportive (see Parsons and Bales, 1955), such results are surprising. Our husbands seemed the more emotionally supportive and conciliatory. The results do not suggest that husbands are more emotional than wives—appealing and coercive categories encode highly emotional responses. They do, however, indicate a tendency for these newlywed wives to use emotional pressure on their husbands more than the husbands used it on them. Moreover, at this stage at least, these husbands tended to be more susceptible than their wives to this kind of pressure; indeed, in response to every category they showed more concern for their wives' feelings, reassured them more, sought forgiveness more, attempted to compromise more, and so forth. These differences are more graphic in Table 8, which compares the consequent acts of husbands and wives for each antecedent category but groups the responses into only two categories: conciliatory (resolving and reconciliatory acts) and pressuring (appealing and coercive acts). In response to every category wives put more pressure on husbands while husbands are more conciliatory.

It is especially instructive to note the response distributions to a reconciling act (Table 7). While both sexes respond in kind above expectation, for husbands this response is the mode; they are much more likely than wives to respond in kind and thus keep the interaction in the reconciling mode. Wives are more prone than husbands to use coercion or personal attack as a response to reconciling behavior. Indeed, in response to a reconciling act wives use the pressuring categories (appeals and coercion) about one-quarter of the time (26.3 percent), while husbands use them only 15.5 percent of the time (and of this only 1.8 percent is coercion). These husbands apparently are more constrained by a reconciling act to respond in kind and thus end the conflict; wives tend more than husbands to follow reconciling behavior on the part of their husbands with efforts to attain their own aims. It is tempting to interpret these data on wives as an indication that wives tend to take reconciling behavior by their husbands as a sign of weakness and

Table 7.

PERCENTAGES OF CONSEQUENT ACTS FOR EACH ANTECEDENT ACT OF HUSBANDS AND WIVES IN ISSUE-ORIENTED SCENES

Consequent Categories

Antecedent Categories	Sex	Cognitive	Resolving	Reconciling	Appealing	Rejecting	Coercive	N
Cognitive	H	64.2	13.2	5.6	8.8	1.9	5.6	1597
	W	65.3	9.9	2.9	11.5	2.5	7.8	1639
Resolving	H	46.6	24.9	14.7	8.3	2.1	3.4	326
	W	47.6	20.1	-8.9	11.7	4.6	7.1	437
Reconciling	H	30.9	13.1	40.5	13.7	0.0	1.8	168
	W	33.6	10.5	-25.9	18.2	3.6	+8.1	247
Appealing	H	56.3	13.3	8.4	11.7	4.9	5.4	368
	W	51.7	-8.1	7.0	+19.2	4.4	9.6	271
Rejecting	H	27.3	16.4	7.3	17.3	10.0	21.8	110
	W	29.1	-7.3	-0.9	19.1	-4.5	+39.1	110
Coercive	H	43.4	11.7	5.5	7.9	17.2	14.1	290
	W	38.7	8.6	2.7	11.3	13.4	+25.3	186
N	H	1601	415	261	276	117	189	2859
	W	1606	323	175	379	112	295	2890
Percent	H	56.0	14.5	9.1	9.7	4.1	6.6	
	W	55.6	11.2	6.1	13.1	3.9	10.2	

NOTE: Plus (+) = W higher by 5 percent or more; minus (−) = W lower by 5 percent or more.

Table 8.
PERCENTAGE DIFFERENCES IN HUSBANDS'
AND WIVES' CONCILIATORY AND PRESSURING RESPONSES
IN ISSUE-ORIENTED SCENES

Antecedent Categories	Consequent Categories	
	Conciliatory[a] (− indicates W < H)	Pressuring[b] (+ indicates W > H)
Cognitive	−6.0	+ 4.9
Resolving	−10.6	+ 7.1
Reconciling	−17.2	+10.5
Appealing	−6.6	+11.7
Rejecting	−15.5	+19.1
Coercive	−5.9	+14.6

[a] Conciliatory combines resolving and reconciling categories.
[b] Pressuring combines appealing and coercive categories.
NOTE: Reading the first row of the table, to their husbands' cognitive acts wives are 6 percent less often conciliatory and 4.9 percent more often pressuring than husbands are to wives' cognitive acts.

to use it as an opening to attain their own ends; one must be careful, however, to avoid too quick an interpretation, since wives generally use more pressure on husbands in response to any act.

The response distributions to rejection also merit special attention, since both sexes use rejection as an antecedent the same number of times. Wives use almost twice as many coercive responses as husbands; indeed, for wives this response is the mode. Husbands use about three times as many resolving and reconciling acts in response to rejection as wives (although they also use rejection acts more).

Thus, in the two issue-oriented scenes husbands show relatively greater concern for actually resolving the problem and keeping the relationship harmonious; wives appear to behave in ways designed to enforce their own point of view.

The relationship-oriented scenes, in which one partner is instructed to maintain distance and the other to achieve closeness, embody more fully the issues of separateness and connectedness (Hess and Handel, 1959) or the extent to which individuality versus mutuality will obtain in the relationship. The instructions to maintain distance attempt to arouse in one partner the desire to isolate himself from the other, to assert his own interests over those of the dyad. The instructions to achieve closeness attempt to mobilize a reaffirmation of attachment. The inherent dilemma of the unity of separate individuals is further complicated by the Improvisations in that outsiders have entered the situation. Any mutual resolution requires one of the parties to break with the instructions. Moreover, the instructions to maintain distance may be presumed to run counter to the newlywed's desire for union; the partner striving to get close thus has extra leverage in the conflict.

Husbands and wives responded very similarly in the closeness-distance scenes. To what extent the similarity in these scenes was related to the temporal contiguity between the husband distant and the wife distant scenes and the fact that the wife distant always followed the husband distant we cannot know. Comparisons of contingencies between antecedent acts by one partner and consequent acts by the other add but little to the above picture of husband-wife differences. In general the directions of differences correspond to those found in the issue-oriented scenes. Thus, husbands, while maintaining distance, are more likely than are wives in that role to respond to their partner's appeal with approaches toward reconciliation; and wives are more likely than husbands to respond to appeals with rejection. In trying to get close, husbands are more likely than wives in that role to respond positively to any efforts at resolution or reconciliation by the distancing spouse; wives are more likely to counter such efforts with further argument and coercion. A seemingly discrepant finding, compared to that in other situations, is that in the distancing role wives are more apt than husbands to respond in kind to resolving or reconciling acts by the spouse seeking closeness.

Thus, generally husbands behaved in more pacifying ways than wives even in the closeness-distance scenes. Wives showed a fairly consistent tendency toward greater use of emotional pressure. It is interesting, however, that when sanctioned by the instructions husbands are more persistent than wives in maintaining distance in the face of resolving or reconciling acts.

Male-Female Similarities in Communication

It seems time to put to rest once and for all the sex-role differentiation theory of Parsons and Bales (1955), at least as far as dyadic interaction goes. Even those studies that tend to confirm the theory in finding men more instrumental and women more expressive note great similarities in the behavioral repertoires of the sexes (see Kenkel, 1957, 1961; Kenkel and Hoffman, 1956; March, 1960). Other studies have not even found small differences when the subjects were intimates (see Heiss, 1962; Leik, 1963; O'Rourke, 1963; Levinger, 1964). Levinger argues that there is task specialization (division of labor) within marriage, but that socioemotional behavior must be reciprocal to maintain the dyad. As expected, he finds task specialization and socioemotional mutuality among his couples. Rossi (1968) agrees; she prefers to see the instrumental and the expressive as two dimensions of all roles. It certainly seems more fruitful to assume that instrumentalism is one mode of action and expressivism another, rather than that they are poles on a single continuum. One can then define what is meant by instrumental and expressive behaviors and establish criteria for judging whether a person is high on both, low on both, high on one, low on the other, and so forth. One could then distinguish among families on the basis of the quality of their interaction and the appropriateness of their mode of interaction to the situation.

Certainly husbands and wives must develop both instrumental and expressive components. Parsons himself notes the instrumental component in traditional child care, and, although no similar discussion is given to the place of expressive components in traditionally male functions, the man who failed to recognize and respond to his own and others' feelings would probably experience serious difficulty in all interpersonal relationships, in tension management, and in finding the emotional support he needs to function adequately in a social world.[2]

[2] An example of such failure is the teacher in Bel Kaufman's *Up the Down Staircase* (Prentice-Hall, 1964) who, on receiving a love letter from one of his students, proceeds to correct her grammar.

An intimate relationship seems especially to require a balance between complementary and similar instrumental and expressive behavior. One partner may at times depend on the other to counter an emotional impulse with a cognitive task orientation and vice versa. But most spouses also depend on their partners to respond at times in kind. Partners with differentiated and flexible schemata would have the facility to alternate between instrumental and expressive modes depending on their own needs, the situation, and the needs of their spouses. In contrast, persons with undifferentiated or rigid schemata would probably be more consistently instrumental or expressive in their interactions, and would demand more stereotyped instrumental or expressive actions from others.[3]

Male-Female Differences in Communication

Given the assumption (based on research findings) that husbands and wives share responsibility for instrumental and expressive acts, we are still left with the need to explain our findings. Why is it that our newlywed husbands exhibit a greater proportion of positive expressive acts and seem more inclined to resolve the conflict and reconcile differences, while their wives are more inclined to engage in negative expressive acts and more readily apply emotional pressure as a means of handling conflict? We believe that the differences we found are consonant with what is generally known about the behavior available to persons of greater or lesser power.

Power. Deutsch (1969a) argues that the ability to engage in authentic cooperation in the midst of conflict presupposes a power base from which to operate. In effect, cooperation requires that both parties be capable of independent action; each must know that he is able to "go it alone" should the occasion arise. Empirical confirmation comes from Solomon (1960), who reports that a subject is more likely to engage in trusting behavior, if he has greater power relative to the person against whom he plays.[4]

[3] Thus "authoritarian personalities" have more stereotyped notions of male-female roles and behavior (Frenkel-Brunswik, 1964).

[4] In the particular experimental game, trusting behavior meant choosing to cooperate, which could cost money if the other did not cooperate in kind.

Thus, the more powerful member seems able to afford cooperation.

Power is a difficult concept to define. It makes sense to us, however, to tie the definition to the notion of interdependence, as Deutsch (1969a) suggests. Assume that two people are related to one another in such a way that the attainment of the individual goals of each is somehow dependent on the other. Independence of the other does not mean power over the other. Power can be defined by the (relative) independence of one party from the other and the other's dependence on him for the attainment of goals.

Male Chivalry and Female Vulnerability. Our cultural and ancestral tradition is patriarchal. For a long period of Western history men had almost complete authority, and women were often treated as possessions. It is interesting to note that out of this condition of imbalanced power seem to have grown notions of chivalry and gallantry—codes of masculine behavior toward the "weaker" sex that presage Deutsch's (1969a) findings on trust and cooperation. A gentleman, according to the code, treats a woman with care, respect, and tenderness, regardless of situation or circumstance. While we do not see as much of this chivalry today (men rarely offer women their seats on subways and buses anymore), there still are many signs that supportiveness and nonaggressiveness toward women are not only expected but also shown. Indeed, males may refuse to become overtly aggressive toward females even under extreme provocation (Taylor and Epstein, 1967).[5] The traditional masculine role thus includes not only the image of independence but also the image of protector. The role of the husband is to support and care for his wife, and our husbands are doing that.

Many studies have suggested the greater dependence of women on familial and marital ties (Blood and Wolfe, 1960; Komarovsky, 1955; Gurin and others, 1960). Compared to men, women placed a greater investment in marriage and were more vulnerable to the exigencies of the marital relationship. Traditionally, a woman's status as an individual and her self-worth depended on how

[5] It is interesting that males reciprocated when males were aggressive and that females reciprocated against aggressive males but not aggressive females. While we do not want to press one study too much, we wonder whether neither sex feels exhilaration in conflict with an opponent perceived as weak—a female.

she fared as a wife and mother. Her identity was bound up in her husband and in her marriage: as a bride she abandoned her maiden name, took on the family name of her husband, resided with him at his residence, followed where his career led, and accustomed herself to his life-style. Marriage research indicates that women had to make by far greater adjustments in marriage than men (Burgess and Cottrell, 1939; Landis, 1946; Burgess and Wallin, 1953; Bernard, 1964). Moreover, only by marrying could a woman legitimately realize her biological femininity through childbearing. Only thus—with the possible exception of the religious life—did she generally attain full acceptance in society. Having a highly successful career did not, in most people's eyes, make a woman admired as a woman but rather made her something of an oddity. In short, and with exceptions understood, a woman's acceptance by society has come from being the wife of a particular man and the mother of their children.

Men also depend on their wives for the attainment of mutually desired outcomes. The desire for sexual fulfillment, emotional attachment, companionship, security, and care is not limited to females. But the male identity has been less fused to the status and quality of his marriage and family. He has enjoyed an alternative mode for identity-formation and ego-gratification; occupational achievement and success, over which he himself might exercise some control, enhanced his self-esteem and guaranteed his place in society.

Growing Up Male and Female. Such male-female distinctions have been a part of growing up in America, at least among the middle class. Douvan and Adelson (1966) report revealing differences in the ways in which adolescent males and females orient themselves toward the future. Boys are preoccupied with decisions about future occupations; they show sophisticated and differentiated knowledge of possible jobs that might interest them and are working on plans that bridge their present situation and their anticipated future. Their self-esteem depends on work, skill, and achievement. Adolescent girls also discuss future work plans, but their ideas are more vague, they are less settled on jobs they might like, and they show a less realistic view of the steps they might take toward the jobs mentioned. Adolescent boys are able to control experiences that enhance a sense of self; who they are is measured in terms of what they do, and thus their choices about activities, training, and experience directly contribute to their self-definition. Adolescent girls, on the other hand, are less in control of who they may become; their future orientation is necessarily less differentiated, since their identity depends on the man they will marry. Lacking the means to coordinate experiences of their talents and interests directly with activities projected toward a selected future, girls exhibit a remarkable similarity in their fantasies about their future selves.[6] Their adult possibilities are dictated by the cultural image of the ideal American homemaker disseminated through the mass media. When the woman actually marries, she begins the process of concrete self-definition (which her husband began much earlier). She now works out the details of her unique fit with the cultural image to which she aspires, given the individuality, desires, and limitations of the man who has become her husband.

Even then, we believe, she is still unable to consolidate a large, but salient component of her identity. Fulfillment as a whole woman depends on motherhood. Her notions of herself as a mother remain embedded in cultural fantasies and are no doubt surrounded by fear and anxiety.[7] In many ways, however, motherhood is the point of emancipation of women from their families of origin. Whereas a boy may be seen as a man when he enters the service, obtains his first full-time job, or gets married, a young wife or female worker is often still viewed as immature. She is not a woman, has not gained adult status, until she bears a child.

Power, Security, and Male-Female Interaction. For all these reasons we assume that husbands have more power than wives and that wives are more dependent. We also assume that being a newlywed is more stressful for women than for men, and that lacking a stable, comfortable self-image, women are more anxious and insecure than their husbands. Men entering marriage thus have greater power than their wives, and this power differential can

---

[6] Data gathered by Susan M. Ervin and presented in Douvan and Adelson (1966, p. 235).

[7] Rossi (1968) notes that in our society women are ill-prepared for motherhood by the training they have received; fear and anxiety are, therefore, expectable.

account for many of the sex-linked variations in behavior. We think that our findings reflect these conditions and that the greater supportiveness shown by our newlywed husbands in the Improvisations is necessitated by and a response to their wives' needs. Since they are the ones with power, they can afford to be more magnanimous.[8]

The wives' greater use of appeals and coercion or personal attack may reflect their insecurity and anxiety, They need the relationship more and so exert more pressure to end conflict. It may be too that, because of their greater insecurity, winning is more important. Rapoport and Chammah (1965) found interesting but unexplained sex differences in long runs of repeated plays of the Prisoner's Dilemma game. College student men cooperated far more than women in the game. Men playing against men were somewhat more likely to cooperate following the other's cooperation than to retaliate following the other's defection. Women playing against women, on the other hand, were more likely to retaliate against the other's defection than to cooperate following the other's cooperation. Thus, men tended more toward reciprocation of cooperative acts, women toward reciprocation of noncooperative acts. Moreover, whereas the men tended to end the long runs of the game locked in on mutual cooperation, women tended to end up locked in on mutual defection. It may well be that both these results and our own are signs of differences in the sense of inner well-being and security of the sexes.

Marital "Success" and Male-Female Differences. In the first chapter we noted a number of unexplained correlates of marital "success." After reviewing the extensive literature on marital adjustment, Barry comments: "A pattern seems to be emerging from these data. Factors pertaining to the husband appear to be crucial to marital success. Background factors generally considered to lead to a stable male identity, such as happiness of the husband's **parents'** marriage and the husband's close attachment to his father, are related to happiness in marriage. The higher the husband's socioeconomic status and educational level, the greater the marital happiness. The more stable and nonneurotic the husband portrays

---

[8] That the husbands may also be acting out the cultural stereotype (the chivalrous male) in front of observers does not change the interpretation appreciably.

himself on personality inventories at the time of marriage and the more consistent he is in such self-portrayal over the course of the marriage, the happier the marriage. The higher the wife rates him on emotional maturity as well as on fulfilling his role as husband in conformity to cultural expectations, the happier the marriage. . . . It would appear—to generalize a bit—that a solid male identification, established through affectional ties with the father and buttressed by academic and/or occupational success and the esteem of his wife, is strongly related to happiness in marriage for the couples" (1970, p. 47).

An explanation in terms of differences in male and female power is consonant with findings of both questionnaire studies (as noted by Barry above) and research on cooperation in experimental games.

Power and Interpersonal Strategies. There is a further element in the power-dependence relationship that should also be considered in our explanation. Deutsch (1969a) comments on the lack of knowledge concerning the influence that groups of lower power have on those of higher power. He does, however, suggest that several strategies are available to a low power group attempting to bring about a change in a defensive, uninterested, or intransigent high power group. Two of these strategies, moral persuasion (an attempt to influence the high power group by emphasizing the congruence between the desires and interests of the low power group and the values and attitudes of the high power group) and harassment (an attempt to change the behavior of the high power group by increasing the costs of adherence to the status quo) seem analogous to our wives' use of appeals and coercion. In an appeal the wife tries to evoke her husband's sense of fairness, his love for her, the possibility of gratifying his own wishes, and the like. Guilt-induction, the predominant type of message coded as coercive, is designed to make the recipient painfully aware that his behavior fails to measure up to his own standards. It thus serves both purposes. Other coercive acts (disparagement, threats, commands, demands for compensation) extract a price for continuing present behavior.

The use of words as strategic devices for gaining an end have, it seems, been employed by women throughout history. A female's reputation as a scold, a shrew, a nag attest to the costs incurred from crossing her desires. We are not suggesting that the wives in our sample are nags, but we are pointing to the possibility that women, as a low power group, may learn a diplomacy of psychological pressure to influence male partners' behaviors. Men— more powerful because they have more readily available outlets other than marriage for growth, development, and satisfaction— can from their strength support and care for others dependent on them (women and children). Women and women's needs are given less legitimacy, since they are in a weaker position. To attain gratification they have mastered techniques of manipulating emotional communication.

Male-Female Schemata. Interpersonal conflict between a man and a woman impinges on and redintegrates schemata of masculinity and femininity. In the process of growing up, men develop organized structural images defining what it means to be a man in relation to a woman and of how a woman is expected to be in relation to a man; women develop corresponding schemata for their sex. These schemata evolve from interactions with others of both sexes, experienced relationships, and cultural lore. In a society where homogamy (like marrying like) is the rule, where cultural traditions are firm and change is slow and gradual, male and female schemata for masculinity and femininity are likely to be shared by men and women and by marital pairs. Where homogamy and tradition are less firm and where cultural change is rapid, schemata are less likely to mesh. Moreover, in times of rapid change, the schemata developed on the basis of earlier experiences, primarily with one's family of origin, may no longer be appropriate by adulthood.

Our couples, married in the late fifties and early sixties, are oriented toward a symmetrical mutuality. Consciously, they see themselves as coequals in the marriage, with equal rights and status. For the most part they act that way with one another when confronted with conflict. But some less conscious aspects of schemata relating to masculinity and femininity also emerge and are enacted on the testing ground of interpersonal conflict. The dimension of power emerges, and the interactions of the marital pair suggest shared images of male power and female powerlessness. One may argue that these images reflect status realities as well as role inductions from childhood training. If and when status equality between men and women becomes genuine, we may expect a gradual accommodation process whereby even the small sex differences we find in interactive modes would be supplanted by individual differences.

Summary

Our studies of newlyweds suggest that interactive styles of husbands and wives in handling conflict are in general much alike. Where differences occur they are in directions that imply a complementary power relationship: the husbands, in the male tradition, are independent and supportive; the wives, in the female tradition, coerce and appeal to their husbands from a position of weakness. An interpretation in terms of the power differential—actual or perceived—between men and women also helps explain results of questionnaire studies of marital "success" and some experiments on male-female differences.

Whether the relationship between husband and wife and the techniques each employ in coping with conflict between them shift as the marriage progresses in time and with pregnancy and childbirth is the subject of Chapter Fourteen. Before turning to longitudinal development, however, we look at some differences among couples.

The Couple Context: Harmony and Discord

In discussing modes employed by couples in coping with conflict we have, particularly in Chapters Seven and Eight, noted our impressions that individual couples form distinctive systems. The multivariate informational analyses confirm these impressions. Except for the instructional set in the closeness-distance scenes (see Chapter Fourteen), couple differences are the major single source of response variation. Couples differ from one another not only in the degree to which they use different response categories but also in the way they pattern their interactions. That is, Bob and Sue not only act more coercively toward each other than do Tom and Mary, but also respond differently to each other's coercive acts from the way Tom and Mary respond to each other's. This is shown in Table 3, where P;C is 4.7 percent while P_A;C is 7.6 percent. The comparison between the Harrises and Vreelands in Chapten Ten exemplified these general findings.

The Improvisation data reveal great differences in the ways couples handled conflict. Independent assessments of the couples in the form of factor scores, based on an analysis of the interviews, questionnaires, and other data gathered from the couples at the newlywed stage, provide a means of grouping couples so as to compare them and interpret differences in the interaction data.

Factor Analysis of Couples

Goodrich and others (1968) and Ryder (1970) present the results of the factor analytic study of all the data from interviews, questionnaires, interviewer ratings, and a Color Matching Test (Goodrich and Boomer, 1963). Unlike the usual factor analytic study, this one was designed to maximize simple structure among couples rather than tests. In other words, the aim was to maximize the tendency for each couple to have an extreme score on one and only one factor and to be middling in all the others. Thus, ideally one would have couples grouped on the basis of extreme scores on the factors. The procedure worked well enough, although there are a number of couples who have extreme scores on more than one factor.[1]

Of most immediate interest to us is the factor Goodrich, and others (1968) label Factor III, which is heavily loaded with items of reported or judged evaluation of the marriage. Husband's empathy, both partners' support of one another, wife yielding in disagreements, ease of decision process, couple (versus individual identity) orientation, and positive interviewer evaluation of the marriage are all inversely related to this factor. Positively related to this factor are reports of disagreement, of unhappiness, and of doubts about the marriage, and the wife's recollection of troubles with her family of origin. In other words, couples scoring high on the negative end of this factor might be judged to be happily married; those scoring high on the positive end would be judged to be unhappily married.

For purposes of grouping couples we chose one standard deviation above or below the mean factor score as a cutoff. There

[1] In an attempt to develop a taxonomy of marriage, D. W. Goodrich (1968) speculates on the factor patterns from a psychoanalytic point of view.

were six couples whose Factor III scores were at least this much above the mean; five of these scored more than one and one-half standard deviations above the mean. These six couples, who apparently experienced a relatively great amount of discord after only four months of marriage, we called *discordant* couples. Seven couples had Factor III scores at least one standard deviation below the mean, three of them at least one and one-half standard deviations below; these couples we labeled *harmonious*. Evidence for the validity of the discordant grouping came from follow-up of the original forty-six couples: four to seven years following their marriage, only three of all the couples were known to be separated or divorced, and all three were in the discordant group.

Discordant Couples

First Impressions. The two groups differed markedly in the amount of time spent enacting the Improvisations. The discordant couples averaged 472.8 acts per couple, the harmonious couples 249.9, whereas the mean number of interactions per couple for the whole sample was 329.0. Obviously, the discordant couples engaged in much longer conflict scenes than average, the harmonious in much shorter ones.

Table 9 allows a summary comparison of the discordant couples with the other couples in the sample. It is immediately evident that the discordant wives differ very little from the other wives; indeed, the matrices of antecedent-to-consequent response relationships with all scenes combined are also very similar, only three cells differing by 5 percent or more (Table 10). Discordant husbands, however, do differ from other husbands. They are more coercive (by 11 percent) and less cognitive (by 8 percent) in their behaviors with their wives than are the rest of the husbands. Indeed, the discordant couples reverse sex differences in the relative use of coercion (see Chapter Twelve): the discordant husbands are more coercive than their wives. Five of the six discordant couples show this reversal while only six of the other forty couples show it. A comparison of the antecedent-to-consequent matrices of discordant and all other husbands (Table 11) reveals that in response to every antecedent message from their wives the discordant husbands are

Table 9.

Comparison of Discordant and Other Couples in Four Scenes Combined

| Group | Consequent Categories | | | | | | |
	Cognitive	Resolving	Reconciling	Appealing	Rejecting	Coercive	N
Discordant H	38.1	10.0	8.6	8.6	12.5	22.2	1417
Other H	46.0	9.8	11.5	10.5	10.9	11.4	6132
Discordant W	40.7	7.5	7.8	13.2	11.7	19.2	1420
Other W	44.4	8.0	8.0	12.0	12.4	15.3	6163

Table 10.

COMPARISON OF DISCORDANT AND OTHER WIVES IN FOUR SCENES COMBINED

Antecedent Categories	Group	Consequent Categories						N
		Cognitive	Resolving	Reconciling	Appealing	Rejecting	Coercive	
Cognitive	Discordant W	54.8	5.9	4.8	10.9	7.2	16.3	558
	Other W	57.0	7.2	5.2	9.8	7.7	13.2	2866
Resolving	Discordant W	39.4	14.8	7.7	12.7	7.0	+18.3	142
	Other W	42.4	19.1	7.9	8.8	11.6	10.2	606
Reconciling	Discordant W	28.3	7.5	29.2	-5.8	13.3	15.8	120
	Other W	28.7	7.6	26.5	11.0	11.5	14.7	694
Appealing	Discordant W	30.3	8.4	1.7	9.2	25.2	+25.2	119
	Other W	35.2	6.8	4.4	10.9	28.9	13.7	633
Rejecting	Discordant W	22.7	5.8	7.6	29.1	8.7	26.2	172
	Other W	27.1	5.3	6.9	27.1	11.1	22.4	664
Coercive	Discordant W	34.6	7.4	7.4	12.9	17.8	19.7	309
	Other W	34.6	5.6	5.7	11.6	19.4	23.1	700
N	Discordant W	578	106	111	187	166	272	1420
	Other W	2735	491	495	739	763	940	6163

NOTE: Plus (+) = discordant higher by 5 percent or more; minus (–) = discordant lower by 5 percent or more.

Table 11.

COMPARISON OF DISCORDANT AND OTHER HUSBANDS IN FOUR SCENES COMBINED

Antecedent Categories	Group	Consequent Categories						N
		Cognitive	Resolving	Reconciling	Appealing	Rejecting	Coercive	
Cognitive	Discordant H	-50.8	11.3	4.9	7.1	7.3	+18.7	577
	Other H	58.6	9.2	7.8	8.4	6.3	9.7	2744
Resolving	Discordant H	38.1	20.3	-11.0	9.3	5.1	+16.1	118
	Other H	39.9	20.5	16.6	8.8	8.0	6.3	464
Reconciling	Discordant H	-18.7	9.3	37.4	2.8	15.0	+16.8	107
	Other H	28.9	8.3	35.1	7.5	11.0	9.2	481
Appealing	Discordant H	-30.1	10.2	8.1	5.9	20.4	+25.3	186
	Other H	41.5	8.0	9.1	7.7	23.0	10.8	740
Rejecting	Discordant H	-23.6	3.6	7.9	23.0	14.5	+27.3	165
	Other H	28.9	8.5	9.8	24.7	10.6	17.6	757
Coercive	Discordant H	-33.0	6.8	-4.9	6.8	19.3	+29.2	264
	Other H	38.2	9.6	10.8	6.9	16.1	15.4	946
N	Discordant H	540	142	122	122	177	314	1417
	Other H	2819	602	703	645	666	697	6132

NOTE: Plus (+) = discordant higher by 5 percent or more; minus (−) = discordant lower by 5 percent or more.

markedly more coercive and less cognitive than other husbands; they also use fewer reconciling acts in response to resolving messages or coercive messages. In response to coercion, the discordant husbands respond in kind considerably more often than their wives (29.2 percent versus 19.7 percent of the time), which again is a reversal of the sex difference noted in the last chapter; that is, among these discordant couples the husband rather than the wife leads in coercive tit-for-tat exchanges. Correspondingly—though the differences are small—the discordant wives use relatively more resolving and reconciling responses to coercion than their husbands do, again a reversal of the sex differences found for the whole sample.

Thus, in these couples the husbands are the ones who differ most from the rest of the sample, and they differ in the direction of greater punitiveness. These husbands seem to charge conflict with coerciveness, personal grievances, and disparagement.[2]

Barry's (1970) review of marriage research noted that variables relating to husbands correlate with marital "success," whereas variables relating to wives do not. The husband's socioeconomic and educational background, his positive relationship to his parents, his personality strength, his wife's positive view of him as a mature man and husband—all these correlate with marital success. On surface examination it appears that our findings on the discordant couples fit this mold, since it was the husbands who differed from the rest of the sample, not the wives. As in Chapter Twelve, however, a closer analysis reveals a more interesting pattern.

A Closer Look—Lambs and Tigers. Table 12 compares the matrices of the discordant husbands and wives for the issue-oriented anniversary and television scenes. These matrices seem totally different from the matrices for all four scenes combined. In these scenes, the wives are far more coercive overall and in response to every category; they not only are more coercive than their hus-

---

[2] To assure ourselves that the discordant couples' matrices could not have occurred by a chance grouping of couples, we randomly drew four sets of six couples and compared these sets to the discordant couples. The discordant couples differed from these random groups in the ways already indicated in the text. We conclude that the discordant couples differ systematically and not randomly from the rest of the sample.

Table 12.

COMPARISON OF DISCORDANT WIVES AND HUSBANDS IN ISSUE-ORIENTED SCENES

Categories Antecedent	Sex	Consequent Categories						N
		Cognitive	Resolving	Reconciling	Appealing	Rejecting	Coercive	
Cognitive	H	64.5	17.0	6.0	7.8	1.1	3.7	282
	W	59.9	−8.5	2.3	+14.0	4.9	+10.4	307
Resolving	H	44.3	30.0	14.3	11.4	0.0	0.0	70
	W	43.4	−14.2	−5.7	15.1	+6.6	+15.1	106
Reconciling	H	12.5	20.8	58.3	8.3	0.0	0.0	24
	W	+34.4	−11.5	−19.7	9.8	+11.5	+13.1	61
Appealing	H	52.6	21.1	13.2	10.5	1.3	1.3	76
	W	−37.7	−5.7	−0.0	+18.9	+15.1	+22.6	53
Rejecting	H	30.0	10.0	12.5	27.5	12.5	7.5	40
	W	+25.0	−3.6	−0.0	−0.0	−7.1	+64.3	28
Coercive	H	33.0	11.7	5.3	9.6	22.3	18.1	94
	W	+26.7	−3.3	3.3	−3.3	−6.7	+56.7	30
N	H	299	105	61	60	30	31	586
	W	286	53	26	76	41	103	585
Percent	H	51.0	17.9	10.4	10.2	5.1	5.3	
	W	48.9	−9.1	−4.4	13.0	7.0	+17.6	

NOTE: Plus (+) = wives higher by 5 percent or more; minus (−) = wives lower by 5 percent or more.

bands but are also more coercive than the rest of the wives in the sample (18 percent versus 10 percent). In response to a rejecting or coercive message from their husbands, the discordant wives respond coercively over half the time, a response level higher than that in the distance-maintaining role for the sample as a whole.

The discordant wives are very prone to tit-for-tat reciprocation of negatively affective messages from their husbands in these issue-oriented scenes. Their husbands are much more likely than they to respond to all messages with resolving or reconciling acts. The matrices indicate that in the first two scenes the husbands in the discordant group receive a good many more negatively affective messages than do the rest of the husbands and that they take it rather mildly.

But these Caspar Milquetoasts seem suddenly to turn tiger when they receive the distance-maintaining instructions. Table 13 compares the response distributions of the discordant husbands and wives in the distancing role. The wives now look like the rest of the wives; they are only slightly more coercive and are slightly less rejecting than the other wives in this role. Their husbands, however, do an about-face; coercion now is their modal category, and almost 70 percent of their responses are rejecting and coercive acts (as against 43 percent for the rest of the husbands and 53 percent for the discordant wives). They use far fewer cognitive acts and fewer resolving and reconciling acts than the rest of the husbands. The change in the mode of interaction is, indeed, striking.

Nor does the tiger retreat before a distance-maintaining wife, as Table 14 shows. First let us concentrate on the wives. For them, the closeness role came immediately after the issue-oriented scenes in which they were coercive and their husbands conciliatory. Given the set to achieve closeness, they show themselves actually slightly less coercive and rejecting than the rest of the wives and far less than their husbands. Apparently something happens to create such a remarkable shift. It could be that for some reason the instruction to achieve closeness has a much greater effect on them than on the rest of the wives; but it could also be that they are taken aback by the exceedingly strong tack taken by their husbands in the husband distant scene.

Indeed, an analysis of the distribution of these wives' re-

Table 13.

Comparison of Discordant and Other Couples in Distance-maintaining Role

Group		Cognitive	Resolving	Reconciling	Appealing	Rejecting	Coercive	N
					Consequent Categories			
Discordant	H	23.5	1.5	4.8	0.5	28.3	41.4	396
Other	H	40.0	6.2	8.0	2.9	26.1	16.8	1781
Discordant	W	32.0	5.2	6.1	3.6	25.9	27.0	440
Other	W	33.6	6.3	7.0	2.6	27.7	22.8	2083

Table 14.
COMPARISON OF DISCORDANT AND OTHER COUPLES IN CLOSENESS ROLE

Group	Cognitive	Resolving	Reconciling	Appealing	Rejecting	Coercive	N
			Consequent Categories				
Discordant H	33.7	7.1	9.6	13.7	8.9	27.1	439
Other H	38.8	8.8	17.4	18.2	5.4	11.5	2074
Discordant W	38.2	7.6	14.7	24.1	2.8	12.7	395
Other W	40.3	5.0	11.3	21.5	6.5	15.4	1775

sponses to coercion by their husbands tends to substantiate the latter hypothesis. In the husband distant scene, as we just saw, these husbands use coercion very frequently. Where the discordant wives tended toward tit-for-tat reciprocation to coercion in the issue-oriented scenes, here they do not; in fact, they reply with rejection or coercion only 14 percent of the time compared to 33 percent for the rest of the wives in the same role. The discordant wives try resolving acts 7 percent more often and use cognitive messages 10 percent more often than the rest of the wives. Apparently, when the tiger roars, these wives become lambs. Indeed, the response matrices for these wives in the husband distant scene seem to indicate shock and an attempt to cool their husbands down.

If this is their aim, it seems not to work. We already saw how coercive the husbands were in that role. Again in the closeness role the response distribution of the discordant husbands (Table 14) suggests the image of a genie let out of the bottle. In spite of the set to achieve closeness these husbands continue to use coercion. They use it as much in this role as do their wives whose set was to maintain distance. In response to coercion they use much less reconciling behavior and fewer appeals than the rest of the husbands and much more rejection and coercion. Since the distance-maintaining wives tend toward the same tit-for-tat, the discordant couples very easily get locked into mutually recriminatory battles. The infrequent use of reconciling behavior by the husbands makes cycling out of such a battle especially difficult.

Schemata for Discord.   Taken as a whole, the Improvisations reveal a great difference between these husbands and the rest of the husbands in the sample. The discordant husbands are more coercive and attacking, less cognitive, conciliatory, and supportive. Since the wives in the discordant group recalled troubles with their families during their own childhood and adolescence, one is tempted to infer a choice of mate who would continue the conflictual interactions they knew as children. But if we look at the development within the Improvisations, we see that the relationship is more complex than this. There is a Jekyll-Hyde quality in both husbands and wives. At first she is coercive and "nasty," he conciliatory; then the roles reverse. Once again, we are reminded that in human communication the whole can be greater than the sum of its parts. How can we explain these findings?

To answer this question we have to allow ourselves to be impressionistic and speculative while basing our impressions on the data. We know that these wives recalled troubles with their families as they grew up. What do we know about the husbands that might help? The interviewers rated all these husbands very low on empathy and supportiveness. The interview material relating to their childhood and adolescence indicated that three of the six experienced early familial disturbance—parental death or separation or father absence. These three also give evidence of a narcissistic self-concern: "I was the favorite because of my athletic ability"; "I was an independent cuss . . . I don't like to compliment others or say I love you." Two of the others make similar comments: "I know my mother admired me very much"; "I was favorite of Dad." The sixth said that he held onto his mother until he became too heavy for her. These indices, along with the low ratings on empathy and supportiveness, incline us to the opinion that these husbands have a need to receive without a corresponding ability to give.

As to the wives, they look like tigers who become lambs when attacked themselves. In interviews, they, like their husbands, reported being unhappy about their marriages. They reported many disagreements with their husbands, and they indicated that they seldom yielded in such disagreements. The interviewers rated these wives especially low in supportiveness. It is tempting to speculate that they are replaying their stormy childhood battles in the Improvisations. Their scenes are reminiscent of the family battles in which a child tests his power but in the end is forced to yield. One might wonder if these women selected husbands who seemed compliant and malleable.

Compliance is often a ground for mounting resentment: the worm does turn. When their wives attacked, the discordant husbands seemed to maintain a benign and bland attitude; when, however, they were placed in a position of power—as in the husband distant scene—they tended to exert power in a crude and undifferentiated way.

Marriage for such couples seems to be seen as a battle of

wills, a struggle over who will get what he wants—with no holds barred. Examination of the Improvisation protocols for the discordant couples attests to the potentials for escalation suggested by the formal analysis of the codings. These spouses became quickly involved in power struggles in which neither seemed very much concerned with what the other was trying to say. Although there may be references to and protestations of love for one another, there were no indications of listening for or concern for each other's feelings. Attacks were highly personal, they were directed at character rather than issue, and insulting references and comparisons to the partner's mother were common. In the closeness-distance scenes suspicion and jealousy were prominent. This group, far more than any other group of couples, projected issues involving accusations of the wife's relation with another man or the husband's relation with another woman. Five of the six couples became seriously embroiled in such jealousy conflicts, compared to only two other couples in the entire sample of forty-six.

As suggested earlier there was a striking sequential aspect to the discordant couples' management of conflict. In the first two scenes the wives attacked while the husbands responded rather calmly and benignly; in the last two scenes the husbands attacked, and their wives tried to mollify them. The husbands thus seemed to be grievance collectors who finally erupted. Because the scenes were presented in a fixed order, we cannot infer that in their daily lives it is the wives who always initiate attack and the husbands who later erupt. It is possible that the order of these roles may reverse. In either case, the data do suggest some consequences to the threatening employment of power, even when there is seeming initial success. Once again our findings with intimate dyadic relationships coordinate with the conflict theory presented in Chapter Four and with suggestions from experimental studies of "game" and "bargaining" situations using ad hoc pairs. Jack Santa Barbara,[3] using the Prisoner's Dilemma game, found that dyads that ended up locked into mutual defection started out showing a marked disparity between partners in cooperation: one partner

[3] Reporting in a personal communication to the authors, October 1970.

tended to cooperate no matter what the other did; the other increased in defection. At a certain point, the high cooperator suddenly shifted to defection and locked in on it. Kelley and Stahelski (1970) report several sets of data that suggest the same phenomenon: the originally cooperative partner of a competitor becomes even more competitive than the competitor. They conjecture that this may occur because the cooperator's frustration at having his goals for the relationship thwarted is translated into extreme aggressiveness. What happens to our discordant couples fits their hypothesis, although we doubt that the discordant husbands would qualify as cooperators in Kelley and Stahelski's terms.

The "martyr" role lasts only so long, it seems—and then, watch out! In reviewing experimental studies of threats in interpersonal negotiations, Kelley refers to a study by McKellar (1949), which found that *"enduring* attitudes of dislike, contempt, and hatred do not arise from mere restraint or thwarting of needs, as would be implied by a simple frustration-aggression view. Instead, they develop from experiences of humiliation, the imposition of physical pain (frequently in the form of bullying by a stronger person), or an encroachment upon one's values, status, possessions, etc. [McKellar's] evidence also suggests the important contribution to these lasting feelings made by hostility that is not given expression because of the higher status or successful dominance of the provoker" (Kelley, 1965, p. 103).

The behaviors of the discordant pairs suggest object relations schemata that interpret relationships in terms of power and threat. Moreover, the behavior of the husbands hints at inflexibility in these schemata. For example, most husbands in the sample shift their actions markedly in accordance with the set given in each of the two closeness-distance scenes. In distancing, coercive and rejecting acts generally predominate over resolving and reconciling acts; for most husbands the order reverses when they are trying to get close. But among discordant husbands this reversal does not occur. Even when trying to get close to their wives, these husbands tend to use coercion and rejection rather than efforts at resolution and conciliation. The data suggest that the carry-over of attitudes from one scene to another is greater for the discordant than for other husbands and that a background of resentment builds up that is not easily mitigated.

Harmonious Couples

At the opposite pole of Factor III are the seven couples we labeled *harmonious*. Interviewers rated such couples as having an easy time with marital decisions and as tending to orient themselves as couples rather than individuals. Factor loadings indicate that interviewers evaluated these marriages positively; they rated both the husbands and wives as high in mutual support and the husbands especially as high in empathy. The replies of these couples to questionnaires seemed to reflect satisfaction with their marriages.

As we noted earlier, this group averaged significantly fewer acts per couple as compared to the discordant couples and even to the sample as a whole. Because there are so few acts it is difficult to analyze each scene individually. Table 15 allows a summary comparison of the response distributions of the harmonious couples and those of the rest of the sample. It is immediately apparent that the harmonious couples tend to keep their interactions in the cognitive realm and to use the rejecting and coercive categories much less often than the rest of the sample. They also use a total of more resolving and reconciling acts. Obviously their Improvisation scenes are much less heated than those of the discordant couples and even than the average of the rest of the sample. It is particularly instructive to note that the harmonious husbands use reconciling acts very much more than do the other husbands or their own wives. The data for the harmonious couples thus point strongly to the supportiveness of the husbands in all four scenes at the newlywed stage and to generally more benign and less heated exchanges.

Avoiders and Engagers. From the analysis of codings plus the factor labeling we might be led to expect that the harmonious couples represent ideal management of conflict. Examination of the protocols lead us, however, to suspect such an interpretation. While it is true that none of the harmonious couples escalates conflict, in sharp contrast to the discordant sample, this is not always because they are especially sensitive to and supportive of one another. The harmonious sample, in fact, seems composed of two

Table 15.

Comparison of Harmonious and Other Couples in Four Scenes Combined

Group	Consequent Categories							
	Cognitive	Resolving	Reconciling	Appealing	Rejecting	Coercive	N
Harmonious H	54.2	8.4	17.0	7.5	6.4	6.4	869
Other H	43.2	10.0	10.1	10.5	11.8	14.3	6680
Harmonious W	53.7	10.6	10.8	9.5	6.4	9.0	876
Other W	42.4	7.5	7.6	12.6	13.0	16.9	6707

kinds of couple relationships. In one subgroup of three couples there appears to be a joining of the conflict in which the partners are sensitive and responsive to one another's needs and statements. These couples resolve the conflicts easily. In another subgroup of four couples issues are dealt with by avoidance. Conflict does not mount intensively, but this is because the interpersonal issue is not confronted directly. What the subgroups have in common is that in neither does conflict escalate.

Harmony and the Marital Relationship.   D. W. Goodrich (1968) speculates that couples at the harmonious end of Factor III may be comparable to Cuber and Harroff's (1965) couples in "intrinsic marriages." Cuber and Harroff note that, in this group, couple identity, rather than individual identity, predominated and that there was deep satisfaction and excitement in mutual sharing. Any disturbance of this mutuality tended to be experienced as such a loss that the marriage itself was threatened. Goodrich believes that greater intimacy requires greater "adaptive work" by the ego and leads to a greater tendency to perceive what are expectable frustrations as threatening to the marriage. Whatever one may think of this rather vague speculation, it is probably safe to say with Boulding (1962) that a threat to a core image provokes anxiety. If these couples so identify with mutual trust and couple solidarity as to make couple identity a core aspect of their self-images, then any threat to the mutual trust and solidarity may provoke anxiety.

Clinical appraisal of the protocols of the harmonious couples suggests that this indeed may be so, at least for some. This appraisal, done without knowledge of the Factor III scores, led us to label four of the seven harmonious couples as avoiders of conflict in Chapter Seven. In that chapter, the Rogerses, for example, illustrate the disruptive effects of anxiety when the harmonious relationship is threatened. Again, we may note that subjective satisfaction with and "success" of marriage is a very mixed dimension. Our harmonious couples claim satisfaction in their marriages, their marriages are rated positively by sophisticated interviewers, and their exchanges in the Improvisation scenes are relatively benign and unheated as compared to other couples. For some harmonious couples—for example, the Birnes in Chapter Eight—these aspects seem to reflect an ease in mutual confrontation and constructive decision-making in a context of empathy and support. For others, the harmony seems to reflect defense against anxiety. Questionnaires on marital satisfaction are particularly likely to confound one group with another. Moreover, our results suggest that success as defined by either stated satisfaction or continuity of marriage is no indicator of specific quality.

Role-Sharing and Role-Segregated Couples

Of the four factors described by Goodrich and others (1968), Factor III is the firmest. The variables contributing to Factor III correlate well with the factor scores, ranging from .55 to .72. The other three factors seem less strong, in that variable loadings on factor scores are considerably lower. Nevertheless, it seemed worth exploring possible relations between performances in the Improvisation scenes and factor data derived from other sources.

Of most interest here was Factor II, which appears to reflect primarily a dimension of role-sharing versus role-segregation and derives mostly from questionnaire items. In the Improvisation scenes role-sharing couples average far fewer acts over the four scenes than the general sample of couples (a mean of 224 as compared to 329); role-segregated couples produce a somewhat greater number of acts (387). This suggests a capacity to extricate themselves more easily from interpersonal conflict. Apart from this, role-sharing couples do not differ appreciably from the remainder of the sample, and husband-wife differences in interactions appear to be no greater for the role-segregated couples than for the role-sharing couples. Clinical appraisal of the protocols suggests that the role-sharers are no less likely than other couples to escalate conflict or to deny or externalize conflict. Comparing role-sharing with role-segregated couples we find that the husbands in the two groups do not differ much. Role-sharing wives, however, tend to be far more cognitively oriented and to make less use of emotional appeals and coercive tactics than do the wives in role-segregated relationships. The role-segregated relationships recall the expressive emotional female stereotype in traditional role-differentiated marriages that was described in Chapter Twelve.

The remaining two factors are more obscure. One has to do

with the couple's involvement with the husband's family; the other has to do with its involvement with the wife's family. Analysis of differences in interactions of groups identified by these factors failed to produce consistent or interpretable findings.

Summary

A group of "discordant" couples identified by factor analysis showed significant and interpretable differences from the rest of the sample in the ways they handled the Improvisation scenes. In the first two scenes discordant wives were "tigers," using a great deal of pressure and coercion to attain their ends; their husbands were like "lambs"—that is, less negatively affective than the rest of the husbands. The relationship-oriented scenes produced an about-face by both partners, and the husbands seemed to change the most. They became far more coercive and attacking than other husbands and than their own wives, even in the role of achieving closeness.

The pattern reminds us of grievance collection, and the about-face in the Improvisations recalls our earlier discussions about dangers in the accumulation of hidden conflict. The reversal also illustrates the danger of the martyr role. Both husbands and wives in the discordant group seem to behave in terms of power-oriented object relations schemata. Conflict is seen as a battle of wills and readily moves into patterns of disruption and escalation.

A group of seven couples with "harmonious" marriages had much shorter interactions and much less heated exchanges, not only than the discordant couples, but also than the rest of the couples in the sample. The harmonious couples seem, however, to be composed of two subgroups, one very adept at expressing and dealing with hostility and conflict, the other engaging in avoidance of conflict. Along with D. W. Goodrich (1968) we conjecture that the latter group may have difficulty later in marriage because of the relative lack of tolerance for conflict.

As a contextual dimension for interaction in interpersonal conflict situations, the *couple* constitutes a system that is a major source of information about the communications that ensue. The analyses of discordant and harmonious couples suggest that couples intermesh not only in the nature of responses and their contingencies but also in a temporal span. Our results suggest that partners may alternate in their modes of interacting with sequential regularity. The sequence is clear only in the case of the discordant couples, where over the four scenes the partners take turns at exaggerated complementary power positions—husbands shifting from "lamb" to "tiger," wives from "tiger" to "lamb." The tactics of interpersonal conflict management are those described earlier as destructive. The discordant couples speak of themselves as unhappy in and doubtful about their marriages. Our results do not indicate whether the poor quality of the relationship "causes" the destructive communication style or whether the destructive communication style has led to the deterioration of the relationship. Perhaps, though, such questions of directional causality are illegitimate in considering systems in which there is continual feedback between the context of the relationship and specific communications.

XIV

The Developmental
Context: Three Early
Stages of Marriage

Fourteen of the forty-six couples became parents during the course of the study. These couples were seen again in the seventh month of the first pregnancy and for a third time four months after their babies were born. Since one couple did not complete the Improvisations for the final stage, we have thirteen couples who constitute what we call the *developmental* group—those couples for whom we can discuss developmental changes in communication and conflict management between the time of marriage and the birth of the first child.

The sample is obviously too small to draw other than tentative conclusions from our findings. Even apart from this and the demographic restrictions noted in Chapter Six, there is another limitation to this discussion of development. Because the time period for data collection was restricted (between January 1961 and December 1964) and because the data collection for the newlywed stage was spread over two and one-half years, not all couples had equal opportunities to become part of this developmental group. A couple entering the study as newlyweds in January 1961 obviously had a greater chance of participating in the pregnancy and child-bearing studies than did a couple entering the study in June 1963.

These timing factors led to a sample of couples who had children relatively early in marriage. Even though couples known to be pregnant were eliminated from the newlywed sample seen four months after marriage, the mean time between marriage and the birth of the first child for the thirteen couples was only twenty-one months.[1] This figure is considerably lower than national figures,[2] and is probably even more so for middle-class couples like those in our sample.

As explained in Chapter Six, for each couple in the developmental group a couple for whom pregnancy did not occur was selected as a match in terms of length of marriage. We will discuss differences between these two groups later. For now we need only note that neither religious preference nor educational attainment differentiated the two groups.[3] As far as we can judge, most of the couples who had children early in marriage did this as a matter of choice; only two of the couples reported that contraception was being practiced when the wife became pregnant. From all indications our developmental group wanted children early in marriage.

The thirteen developmental couples repeated the closeness-distance scenes two more times—during pregnancy and after the birth of the child. We are thus able to analyze the handling of these

[1] The range was from eleven and one-half to thirty-eight months.

[2] National sample data suggest that the average time span from marriage to birth of the first child is twenty-five and one-half months (reported in a personal communication to the authors from David Featherman, 1969).

[3] As indicated in Chapter Six, the mean educational level of the entire newlywed sample was about two years of college, and the sample divided into almost equal thirds of Protestants, Catholics, and Jews. It is interesting that in this sample religious preference bore no relation to early childbearing.

two Improvisation scenes over three early stages of marriage. Table 16 presents an abridgment of the results of two information analyses using the closeness-distance scenes across the three stages.

Table 16.

TWO UNCERTAINTY ANALYSES FOR THIRTEEN DEVELOPMENTAL COUPLES OVER THREE STAGES

Source	%sU(C)[a]	Source	%sU(C)	Source	%sU(C)
A;C	3.94	A_D;C	4.44	R_A;C	5.25
D;C	.67	A_R;C	2.95	R_D;C	6.45
R;C	6.24	A_S;C	4.16	R_S;C	6.33
S;C	.20	A_P;C	6.23	R_{AD};C	5.70
P;C	4.30	A_{DR};C	3.70	R_{AS};C	5.61
A,D;C	5.11	A_{DS};C	4.98	R_{DS};C	5.25
A,R;C	9.20	A_{RS};C	3.44	R_{ADS};C	6.77
A,S;C	4.36	A_{DRS};C	5.11	S_A;C	.43
A,P;C	10.53	D_A;C	1.18	S_D;C	.34
D,R;C	7.12	D_R;C	.88	S_R;C	.29
D,S;C	1.01	D_S;C	.81	S_P;C	1.88
D,P;C	7.70	D_P;C	3.40	S_{AD};C	.87
R,S;C	6.53	D_{AR};C	1.62	S_{AR};C	.78
P,S;C	6.18	D_{AS};C	1.62	S_{DR};C	.53
A,D,R;C	10.81	D_{RS};C	1.12	S_{ADR};C	1.94
A,D,S;C	5.98	D_{ARS};C	2.78	P_A;C	6.60
A,R,S;C	9.97			P_D;C	7.03
A,P,S;C	14.62			P_S;C	5.98
D,R,S;C	7.65			P_{AS};C	10.26
D,P,S;C	11.70			P_{ADS};C	19.61
A,D,R,S;C	12.75				
A,D,P,S;C	25.59				

[a] All results are significant beyond the .001 level.

A   Antecedent act

D   Development stage

R   Role (maintaining distance or getting close)

P   Couple or pair

S   Sex

C   Consequent act

The Continuity of the Contextual System

Before we discuss the influence of the developmental stage, we would like to underline some findings about the developmental sample that are consistent with those for the whole sample at the newlywed stage. The instructions, for example, constrained behavior consistently over the three stages. The role-set accounts for a 6.2 percent reduction in response uncertainty over all three stages $(R;C)$; at the newlywed stage a similar analysis of role showed that it accounted for 5.1 percent of response uncertainty in the last two scenes. If one spouse has a set to maintain distance, this exerts a powerful effect on his behavior whether the partners are newlyweds, the wife is pregnant, or the first baby has arrived. If one knows that a man is trying to keep distant from his wife then one has a good idea of how he will tend to respond to his wife's communications, and the stage of marriage does not seem to make a big difference.

Similarly, the antecedent acts of one partner continued to influence the immediate responses of the other to the same extent over all three stages: 4.2 percent reduction of uncertainty for all newlywed couples, 3.9 percent for the developmental couples over all three stages (see source $A;C$ in Tables 3 and 16). From one phase to another the effects of antecedent messages on responses remain about the same as we described them in Chapter Ten.

Sex differences, though statistically significant at all stages, remain small and fairly constant over the three stages for the thirteen couples.

In Chapters Seven and Eight we commented on clinical impressions of the consistency in couples' approaches to conflict over the three stages, and in Chapters Ten and Thirteen we found that couples showed distinctive patterns of interaction that differentiated them from other couples. That is, the pair behaves as a unit and differs somewhat from other couple units. An informational analysis for the thirteen couples over the three stages shows that the couple maintains consistency as an interacting system (Table 3 shows $P;C$ at 4.7 percent for newlyweds, while Table 16 shows it at 4.3 percent over all three stages). Although couples change differentially over the three stages $(P_D;C)$, from as early as the fourth month of marriage there is stability in their communication styles as couples.

In general, then, the results suggest remarkable continuities of contextual effects on communication and of modes of dealing with conflict.

Influences of the Developmental Stage

We have been discussing consistency and continuity over time in the ways intimates behave with each other when engaged in conflicts concerning their relationship. We are also interested in how they change as they move from newlywed stage to imminent parenthood to becoming parents. First let us note that developmental changes in interpersonal behavior are slight. By themselves, stage differences accounted for only 0.67 percent of response uncertainty (D;C). Like the sex differences—which were also slight—developmental differences, though significant statistically, seem to have been overwhelmed by the effect of the instructions. There are not many ways of maintaining distance or of achieving closeness, so differences in these behaviors that could be attributable to stage differences were few. Nonetheless, the stages do differ significantly from one another in behavior produced, and it is to these differences that we now turn. Because controlling for stage differences did not appreciably affect the uncertainty reduction attributable to antecedent act, we will confine our discussion to the response distributions and the differences among them at the various stages.

The Newlywed Stage

Since the fact of having a child early in marriage distinguished a group of thirteen couples from the rest of the sample, we were led to ask whether and how this group of couples differed from other couples in handling the Improvisations at the newlywed stage. We mentioned in Chapter Six some independent evidence that the developmental couples were different in their orientation to marriage even at the newlywed stage. Raush and others (1970) found that the couples who became pregnant used relatively more "I" references whereas matched couples who did not become pregnant used relatively more "we" references. This finding plus speculation on what it means to want to have children very early in marriage led to the conjecture that the developmental couples were less oriented to the interpersonal aspects of marriage and more concerned with smooth, adequate functioning in marital and familial roles. According to this view the developmental couples tend to a more traditional view of marriage, the institutional pattern of Burgess and others (1963), the child-oriented pattern of Farber (1962), the utilitarian pattern of Cuber and Harroff (1965).[4]

An analysis of the issue-oriented anniversary and television scenes reveals few differences between the developmental couples and the rest of the sample. The developmental husbands use a slightly smaller (by 4 percent) proportion of coercive acts and a slightly larger (by 3 percent) proportion of resolving acts than the rest of the husbands; all other differences are even smaller. In the closeness role, there were again few notable differences. The developmental husbands use 5 percent fewer cognitive acts and 4 percent more appealing acts, thus exerting more emotional pressure on their wives than do the rest of the husbands in this role. The developmental wives are similar less cognitive (by 5 percent) than the rest of the wives; they use proportionally more resolving acts (by 3 percent) and rejecting acts (by 3 percent) and fewer reconciling acts (by 3 percent).

The distance-maintaining role provides a contrast to these findings, as can be seen by inspecting Table 17. Sex differences are reversed for five of the six categories; in other words, the developmental husbands and wives differ from each other in opposite directions to those of the rest of the couples. Most of these differences are small, but those in cognitive acts (developmental husbands less cognitive than their wives) and coercive acts (developmental husbands more coercion) are rather substantial. The developmental husbands use fewer reconciling acts and more rejecting and coercive acts than did the rest of the husbands in the sample. Though they are nowhere near as extreme, the developmental couples look

---

[4] The role-segregation, role-sharing Factor II of Goodrich and others (1968) did not differentiate the developmental and matched couples. As to Factor III, three of the developmental couples and only one of the matched couples were in the discordant group discussed in the previous chapter. On the other hand, two developmental and two matched couples were in the harmonious group. In terms of factor scores the developmental group is mixed.

Table 17.

COMPARISON OF DEVELOPMENTAL AND OTHER COUPLES AT NEWLYWED STAGE IN DISTANCE-MAINTAINING ROLE

Group	Cognitive	Resolving	Reconciling	Appealing	Rejecting	Coercive	N
Developmental H	29.8	5.3	4.9	3.5	31.9	24.6	568
Other H	39.6	5.3	8.3	2.1	24.5	20.1	1609
Developmental W	34.3	8.8	6.8	1.6	30.8	17.7	559
Other W	33.0	5.4	6.9	3.1	26.4	25.1	1964

Consequent Categories

in this role only, like the discordant couples of the last chapter. Interestingly enough, the developmental wives used about 7 percent fewer coercive acts than the rest of the wives.

Are these results interpretable? Except in the distance-maintaining role, the developmental couples seem to differ very little from the rest of the sample. They average fewer acts per couple for the four scenes (288.5 versus 344.8 for the rest of the sample). The husbands are somewhat less coercive, more resolving, and more reconciling than the rest of the husbands except in the distance-maintaining role. In that role these husbands are a bit like the discordant husbands; but unlike them they do not maintain rejection and coerciveness in the closeness role. The developmental wives in response to the distance-maintaining instructions employ a rejecting stance more than do other wives, but they are less prone than other wives to use coercion or personal attack. The developmental partners thus seem to conform more than other couples to the instructors' directions. The differences between developmental husbands and wives in the use of personal attack and coercion suggest that the men tend to establish their distance in a more assertive, aggressive fashion whereas the women tend to withdraw, maintaining distance by insistence on being left alone. We can speculate that these trends may indicate a somewhat more traditional orientation to marriage and male-female relations among developmental couples than other couples.

Time and Stage Changes

Table 18 presents the response distributions of the developmental couples, combining the acts of husbands and wives and the two relationship scenes, for each of the three stages. Two trends warrant attention. Over time there is a consistent increase in the use of cognitive acts (though the major increase occurs between the pregnancy and parenthood stages) and a consistent decrease in the use of rejection. It appears that as marriage progresses through the three stages couples tone down the emotional impact of the conflicts by moving from outright rejection of the partner to a more rational argumentative mode. A more detailed analysis shows that the decline over time in rejection of the other is true for each sex and for each

Table 18.

Percentages at Each Stage for Both Sexes in Relationship-oriented Scenes Combined

Stage in Life Cycle	Categories						
	Cognitive	Resolving	Reconciling	Appealing	Rejecting	Coercive	N
Newlywed	33.5	7.7	9.6	12.3	19.0	17.9	2248
Pregnancy	35.7	8.2	13.9	12.9	13.4	15.8	1857
Parenthood	45.3	7.3	11.2	9.1	10.1	17.0	1809

role (maintaining distance and achieving closeness). It may, of course, be that our couples became somewhat bored with the conflict situations the second and third times around; the decrease in the number of total responses in the latter two stages suggests this. But it may be that over time the couples learned to deal with interpersonal conflict without resorting to rejection. It may also be that they have learned more subtle ways of keeping each other at a distance. Their continued involvement in the scenes might be argued from the fact that efforts at reconciliation did not decrease—if anything, they increased in the later two stages.

Pregnancy

Chapter Twelve indicated that the newlywed husbands tended to make more efforts at reconciliation than did their wives and that newlywed wives tended to use coercive tactics to a greater extent than did their husbands. With the much smaller developmental sample these tendencies are maintained in general at the later stages.

Husbands in Pregnancy. In spite of the overall tendency toward consistency husbands exhibit some striking developmental changes. Even in comparison to their own elevated conciliatory behavior as newlyweds the developmental husbands engage markedly more in such behavior when their wives are in the late stages of pregnancy. In the distancing role the proportion of reconciling acts by husbands went from 4.9 percent at the newlywed stage to 10.1 percent at the pregnancy stage; in the closeness role it went from 17.3 percent to 25.7 percent. Coordinate with the increased efforts by husbands to conciliate is their declining use of coercive tactics in late pregnancy—from 24.6 percent to 15.6 percent under distancing instructions, and from 13.9 percent to 12.1 percent in attempting to achieve closeness. A parallel decline occurred in the proportion of rejecting actions by husbands from the first to the second stage (from 31.9 percent to 26.6 percent in distancing and from 4.7 percent to 1.2 percent in getting close).

Are these changes in husbands attributable to the developmental stage of marriage (pregnancy) or to length of time married? The matched sample of couples seen the second time when married for approximately the same number of months provide some data on the changes that could be due to time rather than developmental stage.[5]

In late pregnancy the developmental husbands differ very significantly from the matched husbands in each role. In both scenes, developmental husbands use proportionally fewer cognitive acts, more coercive acts, and more reconciling acts than their matches. Tests of changes for husbands and wives between the two periods of data collection indicate that husbands of pregnant wives increased in their efforts at reconciliation more than did husbands in the matched sample. The former group increased the proportion of conciliatory acts by 14 percent, whereas the matched husbands increased their conciliatory acts by only 3 percent. Further evidence that this increased use of reconciling acts by developmental husbands is related to the developmental stage lies in the sharp drop in the proportion of such acts after the baby is born.

The other differences between developmental and matched husbands at the second phase of investigation—the lower proportion of cognitive acts and greater proportion of coercive acts of the former group—are more difficult to interpret. Both groups are, however, consistent in some changes over the average of eighteen months. Developmental and matched husbands both increase in cognitive approaches and decrease in rejecting and coercive acts. These changes thus seem to be time-related, in contrast to the change in conciliatory acts.

Wives in Pregnancy.   Despite the fact that it was they who were pregnant, developmental wives did not change as dramatically in their responses as did their husbands. The general increase in

---

[5] The matched couples provide a rough check or indicator, not clear-cut evidence, since the sample was not a control group in any experimental sense. The only "control" was the length of time married. Differences at the second data collection could be due to a number of factors besides the matter of expecting a child or not.

At the newlywed stage the developmental husbands did not differ significantly from the matched husbands in response distributions in either distance-maintaining or closeness-achieving roles. The groups did differ significantly in combined response distributions for the issue-oriented anniversary and television scenes; the main difference was that the developmental husbands used coercive acts proportionally far less than the matched husbands.

cognitive and decrease in rejecting responses have been noted. Other changes in wives during pregnancy were small, but the directions are worth noting. In the distance-maintaining role the pregnant wives were somewhat less reconciling than they had been as newlyweds (4.2 percent compared to 6.8 percent) and more coercive (22.5 percent compared to 17.7 percent). In the closeness role the directions were just the opposite; the pregnant wives become more reconciling (15.2 percent compared to 9.7 percent) and less coercive (12.6 percent compared to 15.2 percent).

Were these changes in wives stage-related (due to pregnancy)? Again we look to the matched couples. At the newlywed stage the developmental and matched wives differed significantly in response distribution only in the distance-maintaining role. The major differences were a far greater use of rejection and a lesser use of cognitive acts by the developmental wives. At the second data collection we find again that the developmental wives' response distributions in both roles differ significantly from those of the matched wives. In both distance-maintaining and closeness-achieving roles the pregnant wives engage in fewer cognitive and more coercive acts. From the first to the second period both groups of wives have decreased their use of reconciling acts in the distancing role and increased their use in the closeness role, so we see this finding as time-related. All other changes in proportions of category use were likewise in the same directions for the pregnant and nonpregnant wives.

The differences between the pregnant and matched wives are (with the exception of reconciling acts) much the same as those found between the two groups of husbands. Compared to their matched counterparts the pregnant couples are less cognitively oriented and more coercive in behavior. Certainly, at the second phase of investigation the two groups differ.

Conflict Management and Pregnancy. The easiest difference to understand is the increase in reconciling acts on the part of the developmental husbands. This difference appears to be related to the stage of pregnancy; husbands seem to be responding to cultural notions about behavior toward pregnant women. Our results agree with verbal reports from wives that husbands are more thoughtful and considerate during the period of pregnancy (McKinney, 1955). There is a great deal of folklore legitimizing increased solicitude by husbands. A husband is supposed to see that his pregnant wife does not become overtired; he is supposed to help more around the house. At the same time there is a general impression that the wife may be more temperamental because of her condition. These attitudes are exemplified even in relatively modern descriptions—such as a chapter entitled "Psychological Rules or How to Live with a Pregnant Wife," in *Husband-coached Childbirth* (Bradley, 1965). The chapter exhorts the husband to be kind and considerate despite the fact that his wife may now be "somewhat neurotic" (p. 116).

There is ample evidence in the literature that women are more emotional during pregnancy. Virtually all who have investigated emotional reactions during pregnancy agree on two things: that all women have both positive and negative attitudes toward pregnancy and that all women experience increased anxiety or tension during this period (Hurst and Strousse, 1938; Thompson, 1942, 1950; Menninger, 1943; American Society for Research in Psychosomatic Problems, 1945; Kavinoky, 1949; Poffenberger and others, 1952; Newton, 1955; Bibring and others, 1961; F. Goodrich, 1961; Loesch and Greenberg, 1962; Brown, 1964). Caplan (1957) believes that certain emotional manifestations run parallel to hormonal and metabolic changes throughout pregnancy. For example, he generalizes that an increase in introversion, passivity, and dependency appears in the middle of the second trimester, reaches a peak at thirty to thirty-five weeks, and does not disappear until a few weeks after delivery. However, any hypothesis that the anxiety and tension experienced by wives during pregnancy result in one particular pattern of behavior is not confirmed by the data presented here. We have no evidence of any general increase in wives' emotionality in handling conflicts with their husbands.

The single unequivocal stage-related change was the marked increase in reconciling behavior by the husbands of pregnant wives. Yet some eighteen months after marriage couples who became pregnant enacted marital conflict situations differently from their counterparts who did not become pregnant. The pregnant couples were more apt to employ coercion and less apt to use cognitive approaches to one another. The matched couples might have been less involved in recapitulation of the Improvisation scenes at the second phase. In each scene, however, they produced more acts than did the pregnant couples.

In both groups husbands and wives at the later phase used fewer negatively toned approaches and more positive ones in trying to reestablish closeness, and in both groups the husbands became somewhat less aggressive in their efforts at maintaining distance. Over time both sets of couples shifted toward more rational, less rejecting, and less coercive ways of dealing with marital partners. But, in general, the shift appeared to be greater for those who did not become pregnant early in marriage. One could argue that the differences between the groups at the later phase suggest that couples who do not get pregnant early deal with marital conflict somewhat less disruptively. Conversely, however, one could argue that couples who become pregnant early are somewhat more able to express hostility directly, without increasing the length of the scenes and without decreasing the possibilities for resolution.[6] It might also be that nonpregnant couples were more threatened by the closeness-distance aspects of the relationship scenes, whereas pregnant couples took these conflicts in a more down-to-earth manner—an interpretation coordinate with the study of pregnant and nonpregnant couples' use of personal pronouns referred to earlier. Each of these interpretations is tenable and coordinate with the differences between the groups at the newlywed stage.

Parenthood

Our last intervention with these families occurred during the fourth month following the birth of the first child. We assumed that by that time the parents would have overcome some initial anxieties about newborns and would have had some experience in meeting the needs of an infant. Moreover, babies by this time have usually acquired some regularities in managing cycles of hunger and sleep, making the establishment of patterns and routines more feasible for parents. The data, then, presumably reflect

[6] Indeed, Hawkins's (1969) analysis suggests that among the pregnant couples, nonresolvers at the newlywed stage tended to become resolvers at the later phase more often than was true for the nonpregnant sample.

patterns of handling relationship conflicts in a small sample of new parents who have already made some crucial adjustments to their firstborns.

Besides other limitations on the data, a major lack at this stage is the absence of Improvisation material from the matched sample of couples who did not have children. We have a sample of thirteen couples studied a third time some six months after they were last seen in the seventh month of pregnancy; there was no matched group of childless couples. There is, thus, no way of accurately evaluating to what extent changes are related to the new stage of parenthood rather than to the continuity of the marriage. Our discussion can be only suggestive.

There are some trends. Both partners in both roles increased the proportion of cognitive acts over the previous stage. Fewer rejecting responses were used by both husbands and wives. These changes between pregnancy and postnatal periods continued the trends noted between newlywed and pregnancy stages. Over the total course of time the change was considerable. For example, in the maintaining-distance role, developmental husbands and wives as newlyweds responded to one another in a rejecting mode some 32 percent of the time; by the fourth month following childbirth the rejecting mode of response had dropped to about 19 percent. Similarly, use of the cognitive category increased from about 32 percent to about 48 percent of responses.

Other changes following the birth of the child are much smaller and less systematic. Both husbands and wives show a slight increase in coercion in the closeness role, with the wives increasing more (4.9 percent increase compared to 2.6 percent). Both also show a decrease in the use of appeals to achieve closeness, with the wives decreasing more (9.6 percent decrease compared to 4.6 percent). Perhaps with time there is a tendency to use stronger methods to bring a partner into line. The major shift, however, and one that seems stage-related, is that husbands become far less conciliatory to distancing wives than they were in late pregnancy (a 7.8 percent decrease). Four months after the baby was born husbands are back to using the same proportion of reconciling messages as at the newlywed stage. Apparently they no longer see their wives as needing special support when engaged in marital conflict. If this finding reflects their actual practice at home, these husbands may be failing their wives just when support is most needed.[7] A recent study by Ryder (in press) finds that wives who have children in the first two years of marriage are more likely to report that their husbands pay insufficient attention to them than wives who do not have children within that period. The results are consistent with our findings: if husbands shift from greater concern and attentiveness during pregnancy to lesser concern and attentiveness after the baby is born, one might expect wives to become more dissatisfied.

Communication and Conflict Management. In spite of the tenuous nature of the results, it is worth examining where husbands and wives stand in relation to one another four months after the first child is born. In general, both handle conflicts less emotionally and more cognitively. Both husbands and wives are less likely to resort to rejection of one another than was true at newlywed or pregnancy stages. The earlier comparison with the matched nonpregnant sample suggested that the decrease in rejecting acts was related to the length rather than the stage of marriage. This time-related trend seems to continue after the baby is born. Changes in coercive behavior after childbearing are not systematic: husbands became less coercive in maintaining distance, and wives became somewhat more coercive in both roles. An analysis by Hawkins (1969) suggests that, whereas rejecting behavior is associated with failure to resolve conflict, coercive behavior shows no such relation. And although one cannot make too much of it, it is interesting that over the three stages the number of scenes that end in unresolved conflict becomes fewer—from eight at the newlywed stage, to six at pregnancy, to three at early parenthood.

In terms of the dyadic relationship and the handling of relationship conflicts, there is no evidence to confirm suggestions from other studies (LeMasters, 1957; Dyer, 1963; Feldman, 1963; Hobbs, 1965) that the transition to parenthood is experienced as a crisis.[8] The present study of couples at this juncture of the life

---

[7] Rossi (1968) makes a strong case for the notion that in our culture women are unprepared for motherhood and so experience this stage as particularly trying.

[8] It is possible that we observed couples too early in the child-rearing stage, when they were still enthralled with what Feldman (1963) calls the

cycle has not clarified the processes underlying the seemingly negative consequences of starting and maintaining a family. If anything,
our findings suggest that parenthood for these couples was a growth-
producing experience. Although the changes may be associated more
with the increased length of the relationship than with parenthood
per se, the directions hint at a greater consolidation of identity for
both partners. That they are less coercive and rejecting when assigned the role of maintaining distance may suggest that husbands
no longer need to assert their manhood so forcefully. Wives' assertions of power in the distancing role may attest to less anxiety about
what is or is not feminine behavior. The data indicate one major
potential problem in the relationship following the birth of the
first child: husbands clearly decrease the supportiveness that characterized their responses to their wives in pregnancy.

Summary

The longitudinal nature of the study allowed us to follow one
group of thirteen couples through the pregnancy and early parenthood stages of marriage. This group, which we designated the developmental couples, differed very little from the rest of the sample of
couples in the ways they handled the Improvisations at the newlywed stage. The major difference occurred in the distance-maintaining role, where the developmental husbands exceeded their wives
and the rest of the husbands in coercive acts, thus reversing the sex
differences found in the larger sample. In the same role the developmental wives were found to be more rejecting than the rest of the
wives. From these two findings we speculated that the developmental couples were apparently more conforming to the instructions,
and that this might indicate a more traditional orientation to
marriage.

At the second data collection we compared the developmental couples to a group matched in terms of the length of time
married but for whom pregnancy did not occur. A time-related
change occurred; both groups of couples behaved in less rejecting
and more cognitive ways the second time they enacted the Improvi-

---

"baby honeymoon," and that later in this stage other changes occur that are
not as favorable.

sations. Since the trend continued into the third stage for the developmental couples, we saw this change as related to length of time married. We tend to think that the change reflects a growing ability to deal with conflict in more reasonable ways.

The one clear-cut stage-related change we found at the second phase was the relatively large increase in reconciling behavior by developmental husbands. We believe the shift reflects cultural norms about how to treat pregnant women. We also found that the developmental couples at late pregnancy behaved less cognitively and more coercively than the matched couples, a finding that may indicate a greater ability on the part of the developmental couples to engage in conflict and resolve it.

The developmental couples were also seen a third time four months after their babies were born. The trend toward more cognitive argumentation and less rejecting behavior continued among both husbands and wives. The reconciling behavior of husbands returned to prepregnancy levels, however. It seems, then, that pregnancy predisposes husbands to a more supportive relationship in arguments with their wives; once the baby is born, husbands no longer see their wives as needing special emotional support in interpersonal confrontations.

Analysis revealed consistency over the three stages of marriage in the constraints imposed on behavior by the partner's immediately antecedent message and by the role-set. Sex differences and stage differences were rather small—no doubt limited by the powerful effect of the distance and closeness instructions. Couples also showed consistency over the three stages in their relationship style as a couple, suggesting that this is established very early in marriage. These areas of consistency do not preclude the fact that couples did change, however, and that different couples changed in different ways.

XV

Summary and Conclusions: An Organization for Complexity

Communication, as Cherry (1966, p. 268) notes, cannot be a determinant process. There is always something to learn by further communications. Nevertheless, it is time for us to stop and review where we have been and where we have arrived.

Orientations

The Questions. Our book began with some questions about intimate human relationships. Our attention was directed basically

194

toward examining how people who are committed to one another go about managing the inevitable differences that arise between them in an ongoing relationship. This question delineated sets of subquestions. One set concerned contextual variables: how and to what extent one partner's actions affect the other's; how and to what extent the specific conflict situation influences how it is handled; whether men and women employ different tactics in their dealings with one another; how the stage and duration of a relationship affect interactions; how and to what extent a couple as a unit establishes a distinctive pattern of interaction; and whether—and if so in what ways—"happy" couples differ from "unhappy" couples in their interactions when faced with conflict. Our findings with respect to these contextual issues may help, we believe, to organize and clarify some of the confusing literature about marriage.

A second group of questions focused on conflict itself. We sought to specify the styles or modes in which partners face or fail to face issues of interpersonal conflict; to identify what escalates or attenuates conflict; and to differentiate the characteristics of destructive and constructive conflict between intimates and of stasis and creativity in relationships. We then sought to relate these findings to marriage specifically.

The third and final subgroup of questions is more abstract and theoretical, relating to our need to conceptualize interactive processes. We have insisted on moving beyond the gathering of multiple isolated facts or the testing of favorite hypotheses toward an approach that does justice to the richness and complexities of our experiences with one another as we indeed know them. Such richness and complexity are more than just a multiplicity of events and influences randomly strung together. Can we conceptualize the organization of complexity?

The Framework. To examine these questions we needed a framework. As a foundation for that framework we chose a thesis of probabilism: that people rarely act in a completely deterministic fashion; rather there are multiple possibilities for response to an event, and we respond to events probabilistically. The thesis thus implies that many causes may influence a single effect and that a single cause may influence many effects. We argued that probabilism provided evolutionary advantages in adaptation, since it maximized the search for and use of information and since it promoted possibilities for change in response to changing circumstances. The data on couples' interactions with one another showed clearly that people behave probabilistically. Moreover, progressive development and creativity in the resolution of interpersonal conflict seemed, to our perusal, especially associated with probabilistic explorations and playfulness.

A theory and a method for investigating how probabilities work in the interrelations of systems were provided by communications approaches. We were thus able to study how one system of events constrains another system, and we could examine the relationships between the messages of partners in destructive and constructive interchanges in varying contexts.

Our studies of communication between couples centered on their handling of interpersonal conflict. From studies and analyses of conflict came the substantive concepts for our framework. We examined modes of engagement and avoidance of conflict, destructive and constructive approaches to conflict, and tactics of negotiation and power as expressed in relationships. We studied the context in which conflict is defined and elaborated. With some data and some speculation we viewed the relations between men and women, and we examined styles of marriages from the standpoint of conflict theory.

With probabilism as a philosophical and theoretical base, communication and information theory as a functional approach to analysis, and conflict theory as a substantive source, we needed yet another stud to our framework for examining the questions posed. Joining the form of communication theory with the content of conflict theory required a concept of structure. From psychoanalytic object relations theory and from Piaget's structural theory we chose the concept of object relations schemata. Schemata organize and give meaning to experience. They may assimilate experiences to their structures, and they may accommodate their structures to new experiences. The balance in these relations is influenced by the differentiation and permeability of schemata; these, in turn, are vulnerable to past and present anxieties. The concept of schemata bridges past and present, personal and interpersonal, and communication and conflict theories in that, although a schema is organized intrapersonally on the basis of past experiences, its activation or transformation requires information from others. The theory helps us understand the circumstances of constructive and destructive conflict, why people respond differently to conflict, and the intermeshing of interpersonal systems.

The framework outlined above did not entirely precede our investigations. An interest in communication, conflict, and marriage did guide the direction of the studies as did biases (discussed in Chapter One) in favor of naturalistic, longitudinal studies of "normal" couples considered as unitary systems. But the framework also evolved, expanded, and developed through interplay with the data. From this interplay between theory and data we (and the reader, we hope) may emerge with increased factual and conceptual understanding of the processes of interpersonal transactions. Before pursuing this matter further, let us briefly review our procedures.

The Procedures. As part of a larger longitudinal study, a relatively homogeneous, group of forty-eight white, middle-class, newlywed couples was asked to enact four situations, called Improvisations, designed to ensure a conflict between the partners. Forty-six of these couples provided usable data for our analysis. At the newlywed stage the situations presented were: (1) an anniversary scene where conflict ensued because each partner had a different plan for dinner; (2) a television scene where the conflict concerned what program to watch; (3) a husband distant scene where the husband's role-set was to maintain distance, the wife's to achieve closeness; and (4) a wife distant scene where the latter roles were reversed. Thirteen couples for whom pregnancy occurred during the time established for the study were seen during the seventh month of pregnancy; to each of these couples a couple for whom pregnancy did not occur was matched in terms of length of marriage, and these couples were also seen. At this stage the couples enacted only the two closeness-distance scenes. Finally the thirteen pregnant couples were seen four months after the birth of the child and again enacted the closeness-distance Improvisations. Tape recordings and transcripts were made of all scenes and these served as sources for the analyses. A Coding Scheme for Interpersonal Conflict was developed and used to code all the Improvisation scenes. Statistical analyses were made primarily using multivariate informational analysis. The Improvisations, in the form of raw protocols of interaction and their codings, constitute the data base for our findings.

Determinants of Interaction

Behavioral Reciprocity. Insofar as people communicate with each other, what person A says to person B constrains person B's response. We find further that among young married couples faced with situations of interpersonal conflict, messages tend to be reciprocal. For example, although there is a modal tendency to respond to any act (interchange) with a cognitively oriented response, cognitive acts by one partner elicit a higher than expected proportion of cognitive responses from the other; approaches to resolution draw similar approaches from the partner; and attempts at emotional reconciliation receive responses in kind; so, too, do coercive tactics and personal attacks receive reciprocal responses. An exception—whether because of the instructions or because of the marital bond—occurs when one partner rejects the other: rejecting acts tend to elicit either emotional appeals or coercive tactics. Mutual rejection, of course, ends conflict: the participants walk out on each other. Responding to rejection with appeals—whether to fairness, to the other's motives, or through pleadings and enticements—gives the partner and the relationship another chance. Although coercive tactics and personal attacks are more aggressive than appeals, they, too, leave an opening for further communication, and it is interesting that coercion, unlike rejection, does not decrease the likelihood of conflict resolution among our couples.

Reciprocation, whether of positively or of negatively toned messages, is a probabilistic tendency and not a foregone conclusion. Were human interactions wholly reciprocal in the one-to-one, tit-for-tat sense (or even if one mode of action inevitably led to another mode of response, which then led back to the initial mode), interaction would become merely the playing out of a ritual whose course is determined from the outset. In fact, the data—even considering unreliability—suggest that there are always possibilities for alternative directions. Coercion does not necessarily lead to coercion; it can be responded to with a conciliatory approach, and such a response may, in turn, shift the direction of following responses. The directional change does not always succeed. Among some couples an attempted shift from tit-for-tat responses seems merely to reinforce prior behavior. For example, among discordant couples a conciliatory act by one partner to the other's coercion seems to foster the continuation of coercion. For most couples, however, a positively toned mode of response by one partner to the other's aggresion evokes a shift in the other's subsequent response. Escape from entrapment in a potentially destructive cycle is thus always a possibility in human communication.

The Situational Context. Bateson argues, "without context, there is no communication" (1972, p. 402), and he suggests a hierarchy of contexts. In our studies we consider successive levels of context in the specific acts of each partner toward the other, the defined conflict situation, and the relationship between the participants. We have commented on the continuing effects of each partner's actions on the other's. We now consider the constraining effects of the situation.

The power of situational influences and the need for including such influences in conceptualizations and studies of individual behavior have received increasing emphasis by psychologists recently (Endler and Hunt, 1968; Mischel, 1973; Moos, 1969). Situational factors exert a major influence on the interactions of our couples. The constraining effects of the specific conflict situation seem in our data as strong as or stronger than the effects exerted by a partner's specific action.[1] Situations induce and maintain the interactions of the participants. They set the tone of the approach to conflict.

Thus, conflicts between marital partners are far easier to resolve when issues of conflict are specific, substantive, definable (and defined) at the situational level. Issue-oriented conflicts are

[1] This differs from results of studies with children (Raush, 1965), in which the immediately preceding acts of participants had far more effect on subsequent acts than did the general situation. It is tempting to suggest that adult interactions are more subject to "higher" contextual levels and that with an increase in cognitive capacities broader conceptual sets come to exert stronger influence. Differences in the methods of the studies make such suggestions mere speculations at this point.

much less heated than relationship-oriented conflicts, and couples who redefine a confrontation about their relationship in terms of a specific focus have an easier time resolving it. In this, our data accord with recent suggestions about family disagreements (Turner, 1970), with experimental studies of bargaining situations, and with examinations of negotiations in international conflict. Conflicts that concern a specific decisional issue orient the participants more heavily toward cognitive approaches than do conflicts concerning the relationship of the participants. When the relationship is at stake, coercion, personal disparagement, and attack become more probable despite their tactical inefficacy in leading to resolution. A similar distinction is evident in positively toned efforts at solution: in issue-oriented conflicts attempts at resolution take a more rational direction, whereas positive attempts to solve relationship conflicts involve more affective approaches, aimed at emotional reconciliation.

The data show that not only do people do different things in different situations, but also the same actions carry different meanings and evoke different responses. As Cherry notes, "words are slippery customers. The full meaning of a word does not appear until it is placed in its context, and the context may serve an extremely subtle function—as with puns or *double entendres*. And even then the 'meaning' will depend upon the listener, upon the speaker, upon their entire experience of the language, upon their knowledge of one another, and upon the whole situation" (1966, p. 10). Bateson makes the same point: "A person responds to the same stimulus differently in different contexts" (1972, p. 289). Our analyses indicate that the nature of the situation affects not only the probabilities of interactive events but also the patterning of the contingencies among them.

The Context of the Relationship. Although the situation is a powerful predictor of the kind of message to expect, participants can transform these expectations. A conflict about a seemingly simple and specific issue can escalate to threaten the entire relationship. The reverse also occurs—a conflict about the relationship may become focused on a specific issue. As Mischel notes, "in life the 'subject' supplies his own instructions and may transform the situation in many alternative (unpredictable) ways" (1973, p. 260), and he suggests that the impacts of situations depend on how they are processed by the person.[2]

The course that conflict takes depends, then, in part on the nature of the conflict, but it also depends on the participants. Our data suggest that, whatever the contributions of the specific partners, the marital relationship forms a unit, and the couple can be thought of as a system. Within our analyses the marital unit was the most powerful source in determining interactive events. Couples function as units, exhibiting their own styles of conflict enactment. Both impressionistically and statistically individual couple patterns were consistent over the first two (and sometimes more) years of marriage. This is especially noteworthy in that the subjects were first studied only four months after marriage. It suggests that, whether through initial mutual selection or through explorations at the beginning of marriage, a couple's style of dealing with interpersonal conflict is established very early in their relationship and remains relatively consistent.

Quite beyond the context of the conflict situations presented them couples act out their own styles, blurring and overriding the situational definitions given in the instructions. Most often we were struck by the almost exquisite intermeshing of individual husband and wife in creating an approach to a conflict between them. Generally, individuals who avoid, deny, or repress conflict are helped in this by their partners and, in turn, help their partners in these same modes. So, too, those who escalate conflict into punitive battles of will assist each other in this. Empathic sensitivity and support by one partner are also generally mirrored by the other. The intermeshing of individual styles in a conjoint approach to the management of conflict (as illustrated in Chapters Six and Seven and in the contingency data of Chapter Thirteen) makes the attribution of individual causality within the ongoing interaction arbi-

[2] This interactionist position relating person and situation is more fully explored in a paper by Bowers (1973). It is interesting that Bowers, whose paper was published after this book was written, independently develops the use of Piaget's concepts of schema, assimilation, and accommodation to integrate personal and situational variables in a fashion similar to the point of view presented here.

trary. Who does what to whom is part of a continuing feedback process in which both partners participate.

For some couples almost any discrepancy in viewpoint seems to impinge on core issues. A disagreement about how to celebrate the first wedding anniversary or a specific remark by the marital partner becomes assimilated into an object relations schema that converts benign and neutral meanings into malevolent ones. Six couples, through a factor analytic study of data other than the Improvisations, were identified as "discordant." Later follow-up found three of these couples divorced, two in spite of becoming parents early in the marriage; after eight years these were the only known divorces in the sample of forty-six couples. At the fourth month after the wedding, the six couples viewed their marriages as unhappy, and interviewers found other evidence of disturbances. Peter DeVries, inverting a line from Shakespeare, notes: "Let us not to the marriage of impediments admit true minds," and our study of the small group of discordant couples illustrates full well how impediments in relationship are mirrored in interpersonal behavior.

The discordant couples engage in much longer scenes than other couples on the average, and the process over the four Improvisation scenes illustrates how conflict may accumulate. The wives in this sample respond to the issue-oriented scenes, which are the first presented, as though the discrepancy in the wishes of the two partners touched directly on schemata relating to power and self-esteem. For example, one wife who has cooked an anniversary dinner, while her husband has made arrangements to go out, says, "You'll eat my chicken or choke!" another wife insists that, if she doesn't get to watch her television program she'll "get very sick." Compared to other wives, the discordant wives employ more coercive tactics in these scenes and are particularly prone to tit-for-tat responses to coercion by their partners.

Deutsch (1969a, 1969b) finds that conflict expands when issues involve power or self-esteem. Yet this is not immediately apparent in the data of the first two scenes. To their attacking wives, the discordant husbands respond relatively benignly—at least at first. But grievances do collect; and in the third scene, where the instructors encourage the husband to isolate and distance himself from his wife, the discordant husbands make the most of their opportunity. They become far more coercive and far less conciliatory than other husbands. Furthermore, their behavior in the final scene, in which they are presumably attempting to achieve closeness to their wives, continues the relatively high level of coercive tactics and relatively low levels of conciliatory acts. Even in this role the discordant husbands seem dominated by object relations schemata relating to power and vengeance for former, unexpressed hurt. It is the wives in the latter two scenes—in contrast to other couples— who enact the more conciliatory and rational parts. The discordant partners thus seem to play out alternating exaggerated power struggles. Suspicion and jealousy are prominent in their interactions, and, in the battles of will that characterize the scenes, indications of concern for the other's communications and feelings are lacking.

A group of seven "harmonious" couples were at the opposite end of the same factor that distinguished the discordant couples as a group. The harmonious group's enactment of the Improvisations was characterized by shorter than average scenes, a lack of heated exchange, and a high proportion of reconciling messages by husbands. We noted that "harmony," like "success" in marriage can mean very different things for different couples. In Chapter Seven we commented that, despite out initial biases, some couples who employed what we would ordinarily think of as "pathological" defenses in evading conflict seemed as happy with their marriages as others. In their lives such couples avoided confronting one another and seemed relatively unconcerned about their relationship. When forced by us into conflict, they defended against confrontation, and their interactions had a static cyclic quality with little interchange. Yet, given a context of mutual affection, avoidance did not seem to contraindicate viable and "happy" marriages. It is interesting, then, that four of the seven harmonious couples had been discussed as avoiders of conflict before the factor scores were known. The other three harmonious couples engaged in the conflicts set by the Improvisations. They dealt with one another directly, yet with sensitivity and empathy. Their approaches to conflict and its resolution showed, even within the space of a single scene, sequential communication exchange, growth, development, and sometimes even creativity. Tolstoi comments in *Anna Karenina* that all happy families resemble one another whereas each unhappy family is unhappy in its own fashion; our findings suggest, on the contrary, that unhappy couples share common styles of interaction more than happy couples do. The harmonious couples seem to be composed of two subgroups: those who manage to avoid conflict and those who deal with conflict constructively. The subgroups share a capacity for avoiding escalation, however.

The Context of Stage and Time. The major determinants of how our couples interact with one another in conflict situations have been discussed above. The stage of marriage, at least within the first two years, tells us far less about interactive events. In the late stages of their wives' pregnancies husbands make far more efforts at emotional conciliation than they did in interpersonal conflicts as newlyweds. Comparison with matched, nonpregnant couples indicated that this change is specific to pregnancy as a stage. There is no evidence that wives become more emotional in dealing with conflict during pregnancy. Following childbirth, husbands no longer seem to feel that their wives require special support in handling a marital conflict. The data thus suggest a stereotype in the male response to pregnancy as a delicate condition. The failure of husbands to maintain their level of supportiveness after the baby is born suggests a basis for the dissatisfaction some wives feel after initial childbirth. Nonetheless, the interactions of the couple yield no evidence that the transition to parenthood is experienced as a crisis.

The data offer mild suggestions that couples who become pregnant early in marriage may be somewhat more conventionally oriented toward traditional male and female roles in dealing with interpersonal conflict, but the findings are not strong. It is clearer that there are some changes over the course of marriage that are associated with length of marriage rather than stage. Both husbands and wives generally decline progressively in their use of rejection and increase in their use of cognitive approaches in argument. Moreover, the enactments tend to be shorter. It is clear that there is less brinksmanship in the interactions, but in terms of coercive tactics the scenes do not seem to be milder.

The changes over time, though statistically significant, are not great. The directions of change through approximately the first two years of marriage suggest that husbands decrease in the assertion of "masculine" power, that wives become less anxious about "feminine" behavior and freer in the assertions of power, and that in general couples take a somewhat calmer, more rational approach to interpersonal conflict. Firmer than these speculations about change is the consistency that couples present over time. Both clinical study (Chapters Seven and Eight) and formal data (Chapter Fourteen) indicated what to us was a surprising stability in couples' patterns of interaction.

The Male-Female Context.   Differences between men and women in dealing with conflict are perhaps most striking in how little they account for the behavior of the participants. Husbands and wives are statistically different in their actions, but the differences are small. Of all variables examined, the sex of the partner tells us least about behavior in conflict situations. Certainly, there is no evidence that in interpersonal conflicts husbands show more instrumental acts and wives more expressive acts as Parsons and Bales's theory of sex differentiation would suggest. In dyadic interaction, husbands and wives tend to respond in much the same ways. Yet, because the topic of male-female differences is important, it is worth noting those differences that do occur, keeping in mind that in our data they are small and seem to be readily overpowered by the effects of scene instructions.

Differences between husbands and wives appear mainly in response contingencies. Thus, newlywed husbands are more likely than their wives to reciprocate efforts at resolution and attempts at emotional conciliation. Wives are more likely than husbands to reciprocate coercive acts and to answer rejection with coercion. In general, newlywed husbands are more likely to use conciliatory approaches than are their wives; this is particularly so when they attempt to achieve closeness to their distance-maintaining partners. In issue-oriented conflicts wives use relatively more coercions and appeals, and husbands use more resolving and reconciling acts.

We noted the marked increase in conciliatory efforts by husbands when their wives were in late pregnancy and the subsequent decrease after childbirth. Yet even in early parenthood husbands lead their wives in the proportion of conciliatory acts. Between newlywed and postnatal periods, wives increase in their proportions of coercive responses, and this is particularly true in their attempts to maintain distance; husbands on the contrary decrease their use of coercive tactics for distancing.

An attempt to interpret these patterns suggests that wives as newlyweds may be somewhat more anxious in confronting conflict than their husbands. The suggestion ties in with experimental findings of sex differences in competitive games (Rapoport and Chammah, 1965) and bargaining situations (Kelley, 1965). Such findings imply that women may feel considerably more uneasy than men about power relationships and competitive interactions. The differences in patterns of communication reflected in our data suggest that despite the conscious orientation toward status equality among these couples married in the late fifties and early sixties, schemata of masculinity and femininity emerged on the testing ground of interpersonal conflict. Husbands were more comfortable with power; they seemed freer to assert independence (as in the distancing scene), while expressing traditional male chivalrous support. Wives employed the strategies of low power groups (Deutsch, 1969a)—moral persuasion through appeals and harassment through coercive tactics. Differences in male and female anxiety with respect to power help explain the findings of questionnaire studies that relate marital "success" to the status and "adjustment" of husbands, not wives. Our studies indicated that husbands more often than wives were agents for escape from negatively toned tit-for-tat communicative cycles, enabling interactions to move into more constructive channels. Within the relationship couples more often depended on the husband to be the reconciler of conflict.

Changing cultural patterns over the coming years may attenuate even the small male-female differences we found. Greater equity between men and women might make conflict between a husband and a wife a less anxious and disruptive experience than it seemed to be for so many of our couples. Yet conflict between intimates with opposing intentions will persist as a condition of relationships with others. We have commented on some aspects of escalation and attenuation of conflict. Let us turn more specifically to modes of handling conflict and their possible consequences.

Styles of Conflict and Marriage

The Psychopathology of Communication. The psychopathology of communication is a subject of considerable recent attention (Bateson and others, 1956, 1963; Ruesch, 1957; Watzlawick and others, 1967). Family and marital disturbances are said to be reflected in disturbed forms of communication. Moreover, some forms of communication, if continued over long periods of time, are said to contribute to the development of severe pathology. The theses and illustrations are potent, though difficult to confirm.

What are surprising in our studies of presumably normal couples are the many instances of what has been described as communicative pathology. In some 15 percent of the scenes couples avoided any confrontation with one another, and some 15 percent of our couples showed a marked consistency in dealing with conflict by avoidance. Although in some instances avoidance seemed a simple matter of discretion, and although one might expect newly married couples to avoid conflict with one another, most cases examined reflected not so much an avoidance of unnecessary conflict as a style of coping with existent interpersonal conflict by avoidance. Clearly, avoidance as a mode of coping fails to resolve issues. Even when there seem to be resolutions of conflict, these have a spurious quality. Nor did avoidance always ensure against escalation of conflict, as illustrated in Chapter Seven. Avoidance often took the form of a piling up of denials, externalizations, and disqualifications that could escalate conflict to a hysterical pitch.

Those who engaged conflict in the situations, who confronted each other with their opposing intentions, were not always better off. In some instances they too exhibited psychopathological forms of communication: disqualifications of their own as well as of the other's remarks; double-binding messages, which present contradictions between communicative and metacommunicative levels while keeping the other bound in an intense field. Engagement too can result in escalation. When schemata involving core issues associated with anxiety are touched on, a specific conflict becomes crucialized, expanding to encompass the entire relationship. As illustrated in Chapter Eight, messages are garbled in sending and receipt, nothing new is heard or sent, and communication becomes an intense, undifferentiated, primitive battle of wills, exemplified by repetitive cycles of "Yes, you will" and "No, I won't."

Stasis in Communication. Both avoidance and engagement can lead to destructive conflict. Both can also lead to a less destructive stasis. In the case of avoidance, even when there is no escalation, and the relationship remains at a benign level, there is a static quality to the interactions. They lack a progressive development and form that continued informational exchange is capable of yielding. Conflict tends to eventuate in a recurrent cyclic pattern. There is little evidence of new learning, and possibilities for change from within the relationship itself seem precluded. Engagement too may yield a static quality. When the interactive repertoires of the participants are constricted, although the lack of variety does not seem to be a function of anxiety, there may be no escalation of conflict but there also may be little sense of movement. Under such circumstances, however, unlike the case of avoidance, genuine resolutions to conflict can occur.

Constructive Conflict. Engagement differs from avoidance in that it offers the possibility of constructive and even creative approaches to interpersonal conflict. Couples who engage and resolve conflict constuctively often do so by keeping the boundaries of conflict within a specific issue. Even when, as in the closeness-distance scenes, the instructions invoke conflict about the relationship, couples may transform the conflict to focus on a specific problem. The data indicate that by doing so they greatly increase the likelihood of resolution.

Coping with conflict between intimates may go beyond the resolution of a specific interpersonal issue. Constructive conflict can be, as Bateson (1972, pp. 301–306) suggests, a learning for the future, and confrontation can be a creative process enabling a new step in this learning. Creativity in this sense seems to require (a) freedom to engage rather than evade the immediate conflict situation; (b) sufficient freedom from the constraints set by the scene and the instructions so that the bond between the partners takes precedence over the immediate set; (c) freedom from the reciprocal pull evoked by a partner's negatively toned message; and (d) freedom from inflexible, anxiety-based object relations schemata. These conditions, although they emphasize an interpersonal framework, bear resemblance to intrapersonal conditions for autonomy, exploration, and creativity. Thus, Rapaport (1967) speaks of the maturely developed ego as needing to be both related to and relatively autonomous from the id and from the environment in order not to become a prisoner of either one; Bruner (1966) suggests freedom from the intensity of strong immediate drives and incentives as a condition for intrinsic learning; Moore and Anderson (1962) believe that, by virtue of its freedom from immediate demands, social play allows the exploration and testing of alternatives.

Within the conflict scenes some couples are apparently able to express such freedom. In such cases the enactments, despite serious and sometimes intense involvement, take on a quality of mutual play and exploration. For such couples the specific resolution—who wins and who loses—seems far less important than the process of mutual growth and understanding. Scenes that took such directions enabled us to suggest an idealized sequence of steps in conflict resolution. In its early phases the sequence resembles that described in experimental conflict studies with ad hoc pairs (Deutsch, 1969a). But, in a relationship that carries strong emotional investment and that is projected as continuing, the termination of conflict goes beyond specific resolution (see Turner, 1970, pp. 137–138); it moves toward practical planning, followed by emotional reconciliation between the partners, then to reaffirmation and consolidation in discussion of other joint activities, and finally turns toward questions of future coping with similar conflict issues. In the traversal of this sequence, the relationship between the partners is the primary medium for learning.

Communication Styles and Marriage. Despite our initial prejudices, couples who coped with conflict by avoidance had no less stable, compatible, comfortable marriages than those who confronted interpersonal disagreements. The former group's constricted patterns of communication, their inefficacy in joint problem-solving did not, according to our data, preclude relationships that were satisfying to the participants. When conjoint avoidance was syntonic with individual styles of repression, denial, deemphasis on feeling, and introspection, when the marital pair established differentiated role patterns, and when there was a bond of mutual affection between partners, then it seemed to us that avoidance could coexist with "happy" marriages. In fact it would be consistent with their style for avoiders especially to perceive and describe their marriages as happy.

Although it may have no direct bearing on marital satisfaction or stability, engagement opens other potentials to a relationship. The capacity to confront interpersonal opposition without escalation, disqualifications, double binds; to maintain mutual sensitivity and responsiveness in the face of interpersonal conflict; to work conjointly in achieving decisions that take emotional as well as cognitive components into account: these offer possibilities for growth and development.

Marriage is becoming more rather than less complex. Seldom has a culture required so much of a single institution as our own does of marriage. In 1960 Arensburg noted: "Our present small, conjugal type of family, with its minimum kinship entanglement and support, ideally requires each person to find a mate for himself, to love that spouse, to share the upbringing of children with him, to find chief emotional identification in the little family growing up around this spouse and partner freely chosen and freely retained. To carry all these roles is not easy and to put so many eggs in one basket is certainly risky; few other family customs or national cultures seem to require such concentration of emotional effort in individual responsibility for self-directed personal adjustment and for unaided child-training" (p. 61).

These problems have not decreased nor is it likely that they will. For example, Bennis and Slater (1968) believe that the increasing growth of temporary, transitory systems requires rapid development and dissolution of personal relationships. They suggest that this, along with geographic mobility, will place greater reliance and burdens on the primary husband-wife bond.

Moreover, couples seem to be demanding ever more from their relationships. Olson points to recent changes in the criteria used to evaluate the success of a marital relationship: "Increasingly, individuals are seeking a relationship that will provide growth for them as individuals and as a couple. . . . There is a search for an authentic and mutually actualizing relationship" (1972, p. 390). He notes the difficulties of this achievement for two individuals who form a couple. "As a result, many couples today are becoming increasingly frustrated because they have rejected the more traditional definition of a successful marriage and yet are having difficulty achieving the type of mutually actualizing relationship that they are striving to achieve" (p. 390). From a study of unconventional marriages (Kafka and Ryder, 1972), Olson notes that the most vital relationships were often ones that did not last.

The practitioner working to help couples and families is apt to be caught up in this cultural swing. Many couples do indeed demand more of their relationship than a comfortable stasis. And some couples are uncomfortable with communicational styles they recognize as destructive. These groups can be aided toward more open, more effective, less destructive, and possibly more creative interactive approaches. Of further implication for practice is the finding that consistent communication patterns are established early in marriage, suggesting possibilities for early, preventive interventions. Husbands' relative decrease in supportiveness to wives following childbirth may also be of practical concern. It is important, however, to note that our findings also indicate that optimal communication, in the psychologist's sense, is not essential to what is perceived as a good relationship for all couples. To place a demand for a particular style of communication on all couples is an imposition of values.

Despite this latter caution, communication styles that enable and foster conjoint learning and a continued evolution of the relationship offer special scope for the future. Couples capable of this can, we believe, engage more competently in meeting the demands and opportunities of an ever more rapidly changing world. Moreover, they can convey to their children the possibilities of adults communicating, learning from one another, and coping creatively with new situations.

Interacting Systems

It remains to develop an organization that might aid us in further conceptualizing the complexities we have discussed in this book. The phenomena we have described are overlapping and interrelated, complicating our discourse. Each topic seemed to demand consideration of the others. It was, for example, impossible for us to speak of couples' interactions without referring to the situations in which they were placed; nor could we speak of the situations without referring to their different meanings for different couples; so, too, a specific interaction stood in the context of the general relationship; and so on. Without questioning, we accept this interweaving in our daily lives: we are, for example, not surprised that "Hello, dear" means something different coming from a passing stranger than from a returning spouse.

Our habits of simple causal thinking were also confounded when we considered who in our couples did what to whom. Escalation, stasis, and creativity in conflict management were not attributable to a particular partner but rather seemed an outgrowth of a conjoint system involving continued, successive feedback. This too is not discrepant from our ordinary experiences: a couple trying to reconstruct the causes of a quarrel or parents trying to learn which of two children is responsible for a fight face the same dilemma of causal attribution.

In Chapter Two we proposed a probabilistic orientation to conceptualizations and research concerning the relationships between events and between systems. We sketched a diagram (Figure 1) indicating how a network of relationships might work. The diagram suggested possibilities for incorporating into our approaches such concepts as equipotentiality—whereby one variable may substitute for another—and multidetermination—whereby several variables may contribute to a single effect. Our analytic methods and findings now lead us to think that that sketch is too simple—particularly, in its inference of linear causality.

Consider instead an alternative conceptualization: an overlapping network of elipses (see Attneave, 1959, pp. 56–60), each representing a variable set—for example, cognitive, personality, relationship, situational, and stage variables. The overlap represents information shared or transmitted between the sets; situations thus "inform" persons, selecting segments of personal experience; persons also inform situations, selecting segments to respond to. The overlap need not be symmetrical; that is, a given situation may have more selecting power in transforming a person's actions than the person has in transforming the situation. When more than two elipses overlap there is redundancy in the information transmitted from different sources. Consider, for example, that a situation of interpersonal conflict selects a segment from partner A's potential repertoire of actions; it also selects a segment from partner B's potential repertoire; each partner's specific actions also, however, select from the repertoire of the other partner; to some extent it is likely that the selection by the situation and by a specific action will overlap. Such redundancy, though not maximally efficient, serves to confirm interpretation and action. In addition to shared information and redundancy, our findings point to an amplifying effect in the relationships among variables—what has been referred to as interaction (Attneave, 1959, p. 58), patterning, or organization. Something new is added, so that from the interaction of two or more systems there evolves something more than their summative components. Hoffman (1971) associates such amplification with positive as compared to negative feedback processes, and she implies that amplification mechanisms can, in shifting systems relations to new levels, have especially constructive or destructive effects.

The authors hope that our theoretical considerations, findings, and speculations have not only informed the reader, but have amplified beyond that input—to foster what we have not expressed and to enable new and constructive steps in the understanding of human relationships.

A Coding Scheme for Interpersonal Conflict

General Introduction

Acts

    I.   An act is defined as the statement or action of one person bounded by the statement or action of another. Except for the last act in a series of interchanges, an act is initiated by the actor's statement or action and it terminates when the statement or action of another begins. Thus, an act may be a lengthy statement, a sentence, a phrase, or a word; it may end at a natural termination point or it may be interrupted by the act of another. In our present work we have coded primarily verbal acts, but acts may also be gestures, expressions, or other physical motions.

    II.   Each act receives two labels: a coding for *action category* and a coding for *phase*.

Action Categories

I.   Category coding involves specific acts. The position taken by the coder is that of the generalized other. The question he must answer is: What would I feel was being done to me if I were the recipient of this particular act? The coder must judge this in two contexts: (1) the actor's knowledge of the setting, including any instructions he may have received about the conflict situation; and (2) what has gone on in the interchange up to the specific act now being coded. In other words, an action category coding may be influenced by preceding codings, but the coder must avoid special knowledge of or influence by subsequent events. He therefore avoids reading or listening ahead of the act he is coding. A particular danger is that coders may try to interpret an act too deeply. The judgment must be at a relatively, but not completely, naive level: how would the recipient judge what was being done to him? Thus, for example, a statement in the form of a question might represent a request for information, an expression of personal concern, an attack, or some other response. The coder must differentiate among these, irrespective of the form of the statement, by taking the position of the recipient.

II.   There are thirty-six action categories. These presumably cover the potentialities for the interactions of two participants in a conflict situation. The categories may be roughly classified as either cognitive, affiliative, or coercive, and they are listed as such in the body of the manual as an aid to the coder. Within this rough classification the categories are ordered roughly according to their *intensity* (discussed below). Each act is coded by selection from the thirty-six action categories. Following coding, data may be lumped according to any of several schemes (discussed below).

Phases

I.   Each act is also coded according to the *phase* of the conflict situation in which it occurs. The phase coding indicates the general position of the participants with respect to the flow of the conflict situation. There are three phases:

(1) *Introductory:* acts prior to the introduction of the conflict issue;

(2) *Conflict:* acts beginning with the first statement of the

conflict issue and continuing until the introduction of an agreed on resolution;

(3) *Resolution and postresolution:* acts beginning with the achievement of a resolution and subsequent discussion.[1]

II.   The judgment of phase is taken from the vantage point of the coder. The coder must judge the position of the participants with respect to the conflict: is this act before, during, or after the conflict? In contrast to action category coding, the coder does *not* take the position of the generalized other. He is thus permitted to revise his coding of phase if additional information leads him to alter his judgment.

Double Coding

I.   The general policy is to minimize double codes. Double codes may be used in the following cases:

(1) when there is a change of phase within a single act; for example, the act may follow an introductory remark with the statement of the conflict issue, or a conflict statement may be followed by a suggestion for resolution;

(2) when the first part of an act is in response to the other's statement, while a later part initiates an event requiring another coding;

(3) when there is too much information in the act to handle with a single coding; for example, tone may change from coercive to affiliative or from cognitive to coercive.

II.   Acts are *not* double coded in the following cases:

(1) when they are ambiguous to the coder—a decision must be made as to the best single code;

(2) when there is disagreement among coders—again the best single code must be selected (see the discussion of consensus coding below).

Triple codes are *never* used.

---

[1] The initial scheme for phase coding consisted of six phases; phases for tempering the conflict and for avoidance of conflict were eliminated, partly because of infrequency of occurrence and partly because these aspects were sufficiently reflected in the action category codings. A differentiation between resolution and postresolution was eliminated because the resolution phase usually consisted of no more than three acts.

III. By convention (because of our data analysis requirements), there cannot be two successive double codes; that is, at least one single-coded act must appear between any two acts that are double-coded. If the rules do not allow the coder to double code in a situation where double coding seems warranted, he must judge which single aspect of an act is most important and code accordingly.

Procedures

I. In coding, a column of the coding sheet is designated for each participant. Acts are numbered successively at the left hand margin, beginning with 1. The coder codes each act successively without listening or reading ahead. As noted above, phase codes may be modified by subsequent considerations, but *not* action category codes.

II. We have used a procedure involving two steps: independent coding and consensus coding.

A. *Independent coding:* Each coder codes the material independently. He proceeds successively through the series of acts, coding each act into one of the three phases and into one (or, if necessary, two) of the thirty-six action categories. In our own work we used tape recordings and typed transcripts simultaneously. Two or three independent coders coded each set of materials.

B. *Consensus coding:* Consensus coders work conjointly. They repeat the procedures of the independent coders, but have available to them not only the raw materials (tapes and transcripts) but also the codings of the independent coders. Using the independent codings as a basis, the consensus coders together arrive at a judgment for coding of each act. This judgment becomes the *standard* code. Consensus requires at least two coders. In some of our work consensus and independent coders overlapped—that is, one of the independent coders also coded in the consensus procedures; later, consensus was done by coders other than those who did the independent codings. The more experienced coders should be used for consensus.

Coder Training. Initially new coders are familiarized with the coding categories. They need not memorize the scheme, since a list of the action categories and phases is always available. If experienced coders and previous *standard* judgments are available, as a new coder begins to code material, an experienced coder should work with him, helping him compare his judgments with the previous consensus. When a coder begins to feel comfortable with the procedures, he can undertake independent coding; he then meets with other new coders, and, under the guidance of an experienced coder (if available), they discuss consensus, comparing their final judgments with the previous standards (again, if available). The final training step is for new coders to work together establishing the standard codings without supervision. Their standard codings are then compared to the standard codings established by experienced coders (if available). We found that, after sixty to one hundred hours of training, spread over three to four weeks, standard action category codes of new coders agreed 67 percent with the standard codes of experienced coders. This compares reasonably well with the reliability of experienced coders (approximately 70 percent absolute agreement).

Lumping. The action categories are comprised of thirty-six discrete units. These presumably cover all possible acts in a conflict situation. The number is, of course, arbitrary; in fact, the original scheme consisted of more than forty categories. The present thirty-six seem, however, reasonably discriminable.

For some purposes this differentiation is too fine. Either theoretical considerations or practical limitations in frequencies may suggest a need for lumping. We have already noted that the categories may be roughly divided into cognitive, affiliative, and coercive groupings. Such a division is, however, too crude. One compromise lumps the thirty-six categories into twelve. These are noted in the final section of the Manual together with the specific categories of which they are comprised. A second scheme, lumping the thirty-six categories into six, is also noted in the final section of the Manual. Other forms of lumping are, of course, possible. The lumping does not affect the coding procedure, since the data are grouped after coding. With lumping, reliability shifts from about 70 percent absolute agreement using thirty-six categories, to about

75 percent absolute agreement using twelve and about 77 percent absolute agreement using six.

Action Category Coding

Cognitive Acts

0. *Conventional remarks*

   Used for: remarks that are ritualistic, cultural, or "social" in implication. Conventional remarks rarely convey information. Obvious conventional remarks are used in greeting and parting (see examples).

   Conventions and confusions: The coder must judge that the remark is purely conventional and not intended to convey or elicit information. For example, "How are you?" as a greeting is coded 0 rather than 2.

   Examples:
   "Hello, dear."
   "How are you?"
   "Happy anniversary."
   "Nice day isn't it?"
   "See you later."
   "So long."

1. *Opening the issue or probe*

   Used for: a move toward bringing an issue or problem into the open. This code represents a preliminary step before overtly facing an issue. It says, in a sense, "there is something to be talked about," or primes the other for a course of action, but the substantive issue is not stated.

   Conventions and confusions: At times a code 1 act may be mistaken for 0, 2, or 3. It appears frequently as the first communication to break the conventionality barrier. It is very important for the coder to keep the set of the "generalized other." The coder may know the purpose of the speaker, but the one to whom the speaker speaks may not. Hence, code 1 should be used only when the listener without special knowledge would know that the speaker is probing or opening the issue.

Examples:

"I have a surprise for you."

"Honey?" (Said in tone of "I have something to say.")

"Something on your mind?"

"What's that smile for?"

2. *Seeking information*

Used for: attempts to find out *factual* information. It cannot be emphasized enough that this is solely to elicit factual information.

Conventions and confusions: A question does not necessarily indicate a 2, and not all 2s are in the form of a question. The function of the statement is the essential determinant.

Examples:

"What time is it?"

"What are you making?"

"Tell me more."

(Examples ordinarily *not* code 2: "How are you?" is usually 0; "What's the matter with you?" is usually 21.)

3. *Giving information*

Used for: presentation of *factual* information.

Conventions and confusions: A 3 act does not necessarily have to be in answer to a question. Generally 3s are well differentiated from the other categories, though at times they are confused with 5s, especially if a move toward action is implicit. If statement is for any purpose other than to give information, another coding should be used. Again the coder should take the position of the "generalized other" who is not privy to special information.

Examples:

"It's 10 o'clock."

"I'm finished with the dishes."

4. *Withholding information*

Used for: an attempt to conceal or disguise plans or feelings that the other wishes to know about, but without implying rejection of the other.

Conventions and confusions: The coder must find that the refusal to answer the other's questions is not rejection of other but merely an unwillingness to answer, without strong emotional impact. When, in response to "What's the

matter?" the speaker replies "Nothing," the context and
tone are important for making a judgment of code. The 4s
should be discriminated from 45s.

Examples:

(A: "I've got a surprise." = 1)

(B: "What's the surprise?" = 2)

A: "I'm not telling."

Other examples are not presented because they depend
too much on context and tone.

5. *Suggesting a course of action*

Used for: suggestions for action, whether in the form of a
declaration or a question.

Conventions and confusions: Code 5 acts can be differentiated
from 47s by the tone of voice and the context.

Examples:

"Let's stay home."

"How about going out to dinner?"

"Why don't you go wash up?"

"Come on over and sit down."

6. *Agreeing with the other's statement*

Used for: the verbal equivalent of a behavioral nod.

Conventions and confusions: This code represents a fairly
cursory agreement, saying, in effect, "Go on; tell me more."
It must be discriminated from 23, which is a real acceptance
of what other has said; 6 is more cursory and conventional.
"Yes, but . . ." is usually 11, not 6.

Examples:

"Okay." (cursory)

"Uh huh."

"Mm hm."

(A: "Let's go to the show." = 5)

(B: "Okay." = 23)

A: "Okay."

7. *Giving cognitive reasons for a course of action*

Used for: statements of reasons most frequently in support
of one's own intention but can also be those for following
other person's course of action. The category reflects rational arguments.

Conventions and confusions: When emotional elements enter,

the coding is no longer 7. If the statement is made supporting one's own argument in denying the other's argument, it is coded 11. If it is merely sustaining one's own position, then it is coded as 7. A suggestion for a course of action (5) that is nested within arguments for such action tends to be coded as 7.

Examples:

"Let's go because I already have the tickets."

"There are three reasons why we should do this."

(Example not coded 7: "That's true, *but* I've already cooked the dinner" is 11)

8. *Exploring the consequences of a course of action*

Used for: a cognitive exploration of "What will happen if . . ."

Conventions and confusions: Code 8 tends to appear when people are close to agreeing on a course of action and are ready to explore the implications of their decision. It is the cognitive counterpart of 21 and 24. If elements of concern for the other's feelings (21) or the seeking of reassurance (24) appear, these take precedence. Compared to 29, which is concern with the general relationship and has an affiliative component, 8 is oriented toward a specific course of action and is more cognitive.

Examples:

"Will the food keep if we go out to dinner?"

"What will happen if we do _____?"

(Examples often confused with 8: "Would you be upset if we do this?" = 21; "Are you angry at me for this?" = 24; "Well, how shall we settle this?" = 29.)

10. *Giving up or leaving the field*

Used for: statements received by the other as a genuine "I give up" rather than as a tactic to induce or force the other to give in to one's demands.

Conventions and confusions: Code 10 acts should be distinguished from rejection (45) and guilt-induction (51). A 10 act signifies leaving the field of interaction.

Examples:

"I give up."

"I quit."

"I'm going to bed."

"I don't know what to do."

11. *Denying the validity of other's argument with or without the use of counterarguments*

Used for: cognitively oriented rational arguments.

Conventions and confusions: If there is any element of negation of the other's argument, the act is coded 11, not 7. This code is distinguished from 45, which is stronger, more abrasive, and more emotionally charged, and from 51, which is an assault of a more personal and emotional nature.

Examples:

"Yes, but . . ."

"I see no reason for _____."

"Yes, I did _____."

"No, I didn't _____."

"I don't agree with that."

13. *Changing the subject*

Used for: attempts to delay or effect a temporary pause in the conflict by shifting the topic of conversation. The recipient perceives this as a diversion from the topic under discussion, rather than as an attempt on the part of the sender to win the argument.

Conventions and confusions: In contrast to a 13, a 26 would be received by the generalized other more as a manipulative technique by the sender to win his point.

Examples:

"Look at that cat."

"Let's talk about something else."

(In the midst of an argument) "Did you put the dog out?"

Affiliative Acts

15. *Using humor*

Used for: acts in a humorous tone whose function, as perceived by the other, is to temper the conflict.

Conventions and confusions: The content may be diverse, but the generalized other would receive the statement (because

of tone and phrasing) as an attempt to lower the tension
level.

Examples:

"You're a stinker! That's a footnote by the way."

"Well, I never knew him [Shakespeare], but I enjoy his
plays."

"I'm going to trade you in."

19. *Avoiding blame or responsibility*

Used for: acts casting blame onto someone or something else
with the intent of making the other realize "it's not my
fault," or "I've no control over it."

Conventions and confusions: 19 is affiliative and conciliatory
in tone, in contrast to 41, which would be received as
coercive.

Examples:

"I didn't want to bring work home, but I can't help it."

"My mind was on something else."

"Well, there are circumstances that just don't allow me
to make a phone call."

"*I* didn't bring it up; *he* brought it up."

(Example not coded 19: "I've got to get this work done
tonight so leave me alone" is 41.)

20. *Accepting blame or responsibility*

Used for: a conciliatory or affiliative gesture, often an appeal
for forgiveness.

Conventions and confusions:—

Examples:

"I don't mean to be rude."

"I'm sorry."

"I admit I'm wrong."

21. *Showing concern for the other's feelings*

Used for: acts exploring the other's affect and/or emotional
investment in relation to an issue or goal.

Conventions and confusions: In contrast to 24, which emphasizes concern about oneself, 21 emphasizes concern for the
other person. An expression of concern continuously repeated becomes a nagging or coaxing (40); the convention

we have used is that after one repetition of a 21, subsequent repetitions are 40s.

Examples:

"What's bothering you, honey?"

"Do you really want to do that?"

"I want you to be happy."

"Are you really satisfied?"

23. *Accepting the other's plans, actions, ideas, motives, or feelings*

Used for: acts indicating real acceptance of what the other has said.

Conventions and confusions: See category 6.

Examples:

"That's a good idea."

"We will do just what you wanted to do."

"You have a point there."

"Okay. That would be fine with me."

24. *Seeking reassurance*

Used for: an attempt to evoke reassurance from the other either directly or indirectly (such as by self-deprecation, calling on the other to deny the remarks—see examples).

Conventions and confusions: At times it is very difficult to distinguish 24 from 21. A judgment must be made whether the statement shows concern for *oneself* (24) or for the *other* (21). It may be confused with 2, because 24 is very often in the form of a question; however, the request is not for a factual but rather for an emotional response.

Examples:

"You're not mad at me, are you?"

"You do love me, don't you?"

"I've been pretty stupid, haven't I?"

"Now I feel like a little baby."

"Forgive me?"

A: "I do love you." = 28)

B: "Do you really mean it?"

25. *Attempting to make up*

Used for: an attempt to soothe and smooth emotional differences, perceived as an attempt to restore good feelings in the relationship.

Conventions and confusions: A 25 act would not be perceived by the other as seeking reassurance or forgiveness, but as restoring the relationship to a preconflict level.

Examples:

"Now give me a kiss, and let's forget it."

"Maybe we're both wrong."

"Shake?"

26. *Diverting the other's attention as a maneuver to gain one's aim*

Used for: an act perceived by the recipient as a diversionary attempt on the part of the other to win his point. The emphasis is on the diversionary aspect and the manipulative aspect is often so obvious as to be ineffective. In the context of an argument, when the other person is on the offensive with good arguments, the speaker suddenly changes the argument.

Conventions and confusions: See category 13.

Examples:

"Where did you learn to argue so well?"

(In the midst of deciding which television show to watch) "Why don't you go get me a coke?"

(In the scene where the wife is maintaining distance)   H: "Well, you are cute." H: "Did anyone ever tell you you're beautiful?"

"You're cute even when angry."

"You certainly express yourself well on that point."

27. *Introducing a compromise*

Used for: an attempt to include each person's aim in an overall solution.

Conventions and confusions: The difference between 27 and 35 is that 35 is perceived as an attempt on the part of the other to get his own way by offering something else, whereas 27 is perceived as a genuine attempt to reconcile the differences between the two.

Examples:

"I'll make a deal with you."

"I'll tell you what; we'll split it fifty-fifty."

"Let's do it this way now; next time we'll do it your way."

28. *Offering help or reassurance*

Used for: an assurance through word or gesture of positive feeling.

Conventions and confusions:—

Examples:

"No, no, no. I'm completely happy."

"So long as we can work it out, that's what counts."

"Here—I'll help you with your coat."

29. *Offering to collaborate in planning*

Used for: an offer to help in adopting a solution or to work together to plan a solution.

Conventions and confusions: A 29 act *may* be a suggestion for a course of action (5), but it recognizes that a unilateral solution is not possible.

Examples:

"What do you think?"

"Let's figure it out."

"Well, what are we going to do?"

"Well, let's look at it both ways."

31. *Appealing to fairness*

Used for: an attempt to obtain one's goal (aim) by appealing to the other's sense of fair play.

Conventions and confusions: A 31 statement appeals to the positive sense of fairness and justice in the other. In a 51 act, the other is accused of "bad motives."

Examples:

"We always do what you want to do."

"But that's not fair."

"Do you realize I've had a busy day too?"

"What would you do if I behaved that way?"

33. *Appealing to other's motives*

Used for: an attempt to convince the other that one's plans will give him or both parties as much as or more than his plans will. The recipient perceives this as an appeal to the benefits he would achieve by accepting the sender's plans.

Conventions and confusions: In contrast to 7, the emphasis is on the motives of the other rather than on the rationality of the argument.

Examples:

"You'll really like this, dear."

"It would really make you feel much better."

"Doing_____ would be of benefit to both of us."

35. *Offering something else as a way of winning one's goal*

Used for: an appeal to the other person by offering him something in return for his agreement. It is perceived by the other as having the quality of a bribe.

Conventions and confusions: See category 27.

Examples:

"I'll give you a lollipop if you stop crying."

"You won't get your present unless you do_____."

37. *Appealing to the love of the other*

Used for: a statement perceived as a direct personal appeal. It exerts pressure on the other by capitalizing on the affiliative relationship.

Conventions and confusions: Although an appeal to the love of the other person may have guilt-inducing properties, the judgment must be whether the other receives it as accusatory (51) or affiliative (37).

Examples:

(In the context of a love relationship) "I would appreciate it very much if you would do this."

"Do it for me."

"If you love [respect, think well of] me, you will_____."

40. *Pleading and coaxing*

Used for: an appeal to the other person either passively (pleading) or actively (coaxing and prodding) without making explicit the motivation to which the appeal is made (such as fairness or love). The key is either in the tone of expression or in the continued repetition of the same appeal without adding more to it (see category 21).

Conventions and confusions: Often implicit in this type of statement is an appeal to the love of the other or to fairness, but if that is not made explicit it would be coded 40.

Examples (all depend on tone):

"Please."
"Come on, honey."
"Do it just this once."
(A: "What's the matter, honey?" = 21)
(B: [statement.])
(A: "What the matter, honey?" = 21)
(B: [statement])
A: "Tell me what's the matter, honey."

Coercive Acts

41. *Using an outside power or set of circumstances to induce or force the other to agree*

    Used for: acts that the other perceives as describing external forces or a present set of circumstances that coerce him to yield.

    Conventions and confusions: See category 19. A 19 act is an excuse for something that has already occurred, whereas a 41 is used to force the other person to go along with a proposed course of action.

    Examples:

    "I've had a hell of a day at the office." (Implied: "so do what I want.")

    "We're obligated to do this."

    "The boss is expecting us."

    "I have a terrible headache." (Implied: "so do what I want" or "so leave me alone.")

43. *Recognizing the other's move as a strategy or calling the other's bluff*

    Used for: acts indicating that what the other has just said has been recognized as a strategy and is being challenged or rendered ineffective.

    Conventions and confusions: Like 11, a 43 denies the validity of the other's argument, but 11 is directed toward the content, whereas 43 challenges the strategy. To be coded 43, a remark has to be perceived as a serious challenge, even if it is couched in somewhat humorous terms. If humor is predominant, it is coded 15.

Examples:

"You're not going to get away with that."

"You can't win that way."

"You keep running away [from the issue]."

"Oh, come off it."

(A: "I'm going to leave you." = 55)

  B: "So long."

    or

  B: "I'll see you when you get back."

45. *Rejecting the other*

Used for: a rejection with a strong personal quality, even if it is ostensibly directed toward the ideas, plans, or desires of the other. This category is characterized by very low affiliation and high power. It is often used to maintain interpersonal distance.

Refusal to answer a direct question by silence is a 45 act.

Conventions and confusions: Both 11 and 4 are sometimes confused with 45. The recipient would perceive 45 as a *personal* rejection.

Examples:

"No, I would rather be alone."

(A: "What the matter?" = 21)

  B: (Silence.)

"I don't want to talk with you."

"Go to hell."

47. *Commanding*

Used for: ordering or forcing the other to do one's wishes.

Conventions and confusions: Tone of voice is important in the distinction between 5 and 47. A 47 act would be perceived from its tone and language as coercing, domineering, or dominating, whereas a 5 would be perceived as suggesting a course of action.

Examples:

"I don't care what you want; we're going to do _____."

"Put the book down!"

48. *Demanding compensation*

Used for: an act in which one demands a price from the other for one's yielding. It is the inverse of 35.

Conventions and confusions: A 48 act is coercive, while a 27 is conciliatory.

Examples:

"I'll let you do what you want, but by damn you'll have to _____."

"I'll let you get away with this, but I'm going to _____."

51. *Inducing guilt or attacking the other's motives*

Used for: an act that puts the other on the defensive about his motives or behavior by attacking, uncovering, criticizing, or interpreting them as not matching up to a supposed ideal standard.

Conventions and confusions: See categories 31 and 37. Tone can be misleading in category 51 acts; people can induce guilt in a very "nice" tone of voice.

Examples:

"You don't really want to do _____, you're just being spiteful [mean, stubborn]."

"You're doing things to upset me. You know I don't like this, but you do it anyway."

"You know you have just ruined my whole day."

53. *Disparaging the other*

Used for: an attack perceived by the other as against his person, character, or talents.

Conventions and confusions:—

Examples:

"That's a stupid thing to say."

"Oh, now you're a doctor as well as a psychiatrist."

"You're acting like a dumb jerk."

55. *Threatening the other*

Used for: blunt uses of power.

Conventions and confusions:—

Examples:

"Just try and get away with it."

"I'm liable to get mad—really mad."

"OK, but I'll remember this."

"If you keep acting this way, I'll leave."

Phase Coding

Phase A: Introductory. Acts prior to introduction of the conflict issue. Generally, conventional introductory actions such as greetings and questions, are in phase A. But remarks directed toward bringing up the conflict issue may also be included.

Phase B: Conflict. The conflict phase opens with the first statement of the conflict issue, and it continues until the introduction of an agreed-on resolution. By convention, all participants enter into phase B immediately following a statement of the conflict issue by any participant. There is one exception to this: if one participant brings up the conflict issue and the other never contests it, the first act is coded as phase B, but the rest of the acts are coded as phase A or phase C depending on what goes on.

Phase C: Resolution and postresolution. Resolution is accomplished when participants agree on a solution to the conflict. The solution may or may not be mutually satisfactory to all participants, but it must at least receive verbal agreement for it to be coded as phase C. If a participant rejects a proposed resolution, the acts of all participants, including the proposal, continue to be coded as phase B. In other words, phase C cannot be reached unless all participants are in agreement; if only one is trying for a resolution, then the phase remains at B. Further discussion during phase C may lead to a revival of the conflict, with a return to phase B.

Not all phases need be used in a conflict situation. There may be no introductory phase if the participants enter immediately into the conflict; participants may never enter phase B; or they may fail to achieve resolution and so not enter phase C.

Twelve-Category Lumping Scheme

1 = Introduction: 0, 1, 2, 3, 4, 6
2 = Suggest: 5
3 = Reason: 7, 8, 11
4 = Resolve: 27, 29
5 = Cool: 13, 15, 26
6 = Self-concern: 19, 20, 24
7 = Concern for other: 21, 25, 28

8 = Accept: 23
9 = Appeals: 31, 33, 35, 37, 40
10 = Rejection: 10, 43, 45
11 = Power play: 41, 47, 48, 55
12 = Attack: 51, 53

Six-Category Lumping Scheme

1 = Neutral acts, suggestions,
   and rational arguments: 0, 1, 2, 3, 4, 5, 6, 7, 8, 11 } Cognitive

2 = Resolution of conflict
   (reconciling conflict): 13, 15, 23, 26, 27, 29

3 = Interpersonal reconciliation (reconciling socio-
   emotional status)   19, 20, 21, 24, 25, 28 } Affiliative

4 = Appeal: 31, 33, 35, 37, 40

5 = Rejection: 10, 43, 45

6 = Coercion and attack: 41, 47, 48, 51, 53, 55 } Coercive

Bibliography

AMERICAN SOCIETY FOR RESEARCH IN PSYCHOSOMATIC PROBLEMS, COMMITTEE ON INFANCY AND EARLY CHILDHOOD. "Attitudes of Women toward Pregnancy and the Newborn Baby." *Psychosomatic Medicine,* 1945, 7, 224.

ANGYAL, A. *Neurosis and Treatment: A Wholistic Theory.* New York: Wiley, 1965.

ARENSBURG, C. M. "The American Family in the Perspective of Other Cultures." In E. Ginzberg (Ed.), *The Nation's Children.* Vol. I. *The Family and Social Change.* New York: Columbia University Press, 1960.

ASHBY, W. R. *An Introduction to Cybernetics.* New York: Wiley, 1961.

ATTNEAVE, F. *Applications of Information Theory to Psychology.* New York: Holt, Rinehart, and Winston, 1959.

AUBERT, V. "Chance in Social Affairs." *Inquiry,* 1959, 2, 1–24.

BACH, G. R., AND WYDEN, P. *The Intimate Enemy: How to Fight Fair in Love and Marriage.* New York: Morrow, 1969.

BAKAN, D. *The Duality of Human Existence.* Chicago: Rand McNally, 1966.

BAKAN, D. *On Method.* San Francisco: Jossey-Bass, 1967.

BALES, R. F. *Interaction Process Analysis.* Cambridge, Mass.: Addison-Wesley, 1950.

BARKER, R. G. *Ecological Psychology.* Stanford, Calif.: Stanford University Press, 1968.

BARRY, W. A. "Marriage Research and Conflict: An Integrative Review." *Psychological Bulletin,* 1970, *73,* 41–54.

BATESON, G. *Steps to an Ecology of Mind.* New York: Ballantine Books, 1972.

BATESON, G., JACKSON, D., HALEY, J., AND WEAKLAND, J. "Toward a Theory of Schizophrenia." *Behavioral Science,* 1956, *1,* 251–264.

BATESON, G., JACKSON, D., HALEY, J., AND WEAKLAND, J. "A Note on the Double Bind—1962." *Family Process,* 1963, *2,* 34–51.

BEACH, F. A. "Experimental Investigation of Species-Specific Behavior." *American Psychologist,* 1960, *15,* 1–18.

BENNIS, W. G., AND SLATER, P. E. *The Temporary Society.* New York: Harper and Row, 1968.

BERLYNE, D. E. *Conflict, Arousal, and Curiosity.* New York: McGraw-Hill, 1960.

BERNARD, J. "The Adjustments of Married Mates." In H. T. Christensen (Ed.), *Handbook of Marriage and the Family.* Chicago: Rand McNally, 1964.

BERNARD, J. *The Sex Game.* Englewood Cliffs, N.J.: Prentice-Hall, 1968.

BIBRING, G. L., DWYER, T. F., HUNTINGTON, D. S., AND VALENSTEIN, A. F. "A Study of the Psychological Processes in Pregnancy and the Earliest Mother-Child Relationship." *Psychoanalytic Study of the Child,* 1961, *16,* 9–27.

BLOCK, J., AND BENNETT, L. "The Assessment of Communication." *Human Relations,* 1955, *8,* 317–325.

BLOOD, R. D., AND WOLFE, D. M. *Husbands and Wives: The Dynamics of Married Living.* Glencoe, Ill.: Free Press, 1960.

BOSZORMENYI-NAGY, I. "A Theory of Relationships: Experience and Transaction." In I. Boszormenyi-Nagy and J. L. Framo (Eds.), *Intensive Family Therapy: Theoretical and Practical Aspects.* New York: Harper and Row, 1965.

BOULDING, K. E. *The Image: Knowledge in Life and Society.* Ann Arbor: University of Michigan Press, 1956.

BOULDING, K. E. *Conflict and Defense: A General Theory.* New York: Harper and Row, 1962.

BOWEN, M. "Family Therapy and Family Group Therapy." In H. I. Kaplan and B. J. Sadock (Eds.), *Comprehensive Group Psychotherapy.* New York: Williams and Wilkins, 1971.

BOWERS, K. S. "Situationism in Psychology: An Analysis and a Critique." *Psychological Review,* 1973, *80,* 307–336.

BRADLEY, R. A. *Husband-coached Childbirth.* New York: Harper and Row, 1965.

BROWN, L. B. "Anxiety in Pregnancy." *British Journal of Medical Psychology,* 1964, *37,* 47–57.

BRUNER, J. S. *Toward a Theory of Instruction.* Cambridge, Mass.: Belknap Press, 1966.

BRUNSWIK, E. *Systematic and Representative Design of Psychological Experiments.* Berkeley: University of California Press, 1947.

BUBER, M. "The William Alanson White Memorial Lectures." Fourth Series. *Psychiatry,* 1957, *20,* 95–129.

BUBER, M. *I and Thou.* 1923. (2nd ed.) New York: Scribner's, 1958.

BURGESS, E. W., AND COTTRELL, L. S. *Predicting Success or Failure in Marriage.* New York: Prentice-Hall, 1939.

BURGESS, E. W., LOCKE, H. J., AND THOMES, M. M. *The Family: From Institution to Companionship.* New York: American Book, 1963.

BURGESS, E. W., AND WALLIN, P. *Engagement and Marriage.* Chicago: Lippincott, 1953.

CAMPBELL, D. T. "Methodological Suggestions from a Comparative Psychology of Knowledge Processes." *Inquiry,* 1959, *2,* 152–183.

CAPLAN, G. "Psychological Aspects of Maternity Care." *American Journal of Public Health,* 1957, *47,* 25.

CHERRY, C. *On Human Communication: A Review, a Survey, and a Criticism.* (2nd ed.) Cambridge, Mass.: M.I.T. Press, 1966.

CONSTANTINE, L. L., AND CONSTANTINE, J. M. "Group and Multilateral Marriage." *Family Process,* 1971, *10,* 157–177.

COOMBS, R. H. "Value Consensus and Partner Satisfaction among Dating Couples." *Journal of Marriage and the Family,* 1966, *28,* 166–173.

COSER, L. A. *The Functions of Social Conflict.* Glencoe, Ill.: Free Press, 1956.

COTTRELL, L. S. "The Analysis of Situational Fields in Social Psychology." *American Sociological Review,* 1942, *7,* 370–382.

CUBER, J. F., AND HARROFF, P. B. *The Significant Americans: A Study of Sexual Behavior among the Affluent.* New York: Appleton-Century-Crofts, 1965.

DEUTSCH, M. "Conflicts: Productive and Destructive." *Journal of Social Issues,* 1969a, *25,* 7–41.

DEUTSCH, M. "Socially Relevant Science: Reflections on Some Studies of Interpersonal Conflict." *American Psychologist*, 1969b, *24*, 1076–1092.

DITTMANN, A. T. *Interpersonal Messages of Emotion.* New York: Springer, 1973.

DOEHRMAN, M. G. "The Effects of Coercive Communications upon Conflict Resolution in Newlywed Couples." Unpublished master's thesis, University of Michigan, Ann Arbor, 1968.

DOUVAN, E. A. M., AND ADELSON, J. A. *The Adolescent Experience.* New York: Wiley, 1966.

DYER, E. D. "Parenthood as Crisis." *Marriage and Family Living*, 1963, *25*, 196–201.

DYMOND, R. "Interpersonal Perception and Marital Happiness." *Canadian Journal of Psychology*, 1954, *8*, 164–171.

ENDLER, N. S., AND HUNT, J. MC V. "S-R Inventories of Hostility and Comparisons of the Proportions of Variance from Persons, Responses, and Situations for Hostility and Anxiousness." *Journal of Personality and Social Psychology*, 1968, *9*, 309–315.

ERIKSON, E. H. "Identity and the Life Cycle." *Psychological Issues.* Monograph No. 1. New York: International Universities Press, 1959.

ERIKSON, E. H. *Childhood and Society.* (2nd ed.) New York: Norton, 1963.

ESTES, W. K. "Toward a Statistical Theory of Learning." *Psychological Review*, 1950, *57*, 94–107.

FANO, R. M. *Transmission of Information: A Statistical Theory of Communication.* Cambridge, Mass.: M.I.T. Press, 1961.

FARBER, B. "Types of Family Organization: Child-oriented, Home-oriented, and Parent-oriented." In A. M. Rose (Ed.), *Human Behavior and Social Process.* Boston: Houghton Mifflin, 1962.

FELDMAN, H. "Development of the Husband-Wife Relationship." Unpublished manuscript, 1963.

FINK, C. F. "Some Conceptual Difficulties in the Theory of Social Conflict." *Journal of Conflict Resolution*, 1968, *12*, 412–460.

FISHER, R. "Fractionating Conflict." In R. Fisher (Ed.), *International Conflict and Behavioral Science: The Craigville Papers.* New York: Basic Books, 1964.

FREEDMAN, M. B., LEARY, T. F., OSSORIO, A. G., AND COFFEY, H. S. "The Interpersonal Dimension of Personality." *Journal of Personality*, 1951, *20*, 143–161.

FRENKEL-BRUNSWIK, E. "Sex, People, and Self as Seen through the

Interviews." In T. W. Adorno and others (Eds.), *The Authoritarian Personality*. New York: Wiley, 1964.

GARNER, W. R., AND MC GILL, W. J. "Relation between Uncertainty, Variance, and Correlation Analyses." *Psychometrika*, 1956, *21*, 219–228.

GOODRICH, D. W. "Recent Research in Early Family Development and Child Personality." In R. H. Ojemann (Ed.), *Recent Research Looking toward Preventive Intervention*. Iowa City: State University of Iowa, 1961.

GOODRICH, D. W. "Psychoanalytic Speculations on a Taxonomy of Marriage." In J. Marmor (Ed.), *Modern Psychoanalysis: New Directions and Perspectives*. New York: Basic Books, 1968.

GOODRICH, D. W., AND BOOMER, D. S. "Experimental Assessment of Modes of Conflict Resolution." *Family Process*, 1963, *2*, 15–24.

GOODRICH, D. W., RYDER, R. G., AND RAUSH, H. L. "Patterns of Newlywed Marriage." *Journal of Marriage and the Family*, 1968, *30*, 383–391.

GOODRICH, F. W., JR. "Psychosomatic Aspects of Obstetrics." *Psychosomatics*, 1961, *2*, 194.

GURIN, G., VEROFF, J., AND FELD, S. *Americans View Their Mental Health: A Nationwide Interview Survey*. New York: Basic Books, 1960.

HALEY, J. *Strategies of Psychotherapy*. New York: Grune and Stratton, 1963.

HANDEL, G. "Psychological Studies of Whole Families." *Psychological Bulletin*, 1965, *63*, 19–41.

HAWKINS, E. "The Effects of Disjunctive Communication upon Conflict Resolution at Three Stages of Marriage." Unpublished master's thesis, University of Michigan, Ann Arbor, 1969.

HAYS, W. L. *Statistics for Psychologists*. New York: Holt, Rinehart, and Winston, 1963.

HEISS, J. "Degree of Intimacy and Male-Female Interaction." *Sociometry*, 1962, *25*, 197–208.

HENRY, J. *Pathways to Madness*. New York: Random House, 1971.

HERTEL, R. K. "The Markov Modeling of Experimentally Induced Marital Conflict." Unpublished doctoral dissertation, University of Michigan, Ann Arbor, 1968.

HERTEL, R. K. "The Application of Stochastic Process Analyses to the Study of Psychotherapeutic Processes." *Psychological Bulletin*, 1971, *77*, 421–430.

HESS, R. D., AND HANDEL, G. *Family Worlds: A Psychosocial Approach to Family Life.* Chicago: University of Chicago Press, 1959.

HESS, R. D., AND HANDEL, G. "The Family as a Psychosocial Organization." In G. Handel (Ed.), *The Psychosocial Interior of the Family.* Chicago: Aldine, 1967.

HEYNS, R. W., AND LIPPITT, R. "Systematic Observational Techniques." In G. Lindzey (Ed.), *Handbook of Social Psychology.* Vol. 1. Cambridge, Mass.: Addison-Wesley, 1954.

HOBBS, D. F., JR. "Parenthood as Crisis: A Third Study." *Journal of Marriage and the Family,* 1965, *27,* 367–372.

HOFFMAN, L. "Deviation-amplifying Processes in Natural Groups." In J. Haley (Ed.), *Changing Families: A Family Therapy Reader.* New York: Grune and Stratton, 1971.

HURST, J. C., AND STROUSSE, F. "The Origin of Emotional Factors in Normal Pregnant Women." *American Journal of Medical Science,* 1938, *196,* 95.

JACKSON, D. D. "The Question of Family Homeostasis." In D. D. Jackson (Ed.), *Communication, Family and Marriage.* Vol. 1. *Human Communication.* Palo Alto, Calif.: Science and Behavior Books, 1968.

KAFKA, J. S., AND RYDER, R. G. "Notes on Marriage in the Orbit of the Counter-culture." Unpublished manuscript, 1972.

KAVINOKY, N. R. "Marital Adjustment during Pregnancy and the Year After." *Pan American Medical Woman's Journal,* 1949, *56,* 1–2.

KELLEY, H. H. "Experimental Studies of Threats in Interpersonal Negotiations." *Journal of Conflict Resolution,* 1965, *9,* 79–105.

KELLEY, H. H., AND STAHELSKI, A. J. "Social Interaction Basis of Cooperators' and Competitors' Beliefs about Others." *Journal of Personality and Social Psychology,* 1970, *16,* 66–91.

KEMENY, J. G., AND SNELL, J. L. *Finite Markov Chains.* Princeton, N.J.: Van Nostrand, 1960.

KEMENY, J. G., SNELL, J. L., AND THOMPSON, G. L. *Introduction to Finite Mathematics.* (2nd ed.) Englewood Cliffs, N.J.: Prentice-Hall, 1966.

KENKEL, W. F. "Influence Differentiation in Family Decision Making." *Sociology and Social Research,* 1957, *42,* 18–25.

KENKEL, W. F. "Husband-Wife Interaction in Decision Making and Decision Choices." *Journal of Social Psychology,* 1961, *54,* 255–262.

KENKEL, W. F., AND HOFFMAN, D. K. "Real and Conceived Roles in

Family Decision Making." *Marriage and Family Living,* 1956, *18,* 311–316.

KOMAROVSKY, M. "Functional Analysis of Sex Roles." In M. B. Sussman (Ed.), *Sourcebook in Marriage and the Family.* (3rd ed.) Boston: Houghton Mifflin, 1968.

KUHN, T. S. *The Structure of Scientific Revolutions.* Chicago: University of Chicago Press, 1962.

LAING, R. D. *The Politics of the Family and Other Essays.* New York: Vintage, 1972.

LANDIS, J. T. "Length of Time Required to Achieve Adjustment in Marriage." *American Sociological Review,* 1946, *11,* 666–667.

LANDIS, J. T. "Marriages of Mixed and Non-mixed Religious Faith." In J. T. Landis and M. G. Landis (Eds.), *Readings in Marriage and the Family.* New York: Prentice-Hall, 1952.

LEAR, M. W. "Save the Spouses, Rather than the Marriage." *New York Times Magazine,* August 13, 1972.

LEARY, T. F. *Interpersonal Diagnosis of Personality.* New York: Ronald, 1957.

LEIK, R. K. "Instrumentality and Emotionality in Family Interaction." *Sociometry,* 1963, *26,* 131–145.

LE MASTERS, E. E. "Parenthood as Crisis." *Marriage and Family Living,* 1957, *19,* 352–355.

LEVINGER, G. "Task and Social Behavior in Marriage." *Sociometry,* 1964, *27,* 433–448.

LOESCH, J. G., AND GREENBERG, N. H. "Some Specific Areas of Conflict Observed during Pregnancy: A Comparative Study of Married and Unmarried Pregnant Women." *American Journal of Orthopsychiatry,* 1962, *32,* 624–636.

MC GILL, W. J. "Multivariate Information Transmission." *Psychometrika,* 1954, *19,* 97–116.

MAC KAY, D. M. *The Science of Communication—A Bridge between Disciplines.* Keele: University College of North Staffordshire, 1961.

MC KELLAR, P. "Provocation to Anger and the Development of Attitudes of Hostility." *British Journal of Psychology (General Section),* 1949, *40,* 104–114.

MC KINNEY, B. M. "The Sexual Aspects of Breast Feeding." *Child Family Digest,* 1955, *6,* 45–57.

MARCH, J. G. "Political Issues and Husband-Wife Interaction." In N. W. Bell and E. F. Vogel (Eds.), *A Modern Introduction to the Family.* Glencoe, Ill.: Free Press, 1960.

242   Bibliography

MENNINGER, W. C. "The Emotional Factors in Pregnancy." *Bulletin of the Menninger Clinic,* 1943, *7,* 15.

MENZEL, E. W., JR. "Naturalistic and Experimental Approaches to Primate Behavior." In E. P. Willems and H. L. Raush (Eds.), *Naturalistic Viewpoints in Psychological Research.* New York: Holt, Rinehart, and Winston, 1969.

MILLER, D. R. "The Study of Social Relationships: Situation, Identity, and Social Interaction." In S. Koch (Ed.), *Psychology: A Study of a Science.* Vol. 5. New York: McGraw-Hill, 1963.

MILLER, G. A. "The Magical Number Seven, Plus or Minus Two: Some Limits on Our Capacity for Processing Information." *Psychological Review,* 1956, *63,* 81–97.

MINUCHIN, S., MONTALVO, B., GUERNEY, B. G., ROSMAN, B. L., AND SCHUMER, F. *Families of the Slums: An Exploration of Their Structure and Treatment.* New York: Basic Books, 1967.

MISCHEL, W. "Toward a Cognitive Social Learning Reconceptualization of Personality." *Psychological Review,* 1973, *80,* 252–283.

MOORE, O. K., AND ANDERSON, A. R. "Some Puzzling Aspects of Social Interaction." In J. Criswell, H. Solomon, and P. Suppes (Eds.), *Mathematical Methods in Small Group Processes.* Stanford, Calif.: Stanford University Press, 1962.

MOOS, R. H. "Situational Analysis of a Therapeutic Community Milieu." *Journal of Abnormal Psychology,* 1968, *73,* 49–61.

MOOS, R. H. "Sources of Variance in Responses to Questionnaires and Behavior." *Journal of Abnormal Psychology,* 1969, *74,* 405–412.

MUNSINGER, H., AND KESSEN, W. "Uncertainty, Structure and Preference." *Psychological Monographs,* 1964, *78* (9, Whole No. 586).

NEWCOMB, T. M. "An Approach to the Study of Communicative Acts." *Psychological Review,* 1953, *60,* 393–404.

NEWCOMB, T. M. "Stabilities Underlying Changes in Interpersonal Attraction." In I. D. Steiner and M. Fishbein (Eds.), *Current Studies in Social Psychology.* New York: Holt, Rinehart, and Winston, 1965.

NEWTON, N. *Maternal Emotions.* Philadelphia: Paul Hoeber, 1955.

OLSON, D. M. "Marriage of the Future: Revolutionary or Evolutionary Change?" *The Family Coordinator,* Oct. 1972, 383–393.

O'ROURKE, J. F. "Field and Laboratory: The Decision-making Behavior of Family Groups in Two Experimental Conditions." *Sociometry,* 1963, *26,* 422–435.

OTTO, L. B., AND FEATHERMAN, D. L. "On the Measurement of Marital

Adjustment among Spouses." Madison: University of Wisconsin, Center for Demography and Ecology, 1972.

PARSONS, T., AND BALES, R. F. (Eds.) *Family, Socialization, and Interaction Process.* Glencoe, Ill.: Free Press, 1955.

PARZEN, E. *Stochastic Processes.* San Francisco: Holden-Day, 1962.

PIAGET, J. *The Language and Thought of the Child.* New York: Harcourt Brace and Jovanovich, 1926.

PIAGET, J. *Structuralism.* New York: Basic Books, 1970.

POFFENBERGER, S., POFFENBERGER, T., AND LANDIS, J. T. "Intent toward Conception and the Pregnancy Experience." *American Sociological Review,* 1952, *17,* 617–618.

RANK, O. *Will Therapy and Truth and Reality* (1936). New York: Knopf, 1968.

RAPAPORT, D. "The Theory of Ego Autonomy: A Generalization." 1957. In M. M. Gill (Ed.), *The Collected Papers of David Rapaport.* New York: Basic Books, 1967.

RAPOPORT, A., AND CHAMMAH, A. M. *Prisoner's Dilemma: A Study in Conflict and Cooperation.* Ann Arbor: University of Michigan Press, 1965.

RAUSH, H. L. "Interaction Sequences." *Journal of Personality and Social Psychology,* 1965, *2,* 487–499.

RAUSH, H. L. "Naturalistic Method and the Clinical Approach." In E. P. Willems and H. L. Raush (Eds.), *Naturalistic Viewpoints in Psychological Research.* New York: Holt, Rinehart, and Winston, 1969.

RAUSH, H. L. "Process and Change—A Markov Model for Interaction." *Family Process,* 1972, *13,* 275–298.

RAUSH, H. L., DITTMANN, A. T., AND TAYLOR, T. J. "Person, Setting and Change in Social Interaction." *Human Relations,* 1959, *12,* 361–379.

RAUSH, H. L., FARBMAN, I., AND LLEWELLYN, L. G. "Person, Setting and Change in Social Interaction, II: A Normal-Control Study." *Human Relations,* 1960, *13,* 305–333.

RAUSH, H. L., GOODRICH, W., AND CAMPBELL, J. D. "Adaptation to the First Years of Marriage." *Psychiatry,* 1963, *26,* 368–380.

RAUSH, H. L., MARSHALL, K. A., AND FEATHERMAN, J. M. "Relations at Three Early Stages of Marriage as Reflected by the Use of Personal Pronouns." *Family Process,* 1970, *9,* 69–82.

RAVICH, R. A. "The Use of an Interpersonal Game-Test in Conjoint Marital Psychotherapy." *American Journal of Psychotherapy,* 1969, *23,* 217–229.

RISKIN, J. M., AND FAUNCE, E. E. "An Evaluative Review of Family Interaction Research." *Family Process*, 1972, *11*, 365–455.

ROSSI, A. S. "Transition to Parenthood." *Journal of Marriage and the Family*, 1968, *30*, 26–39.

ROTH, J., AND PECK, R. F. "Social Class and Social Mobility Factors Related to Marital Adjustment." *American Sociological Review*, 1951, *16*, 478–487.

RUESCH, J. *Disturbed Communication*. New York: Norton, 1957.

RUSSELL, C., AND RUSSELL, W. M. S. *Human Behavior*. Boston: Little, Brown, 1961.

RYDER, R. G. "Two Replications of Color Matching Factors." *Family Process*, 1966, *5*, 43–48.

RYDER, R. G. "Dimensions of Early Marriage." *Family Process*, 1970, *9*, 51–68.

RYDER, R. G. "Longitudinal Data Relating 'Marriage Satisfaction' and Having a Child." *Journal of Marriage and the Family*, in press.

RYDER, R. G., AND GOODRICH, D. W. "Married Couples' Responses to Disagreement." *Family Process*, 1966, *5*, 30–42.

RYDER, R. G., KAFKA, J. S., AND OLSON, D. H. "Separating and Joining Influences in Courtship and Early Marriage." *American Journal of Orthopsychiatry*, 1971, *41*, 450–464.

SEELEY, J. R., SIM, R. A., AND LOOSLEY, E. W. *Crestwood Heights: A Study of the Culture of Suburban Life*. New York: Basic Books, 1956.

SHANNON, C. E., AND WEAVER, W. *The Mathematical Theory of Communication*. Urbana: University of Illinois Press, 1949.

SMITH, J. E. K. "Multivariate Attribute Analysis." Ann Arbor: Engineering Research Institute, University of Michigan, 1953.

SOLOMON, L. "The Influence of Some Types of Power Relationships and Game Strategies upon the Development of Interpersonal Trust." *Journal of Abnormal and Social Psychology*, 1960, *61*, 223–230.

SPOCK, B. *Baby and Child Care*. New York: Pocket Books, 1957.

STRODTBECK, F. L. "Husband-Wife Interaction over Revealed Differences." *American Sociological Review*, 1951, *16*, 468–473.

SULLIVAN, H. S. *The Interpersonal Theory of Psychiatry*. New York: Norton, 1953.

TAYLOR, S. P., AND EPSTEIN, S. "Aggression as a Function of the Interaction of the Sex of the Aggressor and the Sex of the Victim." *Journal of Personality*, 1967, *35*, 474–486.

THARP, R. G. "Psychological Patterning in Marriage." *Psychological Bulletin*, 1963, *60*, 97–117.

THIBAUT, J. W., AND COULES, J. "The Role of Communication in the Reduction of Interpersonal Hostility." *Journal of Abnormal and Social Psychology*, 1952, *47*, 770–777.

THOMPSON, L. J. "Attitudes of Primaparae as Observed in a Prenatal Clinic." *Mental Hygiene*, 1942, *26*, 243.

THOMPSON, L. J. "Prenatal and Neonatal Mental Hygiene." *Digest Neurological Psychiatry*, 1950, *18*, 109.

THORPE, W. H. *Learning and Instinct in Animals*. Cambridge, Mass.: Harvard University Press, 1956.

THORPE, W. H. *Science, Man and Morals*. Ithaca, N.Y.: Cornell University Press, 1965.

"Toward the Differentiation of a Self in One's Own Family." In J. L. Framo (Ed.), *Family Interaction: A Dialogue between Family Researchers and Family Therapists*. New York: Springer, 1972.

TURNER, R. H. *Family Interaction*. New York: Wiley, 1970.

UDRY, F. R. *The Social Context of Marriage* (2nd ed.) New York: Lippincott, 1971.

UDRY, F. R., NELSON, H. A., AND NELSON, R. "An Empirical Investigation of Some Widely Held Beliefs about Marital Interaction." *Marriage and Family Living*, 1961, *23*, 388–390.

WATZLAWICK, P., BEAVIN, J. H., AND JACKSON, D. D. *Pragmatics of Human Communication—a Study of Interactional Patterns, Pathologies, and Paradoxes*. New York: Norton, 1967.

WEICK, K. E. "Systematic Observation Methods." In G. Lindzey and E. Aronson (Eds.), *Handbook of Social Psychology*. Vol. 2. (2nd ed.) Reading, Mass.: Addison-Wesley, 1968.

WIENER, N. *Cybernetics*. New York: Wiley, 1948.

WILLEMS, E. P. "Planning a Rationale for Naturalistic Research." In E. P. Willems and H. L. Raush (Eds.), *Naturalistic Viewpoints in Psychological Research*. New York: Holt, Rinehart, and Winston, 1969.

WILLEMS, E. P., AND RAUSH, H. L. (Eds.) *Naturalistic Viewpoints in Psychological Research*. New York: Holt, Rinehart, and Winston, 1969.

WYNNE, L. C., RYCKOFF, I. M., DAY, J., AND HIRSCH, S. I. "Pseudo-Mutuality in the Family Relations of Schizophrenics." *Psychiatry*, 1958, *21*, 205–220.

Index

246